RACE, TASTE, C

Yuni

First published in Great Britain in 2020 by

Policy Press
University of Bristol
1-9 Old Park Hill
Bristol
BS2 8BB
UK
t: +44 (0)117 954 5940
pp-info@bristol.ac.uk
www.policypress.co.uk

British Library Cataloguing in Publication Data
A catalogue record for this book is available from the British Library.

ISBN 978-1-4473-5347-8 paperback
ISBN 978-1-4473-5349-2 ePub
ISBN 978-1-4473-5348-5 ePdf

Cover design by Lyn Davies
Printed and bound in Great Britain by TJ International, Padstow
Policy Press uses environmentally responsible print partners

FSC www.fsc.org MIX Paper from responsible sources FSC® C013056

For Charlie and Ali, exemplars of commitment.

What are the 21st century challenges shaping our lives today and in the future? At this time of social, political, economic and cultural disruption, this exciting series, published in association with the British Sociological Association, brings pressing public issues to the general reader, scholars and students. It offers standpoints to shape public conversations and a powerful platform for both scholarly and public debate, proposing better ways of understanding, and living in, our world.

Series Editors: Les Back, Goldsmiths, Pam Cox, University of Essex and Nasar Meer, University of Edinburgh

Other titles in this series:

Published

Miseducation by Diane Reay

Snobbery by David Morgan

Money by Mary Mellor

Making Sense of Brexit by Victor Seidler

What's Wrong with Work? by Lynne Pettinger

Contents

List of figures

About the author

Yunis Alam was born and raised in Bradford, a city in the north of England, where he still lives and works. His teaching and research interests include ethnic relations, popular culture and postcolonial literatures. He has previously written novels and short stories and edited anthologies which bridge ethnographic and literary traditions.

Acknowledgements

This book is the result of a long, seemingly unending research interest in car culture, especially that present in multicultural cities. It's a near-impossible task to thank all those who have stimulated and provoked this interest, but I am appreciative of the time and conversation given by Aaliya Bashir, Carole Binns, Ayesha Butt, Ian Daley, Phil Edwards, Mohammed Farook, Jim Goddard, Bana Gora, Tarik Hussain, Yasmin Hussain, Atif Imtiaz, Ansar Jawed, Javed Khan, M.G. Khan, Sajid Khan, Khizer Rehman, Anwar Shah, Yunas Samad, Paul Sullivan, Mohammed Sultan and Nadeem Zeb.

Thanks are also in order to all at Policy Press, particularly Shannon Kneis and Kathryn King, and to the reviewers who gave valuable feedback on an earlier draft of this book. I am indebted to Nasar Meer and Les Back, both of whom have been more than supportive of this book and, indeed, were instrumental in its commission. Beyond this, their sensitivity, knowledge and input relating to the subject matter have always been welcome and appreciated.

Without the time, energy and commitment from the many who contributed to the research as participants, of course, this book would not exist. They have endured my questions, observation and even presence with good humour and openness, producing countless fascinating conversations about the car, its people and the narratives that seem to define, not always accurately, our city. To them, even those whose words may not appear on the pages to follow, I remain humbled and grateful, and I continue to be impressed by their enthusiasm and commitment, not only to their cars, but to Bradford, also. The same applies especially to Ali, who not only happens to be interested in cars, but also invited me to car meets and introduced me to many others who share his passion. And on this note, I am grateful, yet again, to the rest of my family for allowing me to be isolated, segregated and antisocial during some of the more intense moments of this research, particularly the write-up. Razia, Aaisha, Farah and Zuby: thanks for tolerating me when I said I was "busy".

Finally, I am confident that this book would not have been written, nor would the research ever have been conducted, were it not for the presence of my friend and collaborator, Charlie Husband. Charlie embodies what it is to do sociology as a political, but inherently human, empathetic and morally conscious, act. Throughout the time I have known Charlie, he has been consistently available to talk about work, life and other, less pressing matters. Despite not driving a car, Charlie's interest in and zest for this subject matter – and I write this without exaggeration – exceeds my own, and this has proven vital, especially during those moments where necessary energy and purpose are displaced by the encroaching pressures of university life. Charlie's support for this work is worthy of more than a few lines expressing thanks.

Preface

At its heart, social research involves exploring topics and themes, some of which are more pressing than others. In some areas there sit tension, ambiguity and even a stark sense of threat, danger or insecurity for the researcher and those being researched. Regardless, in most cases, researchers mine their participants for data, from which analysis, diagnosis and, on occasion, recommendation flows. There are examples of researchers going beyond this, but the premise dictating the nature of the relationships is that of power dynamics: some approaches aim to harmonise balance between researchers and the researched, whereas in others, this is not a concern. However, for some of us, research is personal and political in terms of our connection with the subject matter, the people who fill in the frames and what we hope the research might achieve. Moreover, every aspect of a research process calls for a decision to be made, and this too can have political dimensions: who does the research, how, why and with whom are all elements of a larger whole in which power and its impacts are present.

This book tries to account for this research context, not only by working through the intersections of ethnicity, class and taste, but also because the normative readings of identities are grounded in the fabric of day-to-day life in which some groups become rendered subjects and objects of debate. In British society, in common with many parts of the West, there has been a rising and falling of problematic Muslim identities throughout the centuries.[1] Today, and once again, British Muslims have been prioritised as a subject of scrutiny, research and remedy: sexual predators, radical terrorists or terrorist sympathisers, particularly passive victims of patriarchy, social and spatial segregationists, not to mention chronic underachievers in the fields of education, employment and culture. There are a host of other markers through which Muslim identity is rehearsed as challenging, particularly and increasingly through political discourse and mass media. In a process underpinned by 'evidence', Muslim identity is shaped by limited, often ideologically grounded and pre-existing narratives that seem to do little more than perpetuate notions of danger, difference and threat.

The previous paragraphs may seem out of place. This is, after all, supposed to be a book about cars. And it is. However, this is also a book about how we, as social beings, construct ourselves and others, at least in part, through our understandings of car culture. Cars signify meaning, with status, wealth and taste being perhaps the most obvious conceptual blocks that can be inscribed upon any and every car we come across. One of this book's aims, therefore, is to pinpoint how identity is carried, presented and finessed by the car. And here, connections between the car and identity result in a need for us to make sense of what we encounter: an expensive car in a seemingly 'deprived' area may elicit the need for some form of logic to explain the car's presence – the driver is a rich landlord, a visiting celebrity, a criminal. Once such imaginative but coherent impressions are unpicked, a more comprehensive, in-depth and grounded understanding of social situations is revealed.

Cultures that flow from the car are nuanced through transmissions of class, ethnicity, gender and – connected to all of these markers of identity – 'taste'.

Cars can be viewed through a sociology that locates human experience as central, connected and varied. This includes not only the voices of research participants, but also informal, acutely non-academic (often abridged) field notes, written over the span of the research. These are included not as a means of somehow trying to demonstrate street credibility or some unresolved creative authorial ambition, but rather to offer an unambiguous form of depth and insight that is not always present in sociological work. Within social science, it is not unusual for researchers to embrace experiences and histories from which develop interpretations. More than that, using formal and informal types of data shows how sociology does not have to be constrained by a set of monolithic traits and elements of style, which dominate some fields of the discipline. If anything, the approach taken in this book is an effort to reclaim and resituate sociology as a public endeavour in which 'the sociological imagination' is given the space and licence to be overtly and usefully present. Of course, much of the discussion here, and throughout the book, may suggest that my own academic identity rests on an overly reflective practice, which overindulges in ethnographic and ethnic insiderness – indeed, this very sentence may acutely demonstrate this. Regardless, while this may hold some validity, for a working-class, 'ethnic minority'-heritage researcher, the structural impacts that correspond with these elements of identity are present: no matter who or what you think you are, others are perfectly able to not only interpret you, but also create impact upon you. Stating at the outset that personal identity feeds into research seems necessary as a means of framing the pages that follow.

ONE

Introduction

The rationale for this book, and the research that underpins it, comes from a long, evolving and deepening fascination with car culture; how we use, react to and live with cars and their infrastructures is something that continues to provoke curiosity and, at times, concern. While some of this interest came through explicit academic avenues, it grew and was refined through a more personal, pre-academic biography involving relationships with cars and how some friends 'felt' about their vehicles, as well as connections with those who made a living working with, and sometimes against, cars. In the spirit of being open, and no doubt open to an array of criticisms, it is important to state that while not exactly a complete exercise in self-indulgence, this book is based on a desire to explore cars[1] through a framing of the experiences, attitudes and dispositions of car users.

Ubiquitous though it is, and despite the harmful impacts it has generated over the decades, the car continues to represent something beyond utility,[2] with freedom, creativity, status and even deviance being signified by this mass-produced object, which, at its core, still has the basic function of enabling and improving movement. As a development of earlier horseless carriages, cars were supposed to help us become more efficient.[3] And yet, even before the mid 20th century, what we could do and see on the road surpassed this function.

On a typical day on a typical inner-city Bradford road, if such a thing exists, a significant, unusual and varied car presence is witnessed. There are standard, ordinary cars, vans and motorcycles, of various ages and conditions. Occasionally, a car manufactured decades ago appears, turns heads and elicits nostalgia-laced conversation or thought. And then there are modern, and much more expensive, models that seem, in some cases, out of place. Range Rovers, Audi Q7s and BMW X5s are visible across the UK, but the same cannot be said of Bentleys, Lamborghinis and Ferraris. Their presence figures heavily in the developing storyline of Bradford as a 'car city':

LR: Bradford's known for its cars, though … got a good following in a way; a lot of cars in Bradford that are nice – expensive cars, vintage cars and done-up cars as well.
YA: Lots of places have that, though.
LR: Not that many.… But what I was saying was it's not known enough because it's better known for being a sort of rubbish place.… It's not rubbish … but that's what they think.
YA: Who?
LR: You know, everyone. Everyone who matters.… What I mean is that if it wasn't Bradford, then it would be like better known for its cars. You get me? (LR, 26, male, 6 August 2017)

Supporting this variety of cars is an evolving infrastructure: traders, accessory stores and mechanics, as well as body shops, wheel refurbishers, valeters, elite vehicle hire companies and retailers. However, Bradford's lively and viable car sector remains obscured by more potent and possibly compelling narratives that signal communities which are, in whatever ways, lacking.

In the remainder of this chapter, which concludes with a brief outline of the book's shape, some discussion of the research origins, the approach taken and the discourse in which the research sits is offered; some attention is therefore paid to existing research and contemporary car discourse, particularly in relation to car-related policy.

Bodywork: cars in context

The car is one of those strange, multidimensional objects, understandings of which are framed not only by us, as subjective beings, but also by broader historical, economic and cultural forces. Cars are significant in terms of their economic impacts, due not just to the aggregation of cars that are made and sold, but also to the astonishing and taken-for-granted infrastructure that supports and aligns with their presence; roads, fuel and garages are obvious aspects of this. Not so obvious is the expanding array of 'forward/backward economic linkages' with the car.[4] The production of fuel and of steel constitute backward linkages, which for the most part are easily recognisable. However, the realms of sport, out-of-town shopping and, of course, mass-mediated content can sit before or after the point of explicit car consumption. Furthermore, governments promote this exemplar of capitalist production,[5] within which is woven an economic – and thus cultural, social and political – presence and potency.

Some of this infrastructure is of course in the process of continual renewal, evolution and cost. Roads are resurfaced, motorways widened, urban streets 'traffic calmed', with new technological advances requiring new physical infrastructure ('smart' motorways and charging points for electric drivetrain cars, for example). At a more mundane level, top-down and usually state-led car interventions are felt on the ground:

> First they were saying *oh no, you don't want petrol because petrol's really bad at polluting so you're better off with diesel; buy diesel* [cars].... So, yes, people bought into diesel. And now, same scenario again, isn't it? *Diesel's really bad so go with, erm, electric or hybrid.* In five years' time, who's to say they won't turn round and say, *electric and hybrid, they're really bad*, as well? In the end, who pays for it all? We do but no, as long as they're seen to be doing something about the mess they've made, it's all good. (AW, 37, male, 26 November 2018)

While there is some connection to global car-related issues, themes and challenges, this book does not dwell on the environmental impact of the car, and nor will it pursue a line of inquiry in which the future of the car, or the world, is focused upon. However, a brief overview of the current car, transport and economic policy intersections that will no doubt have lasting implications is offered next as context for the themes in this book.

Most major car manufacturers are presently producing ultra-low emission vehicles (ULEV), usually with hybrid or electric drivetrains. In 2018, such cars constituted under 3 per cent of all new registrations in the UK, representing a 20 per cent increase over the previous year. While there was a decline in diesel vehicle registrations (30 per cent), petrol cars increased by 9 per cent. Given that there are presently around 30.9 million fossil fuel-based cars in the UK,[6] switching consumers to ULEVs is a priority,[7] but this has its own consequences, some of which feed into policy planning. Once the technology upon which cars have run for over a hundred years (the combustion engine) starts to become outdated, it will be necessary to update or replace existing infrastructures, including resources for teaching and training, around new technologies. Present projections indicate that fairly significant financial and political investment is necessary in order for

> all new cars and vans to be effectively zero emission by 2040.... By then, we expect the majority of new cars and vans sold to be 100% zero emission and all new cars and vans to have significant zero emission capability. By 2050 we want almost every car and van to be zero emission.[8]

There were approximately 3,100 public charging points in the UK in 2018; estimates suggest that over 27,000 will be needed by 2030.[9] Presently, however, 'range anxiety' – consumer concerns that electric cars need to be charged or refuelled more frequently than petrol or diesel vehicles[10] – needs addressing in order to enhance uptake of ULEVs. Meanwhile, driverless autonomous vehicles are likely to be on the roads in the near future,[11] and this too will pose challenges, requiring state and private investment, but also confidence on the part of consumers.

With these changes related to the reinvention of the car's drivetrain and fuelling, it follows not only that associated car infrastructures will require adaptations, but also that cultural practices linked with the car will also evolve. Driverless cars may reduce various, especially problematic, driving behaviours, but for many, their relationships with their cars will be subject to an existential shift; for some, driving is something akin to a birthright. Furthermore, if driverless cars become the norm, how we conceptualise ownership, and how we consume an object that today encapsulates notions of freedom and independence, as well as skill, creativity and taste, will no doubt be subject to similar cultural and economic transformations.

Given the nature of this book, however, the economic impact of car infrastructure, or the efficacy of transport policy and, by extension, debates in which pollution and sustainability are significant, are not pursued in any depth. Similarly, whether electric cars, public transport and alternative modes of urban mobility could be made more accessible, and thus save the planet from at least a century of brutal overdevelopment in the name of capitalism, is certainly important, but not vital in understanding how cars relate to identity-based meaning. It is worth noting that any attempt to overlay broader, global car-related issues onto the empirical data (interviews, observations and so on) would go against the essence of the research aims. This, in turn, would result in a mismatch between the data and the book's scope. Rather, the extent to which the car informs, and is informed by, the cultures in which it sits remains a core feature of this book.

As a symbol and an economic entity, or merely as a piece of machinery to be used pragmatically, the car has grown in relevance over the last 50 years and continues to make inroads across the globe. Partly, this has been made possible by the relative decrease in car production costs and retail pricing, while rises in income have helped ensure car ownership is 'enjoyed' by more people than ever. In the UK, the car features heavily in the management of spaces, and in the economy at national and local levels. Policing, city planning and transport policy are sharply aligned with a global system of automobility,[12] wherein the car has shaped societies in concrete and abstract ways.

No longer a luxury item, the car ties in with pragmatic utility, but also helps confer and project articulations of affluence and status. Cars hold connotations and render interpretations of those who inhabit them, with some evoking readings of class, gender, generation and, in basic and complex ways, ethnicity. The car, then, even in our imaginations and understandings, does more than move us around. But its functionality is often a minor issue when we actually buy one. We all know it aides our mobility, but this comes at a price: fuel economy, insurance and other running costs are often factored into decision-making equations. For many, even more pressing are the less pragmatic and 'sensible' concerns that nevertheless need to be resolved, especially if we are buying a car that we feel we 'deserve'.[13] It has to have the right sound – loud, silent or somewhere in between. It has to be the right colour – a metallic, pearl or possibly less exotic, more anonymous, painted finish. And it needs to have the right level of trim – seriously, what *is* the point if it does not have cruise control, electric windows, heated electric leather seats, A/C, satnav, electric folding wing mirrors or enough cup holders? On top of all that, and no doubt more, cars become sanctuaries where feelings can be evoked:

> I know, this makes me sound like a nutter. I bet that's what you're thinking: I'm a nutcase.... When I'm driving, I'll be listening to the radio and if a song comes on and I know it, I'll sing along. I'd never do that anywhere else – not even at home.... When one of my cousins died, I couldn't cry in public. I just couldn't.... As soon as I got in my car and I was in pieces. (NA, 31, female, 13 June 2017)

The car, therefore, is able to elicit a palette of emotional responses: happiness, anger, sadness, fear and exhilaration are all waiting when we are driving. Even when we are observing other cars and their drivers, we can, and do, react. And it is here where a significant feature within contemporary, especially urban and multi-ethnic, settings comes to life with and through the car. As a public, multifaceted object, the car has been given some sociological attention, but relatively little of this relates to our lived experience, and even less so when it comes to rehearsing and perpetuating ideas linked with ethnicity.

As discussed elsewhere, there is extensive writing around various dimensions of car-related research, including their manufacture, car crime, and the opportunities and challenges posed by globalisation and technological advances.[14] The mobilities paradigm in particular has yielded valuable work in which the study of cars uses the intersections of culture, globalisation, sustainability and consumption.[15] In and among this diverse body of work, public and private spheres are approached through an array of cross-cutting forces and pressures: from how movement and communication impacts and influences social relations, to more pronounced themes involving pollution and sustainability. More generally, research also situates the car with aspiration, leisure, conflict and art,[16] but also addresses the emotions that cars facilitate and convey.[17]

For Urry, the car takes on several forms and functions. It is a manufactured object and therefore subject to economic processes.[18] It is also a mode of individual consumption and movement, impacting everything from the criminal justice system to city planning. In sum, the car informs a dominant social context and discourse, producing a civil society of 'car-drivers' whose presence on the road is privileged in comparison to that of non-car users. As the 'quintessential manufactured object produced by leading industrial sectors',[19] the car enjoys banal but ubiquitous reach: even if the street is empty, much of its fabric is geared toward the needs of automobiles. We see this in the amount of investment that services motorised transport – some of which is closely connected with the pursuit of economic growth, whereas other investments are made under the remit of road and pedestrian safety.

While this book does not aim to develop analysis of a future in which petrol and diesel cars will be less common, it does offer insights that could feed into policy and public perceptions of what the car represents and how it functions, and how it impacts communities and individuals – as owners, drivers and passengers – as well as those who prefer to remain without a car in their lives. Added to this, the nexus of relationships between consumer object and identity is fertile ground in which expressions of power, discrimination and their counters are present.

Scope and depth

This research started, at least formally, in 2011, and in some ways is ongoing. To date, there have been over a hundred interviews, of various lengths, with a broad range of individuals in terms of age, profession or work, and neighbourhood. The majority of participants, however, are male and of Pakistani heritage.[20] The nature of the sample is based on pragmatic and methodological considerations: the car/road/behaviour discourse, certainly in Bradford, is dominated by representations of young Pakistani-heritage males and, furthermore, many who engage with some of the car cultural, and subcultural, practices are of the same background. It is also worth bearing in mind that it was a conscious methodological decision to research principally males given the significance of research insiderness, which involves ethnicity as well as class, gender and locale.

The car is a social object, and therefore warrants a specific, arguably peculiar mode of sociological investigation. At the same time, there is overlap between an ethnic relations discourse and car culture; it is therefore necessary to consider the extent to which ethnic identity influences how cars are consumed, and how cars transmit racialisation as process and outcome. But this also leads to further complications: it is not only ethnic identity that is at play in this sort of equation; so too is gender and, significantly, the textured manifestations of class. Class in turn references and locates economic, geographic, cultural and consumer attributes of identity. Similarly, the process of consumption is more than just owning or using an object; *how* we use the object, *how* we change it and *how* we feel about it are all relevant, and can help demonstrate how identity is performed.

Earlier research conducted with Charlie Husband, while not explicitly tied into car culture, was interested in exploring what it was to be young, male and of Pakistani heritage, born or 'made' in a place like Bradford.[21] The rationale for that particular research was principally to offer something beyond the usual caricatures of Pakistani Muslim males, in which riot, drug-related crime, 'Islamist' radicalisation, educational underachievement and other negative attributes featured heavily and often. During the fieldwork phases of this earlier research, the car seemed to be a key component in the maintenance and performance of self-identity. Indeed, many of the interviews were conducted in cars, but beyond that, quite a few participants talked about their experiences on the road. Those with noticeable or unusual cars talked about receiving admiring nods by fellow car connoisseurs, whereas some recalled being stopped and questioned by the police, or subject to racial abuse from other road users. For many, the car signified who they thought they were, and how they wanted to be seen, a feature that has continued to present itself:

> You wouldn't be talking to me otherwise, would you, so yeah, obviously, my car is saying something.... Well, it's saying something about me, obviously. It's not original, but no car is original once someone has it.... What I mean, I mean, everyone changes something about their car, don't they? Even your car, there'll be something you've done – might not be obvious, but it's not original any more.... With mine, it's the wheels and the paint – obviously the paint – and the number plate. The number plate is, well, me, isn't it? (MS, 27, male, 5 April 2019)

With these thoughts in mind, then, this book is not a sociological examination of car culture through the use of big data, or through explanations of large-scale changes in consumer behaviour. Rather, this book illustrates how humans have the capacity to invest – economically and especially emotionally – in a mass-produced object as a means of refracting aspects of their own identities. As MS suggests, cars give owners a means through which some aspect of identity can be performed, and then, of course, interpreted. The car then becomes a tangible artefact that allows us to read and perceive people, sometimes in very specific ways. These normative understandings of social reality[22] are primed through a broader context in which identities are framed by and anchored in ideological underpinnings. The scope of this book, therefore, extends to car cultural practices, including the process of enhancement and modification, as well as unpicking what it means to have or not have 'taste'.

Real-world sociology

While this book's aims are diverse and no doubt messy, they feed into the uses of sociology: what sociology can, and perhaps should, do. One strand is to make sociology more meaningful, relevant and accessible. Arguably, this kind of statement may cause professional offence in some quarters because it suggests that, at present, sociology is closed, narrow and often interested in speaking only to itself. This is not necessarily a widely held view, but there is no doubt that a significant proportion of sociological output is aimed at discreet and often appropriately distinct audiences. There remains, perhaps, a stereotypical perception that sociology and some other social sciences are somewhat select disciplines – not exactly elitist, but arguably minority-interest, having little ground-level impact or take-up. Similarly, there has been, certainly over the last two decades, a retreat – at institutional levels[23] – from the philosophies of sociological practice in which curiosity, imagination, and civic or public service were central.[24]

Just as importantly, there does not appear to be an accurate and public understanding of what it is that sociologists actually do. In some cases, sociologists may not be as proficient at disseminating their research as effectively as they are at producing it. Indeed, for some of us, marketing or publicising our research is something that is best left to others – but this is perhaps another reason why sociologists do not have a more pronounced profile that is grounded and made real by our own voices and experiences. Often, of course, sociological research is quite rightly intended for very specific audiences, including, for example, other sociologists, policymakers, funders and specific interest groups to whom the research may particularly speak. As a result, negotiating the needs and interests of our stakeholders[25] may hinder sociology from entering the public sphere more wholly and coherently.

That said, there have been, and continue to be, sociologists whose work has a clearly public remit. Through attending to the concept of 'craft' and making their outputs as accessible as possible, sociologists can ensure that their work becomes visibly important and socially relevant.[26] Of course, 'traditional' sociology has influenced a range of perceptions and informed social changes – everything from political ideology[27] to legislation around cohabitation[28] has used sociological insight and evidence. Sociology, therefore, does not sit outside mainstream culture, but it can work toward becoming more appealing and relevant to diverse publics.

This book, therefore, sits against this backdrop. The usual academic convention of explicitly demonstrating a critical appreciation of pertinent research does not get in the way and overwhelm the broader argument being shaped. Of course, linkages with existing research, theory and thought are made, but for the benefit of flow, and perhaps to the horror of some already, not every sentence has a reference at the end of it. This book's main themes, however, are couched sociologically, and are heavily illustrated with field notes, quotations from participants and, on occasion, photographs. Some of the extracts may indicate a degree of hypersensitivity and subjectivity; many of the field note extracts in particular are not particularly 'academic' or factual and at times veer toward polemic.[29] They are frank, certainly, but in and of themselves lack the potency required to maintain an appropriately critical tone. Within the context of this book, however, they serve two purposes: to explicitly integrate the experiences of the researcher/ethnographer, and to situate particular themes and issues through the use of complementing, but usually underused, data.

Bradford: car city

The salience of ethnicity, the virtues and costs of doing insider ethnography, and the ways in which the city of Bradford has been researched have been discussed elsewhere.[30] Rather than offer a similarly in-depth and wide-ranging discussion, it may be more useful to present a more precise, but relevant, overview of some of the more cogent features informing the research approach. There follows, therefore, a selective account of specific moments that have helped portray Bradford as a city with a clear, and occasionally problematic, ethnic identity biography. The following discussion includes necessary contexts that feed into the remaining sections of this book. As will be shown in due course, the themes raised frequently cross-reference the city, its history and its people.

Up until the 1960s and 1970s, Bradford's textile industry had significant economic impact and presence.[31] Like other cities, Bradford recruited for labour from former British colonies in the aftermath of the Second World War. Within a decade, or sometimes two, these initially economic migrants had established families and communities, thus becoming settled. However, the declining textile industry in the 1970s affected the city's workforce in general, producing generations and families in which unemployment and underemployment became noticeable.[32] Regardless of shortcomings in both educational and employment infrastructure, among Bradford's Pakistani-heritage communities there has been resilience, leading to innovation and success, often through entrepreneurship and through making inroads into professional careers. Some of this has been aided through informal support mechanisms[33] and networks,[34] constituting a form of 'bonding' capital. For example, especially in those parts of the city with marked minority ethnic populations, there are similarly high levels of ethnically linked infrastructure – everything from clothing retailers and restaurants to community centres and places of religious worship. Certainly over the last 20 years, there has also been a visible growth in more mainstream business sectors and entrepreneurship: estate agents, legal services and, of course, a noticeably large amount of activity linked with the car. Among many with a similar view, one participant noted,

> Bradford, it's car city.... You wanna see nice cars, you come to Bradford, yeah? We've got everything here – crazy stuff, expensive stuff – you don't see that in other places. We got like big showrooms with cars you might not see anywhere else. Here and there you might see a nice car, but in Bradford, it's every day, they're everywhere. Like I go to Birmingham now and then but they're not a patch on what we got.... There are like Ferraris and Lambos

> and what not, but you don't see as much. (SH, 29, male, 15 November 2016)

Since the 1950s, however, the city has been also viewed through the lens of racial or ethnic difference.[35] This is not unusual, given that the city became home to largely, though not exclusively, South Asian-heritage communities from the late 1950s onward. Into the 1960s and beyond, a curiosity and a desire for insight into British postcolonial cultural life developed and took on different forms, including social science research. By the 1970s, this focus had shifted onto the discriminations that minority ethnic communities faced, but was nevertheless informed by the 'problem' or 'management' of ethnic minorities, a feature that remains consistent with contemporary academic, policy and public discourse.[36]

During the 1980s, a particularly working-class, but 'assertive' Muslim, minority ethnic identity became noticeable, principally through the Honeyford and Rushdie 'affairs'.[37] Unlike their parents, young British Muslims had been brought up in the UK, with some running the gauntlet of an educational system and a world of work in which discriminations were varied but normative. Although experiencing pernicious racism, young people in the 1980s had different levels of social and cultural capital, means through which their identities could become negotiated, actively projected and thus visible. At the time, the arguably schizophrenic practice of British multiculturalism acknowledged that although Britain's ethnic minorities could be protected from types of racism, state-led discrimination endured, with the removal of educational provision for non-English speakers and restrictive immigration legislation. A year before she became prime minister, Margaret Thatcher's response to immigration reveals the limitations of multicultural 'tolerance':

> If we went on as we are then, by the end of the century, there would be four million people of the new Commonwealth or Pakistan here. Now, that is an awful lot and I think it means that people are really rather afraid that this country might be rather swamped by people with a different culture.[38]

The 1990s saw the maturing of a significantly sized generation of British-born, Pakistani- and Muslim-heritage adults, who were already on the road to parenthood. Whereas first-generation migrant citizens had limited capacity to enhance their children's educational journeys, the second and especially third generations undertook parenting through blending British and Pakistani cultures. Today, this can be seen in all aspects of social life: religious, ethnic and cultural identities seamlessly merge into new and unique versions of Britishness through, for example, food,[39] fashion[40] and social spaces.[41] However, extracurricular religious education came to be seen as detrimental and as further evidence of living segregated and insular lives: the role of the mosque and madrasah, it was argued, not only undermined academic potential but helped isolate Muslim children from mainstream British culture. Some of the debate around such forms of religious education does bring into context the broader lack of effectiveness within mainstream educational infrastructure, but at the level of policy and discourse, this has since become another means through which an ethnic minority is deemed in need of remedy.[42]

In 1995, inner-city Bradford hit the news, and also fuelled research interest, when police heavy-handedness spilled over into what was purported to be ethnic riot.[43] Despite legislative prohibitions, direct, indirect and institutional forms of racism continued. In 1997, the Runnymede Trust published *Islamophobia: a Challenge for Us All*, outlining some of the avenues through which Muslims faced discrimination: media representation, racial violence, housing, education and criminal justice.[44] Also in 1997, the inquiry into the murder of Stephen Lawrence concluded, finding that institutional racism had been a key aspect of the police investigation into his death.

During the 1990s, there was also a growing concern around global Islamic terrorism with the rise of terrorist groups and networks. The events of 11 September 2001 in New York, and the 2001 riots (or 'disturbances') in the north of England, further shifted the ways in which minority ethnic groups were conceptualised and perceived.[45] In Bradford, the riots became yet another moment in which ethnicity helped define the city's identity. Explanations for the riots hinged on a failed multiculturalism, resulting in too much bonding capital and not enough bridging capital, which undermined community cohesion. These communities, therefore, were purported to live parallel, insular and self-segregating lives, becoming ever more ghettoised and exiled from 'white' society. Various reports[46] dwelled on this culturally deterministic logic, often discounting or diminishing the impact of white flight, social and economic stratification or even racism.[47] Faith identity became a perceived driver for cultural inertia: due to their faith, British Muslims in general had not progressed and integrated, rendering them at odds with whatever 'Britishness' was supposed to mean. If they had integrated more fully, then they would not riot or be predisposed to radical – often couched as anti-British or anti-democratic – thoughts and actions.

This understanding has now become embedded to the extent that it is fairly normative and common sense: in the spheres of employment, education and even housing, Muslims, and those who are merely perceived to be Muslim, face discriminations.[48] High-level reports, such as *The Casey Review: a Review Into Opportunity and Integration*, maintain investment in the 'community cohesion' deficits model as instrumental in enabling problematic cultures, or, indeed, differential outcomes.[49] Although the word 'assimilation' is rarely used, references to 'citizenship', 'belonging', 'loyalty' and 'Britishness' in relation to British Muslims appear frequently. Spikes in racially aggravated abuse, violence and crime are encountered whenever a (bad) 'Muslim' event – global or local – occurs. More generally, anti-Muslim discourse is ever-present:

> My husband, he listens to that XXXX Radio and they have some right nutters on there.... You should listen to it. Makes your ears burn.... Because they talk about Muslims not all the time, but a lot. Could be about female forced marriage, or grooming or terror.... And if you listen to it – I don't, but if my husband's driving, then I don't have any choice – if you listen to them, you can tell these people who phone are not right in the head.They are very angry people and they are very biased and happy to blame everything on Muslims or refugees or Africans or Eastern

> Europeans.… For Muslims, it's very depressing.… Every time there's a news story about terrorism or sex offending or something like that, I'm hoping, *please God, don't let it be one of us!* (NA, 31, female, 13 June 2017)

Today, Bradford remains diverse in terms of the ethnic, national and class-based heritage of its population.[50] While there are neighbourhoods with distinctive features and characteristics, including those that can be defined as inner-city 'zones of transition',[51] the city has more affluent areas, appealing to those with middle-class forms of social, cultural and economic capital. As would be expected, there is also diversity in terms of services and infrastructure, which in turn yields varying outcomes in education, healthcare and employment. The impacts of racial discrimination, such as economic and educational underachievement, have been supplanted by newer drivers and focal points for policy, including deradicalisation, social or community cohesion, and forms of integration seeking to resolve the purported failings of multiculturalism. This sits against an ordinary, unspectacular and everyday multiculture[52] that is the norm for many of us, but is less potent than racialised descriptions constructed through fear, threat and dangerous difference. Given the frequency of political rhetoric and commentary channelled through mass media, as well as the clichés and stereotypes, all of which continue to inform perceptions of Muslims, many feel a tangible sense of marginalisation and discrimination. Especially in cities where populations are ethnically diverse, there is now a fervent, but mundane, association between cars, young minority ethnic males and various forms of deviant, antisocial and unruly behaviours on the road.

Chapter outline

In Chapter 2, some detail on Bradford's recent social history develops a background against which later themes can be more usefully investigated. Here, links with sociological research in general, and ethnic relations in particular, add to this book's underpinnings. Some attention is also given to the methodological approach, specifically connecting with public sociology, ethnography and insider research.

In Chapter 3, the links between the car and popular culture are covered through a focus on a small selection of mass media, principally television programmes and popular music, although some mention of film as well as new modes of media consumption and production also features. Chapter 4 is driven by relevant theory, particularly Bourdieu's work relating to class, habitus and taste. Here, distinct car cultural practices are discussed within this conceptual space. Following this, Chapter 5 positions car culture as a mode of consumption and also production through various forms of creativity that appear significant on the car modification and enhancement scenes. Chapter 6 introduces additional theoretical insights into the behavioural dynamics between cars, their owners, other road users and observers. These themes feed into Chapter 7, which integrates racialised debates around cars, identity and behaviours. These narratives are fuelled and rehearsed through media reportage, in which criminality and race[53] become linked. The final chapter offers some alternative ways in which some elements of car culture might be co-opted to feature as positive aspects of the city's identity. This adds a practical layer of analysis in understanding how marginalised identities can instead be appreciated and valued. Throughout, field note segments as well as participant quotations add illustrative texture and insight.

TWO

Researching Bradford: putting the 'auto' into ethnography

PG: Can I ask you something.... Why are you doing this?
YA: What? Interviewing you?
PG: No, not just that. Why are you doing this stuff about cars and that?... What's the point?
YA: That is a good question. (PG, 18, male, 29 May 2017)

This chapter outlines the practice of ethnography before moving into some features of insider research. To begin with, however, it is worth situating ethnography within the sphere of public sociology, and the practice of qualitative social research more generally.

Public sociology through ethnography

The purview of social science has grown and reflects the nature of a world in flux, whether its focus is on global and local re-formations through migration, or on the extent to which political movements – marginal and mainstream – influence policy and social relations. At less ostensibly dramatic levels, there is also research that operates at the ground level. Gane and Back, for example, situate sociology with politics, 'craft', morality and professionalism.[1] One driver within their discussion is the need to shift the balance so that research becomes accessible and public, and can therefore reach out, influence and impact in real, lived ways. Similarly, Burawoy writes about a public sociology that ought to enable change through loops between researchers and their publics through inclusive and politically formed research orientations.[2]

The capacity to produce more innovative and 'mainstream' sociological work sits against the shape of funding structures with their priorities and agendas. For some, universities face compulsions toward the commercialisation of knowledge.[3] The spirit of public sociology, therefore, disrupts this drift into translating research into commercial equations. Research that underpins activist, partisan, critical and other forms of public sociology seems out of touch and, in its simplicity and quaintness, is no longer encouraged, even though that form of endeavour is consistent with what we expect universities to be: hopeful, interesting and curious. Here, ethnography is becoming a vital way of resisting, or at the very least accounting for, those forces that undermine intellectual and academic integrity; not only because it may create impact and change, whether in mindset, policy or cultural practice, but also because it can shed light on new, distinctive or taken-for-granted aspects of social and cultural life.

Ethnography taps into the everyday and unusual aspects of a particular culture's patterns, habits and traditions, and how these develop within the settings in which they appear.[4] However, ethnography was not always appreciated within sociology, and at times was perceived as a less serious, arguably less scientific and somewhat marginal endeavour.[5] This is certainly the case when compared with other, more detached and 'systematic',[6] approaches in which the use of subjectivity may be deemed problematic, in that it is perceived to produce biased data, for example.

One reason for ethnography's growing popularity is that it lends itself to the study of humans and their cultures, opening up an unending array of opportunities in which identity is central. Ethnographers need to be immersed in and involved and closely connected with their field of inquiry. It is both demanding and satisfying, adding further layers to its appeal; ethnographers tend to be quite passionate about their methodology and subject matter, in some cases advocating for, or siding with, their research participants.[7] As a result, it is entirely possible, and by no means a by-product, that the research may produce acquaintanceships and friendships that last beyond the formal life of a particular piece of research. In turn, this sense of being within a cultural formation helps us understand not only social and cultural processes in and of themselves, but also how they develop, vary and are rendered meaningful.[8]

So, ethnography is a qualitative methodology that is more interested in gaining textured, substantive and rich meaning than it is in generating numerical or statistical data; it pursues human motivation, experience and insight. A notable feature of ethnography is that it asks researchers to frame their interpretation, analysis and broader representations of their subject matter through combining the micro and the macro. Ethnographers zoom in, on ourselves: our relationships, patterns, habits and identities are all part of the scenes we aim to capture. From these small facets of social reality, we zoom out, framing them within broader historical, cultural and institutional spaces. Ethnographic projects, therefore, call for in-depth engagement with participants and a field, often over extended periods. In turn, this approach helps ensure that when we encounter and interact with participants' lives, we have greater opportunity to co-construct research processes and data *with* them, instead of conducting research *on* them,[9] thereby rebalancing power relationships between the researcher and the researched.

There are countless ethnographies available exploring all manner of cultures, including the far away, remote and exotic,[10] as well as the more familiar and ordinary.[11] Earlier works that helped establish and develop ethnography tended toward newly discovered cultures, in some cases couching them as exotic, primitive or savage.[12]

Like other methodologies, ethnography is subject to the ideological forces within which it operates, with current thought and practice benefiting considerably from postcolonial and indigenous research vantage points. When it comes to ethnographies done closer to home, in this case the UK, however, a sense of being remote, or different, may also apply, especially when ethnic/racial identity is a central feature of the subject matter. In the case of Bradford, some of its minority ethnic communities have been depicted as isolated, exotic and different.[13] Ultimately, research agendas are driven by a myriad of underpinnings and rationales, but some communities, and their repertoire of culture and identity, are worth investigating either because some 'good' or improvement will be achieved by the research itself, or because this is simply what researchers do. As the following interview segment shows, this is not always explicit, or consciously at the fore:

US: I know what you said, and I get it – like you know, people and what they do with their cars, and why people have certain cars and all that … for me, the racial element – you should write about that because no one talks about it or says anything.

YA: Well, yeah but–

US: No, no – it's good, man – a good thing.… But, for me, I don't properly, fully understand it.… I mean, I do but what I don't understand is what you get out of it? Why are you doing it? Me, I'm thinking, there's no point really, is there? Who cares? I can see there's more to it than only just cars but for me, from my point of view, they don't wanna know, do they? (US, 32, male, 23 October 2018)

Ethnography is one of those social science phrases that yields various meanings. For example, while ethnography refers to the process of research (including fieldwork), it is also a noun: we can 'do' ethnography, or we can 'read' an ethnography.[14] However, even among traditionally accepted and widely used forms of ethnography as methodology, there are no clear, rigid and universally agreed-upon boundaries, reflecting and reinforcing the view that 'the humans that do ethnography and the humans that are the subject of ethnographic research are too complicated and "messy" to allow ethnography to be understood in neat and simple terms'.[15]

Researchers inhabit spaces in which some form of exploitation takes place. Of course, this is not especially egregious or malicious, but researchers potentially stand to gain more, and lose less, than their subjects, certainly once the research is written up. At this point, and despite authorial responsibility resting with the author, the researched become portrayed and rendered open to wider readings. In some cases, therefore, ethnographers aim to ensure participants are given opportunities to take greater control and enact agency in the research endeavour. After all, in most traditional forms of research, there is a power relationship wherein one party carries more weight and produces greater impact than the other: crudely speaking, the researcher will design and drive research, while participants are sources of data. Usually, it is the researcher who does the fieldwork, the data selection, the analysis and the write-up. Responding to this, research participants can feed into the research process and outcomes, including ownership of the themes or issues that ought to be pursued.[16] Much of this depends on the ethnographer's skill set, confidence and experience; for some, hanging out and going with the flow might not seem like being in research mode but for others, it can be an important step in gaining access, eliciting trust, fostering openness and being there to notice phenomena as they occur. Ethnography, then, requires attributes that lie beyond a theoretical knowledge base: confidence in approaching strangers, striking up conversations, and being able to listen and thus identify what members of a culture, group or community find especially significant. Similarly, being 'open', 'flexible' and able to listen are attributes that need to be honed and, with other dispositions, coalesce to form an ethnographic identity.

Perhaps one of the most useful ways of looking at ethnography, however, is to approach it as a human and humanising system of inquiry that attracts researchers predisposed to engaging with other humans by taking into account, and responding to, the power-loaded arena of research. However, if ethnographers share elements of identity with the group being studied, there may be a deeper connection and responsibility not only to the integrity of the research itself, but also to those upon whom it is based.

Being inside, being subjective

A key aspect of ethnography is the extent to which the researcher's subjectivity informs the nature of the process (what activities are to be done; why, when and with whom) and the feel of any ethnographic texts that are produced. However, subjectivity can be perceived to be a mode through which weak, unscientific social science research is undertaken:

> There is an implied criticism of 'subjectivity' which is wearingly familiar and one that obscures the complex relationship between subjects, epistemology, politics and research. Being 'too subjective' or 'over-identified' with the research and respondents results in 'bad research' and self-indulgent texts.[17]

Research located within the realms of ethnic relations in particular has produced many researchers whose interest is acutely tied to their personal politics and identities. Here, because researcher identity is invested and located within chosen subjects, obtaining objectivity and impartiality seems inappropriate. However, subjectivity, partisanship and reflexivity can have positive impacts on the nature of the research relationships, and thus on the quality of the data. More generally, subjectivity sits quite comfortably within ethnographic principles and methodological considerations; part and parcel of the ethnographer's toolkit is a capacity to describe what is going on and how it might be explained. If ethnographers want to get insights into peoples' experiences and beliefs, there is no way of discounting their own position in interpreting what they see. The following extract reveals how some of the tendency toward favouring objectivity remains difficult to overcome, arguably because it is instilled into our psyches as a higher-order mode of interpretation:

I gave a lecture today on ethnography.... I mentioned my research and how I did it. That some of it involves simple things, like getting to know people, chatting with them, telling them about me, listening to their stories, holding and funnelling some of it. That the whole thing was a process and it was immersive and it meant being attentive and ready to think about what it is I'm seeing, taking part in, feeling or somehow experiencing.... Lots of researchers, outside of ethnography, are invested in their research area – some of them would even consider themselves as advocates, or representatives.

'What about objectivity?' [a student asked]

How are you supposed to remain objective if you're trying to experience the culture like its members experience it? And if you are from that culture or community or whatever, how are you supposed to be objective about that?... At the end of the session, a couple of students – ones who hadn't said a word throughout the lecture – came up to me:

'You know what, it doesn't seem real enough,' said one, adding, 'it's not like there's any maths in it.' (Field note, 1 December 2015)

One of the points raised here is the extent to which the ethnographer's identity remains a part of the process. The focus, therefore, should not be on how researcher identity can be detached, but that doing so would not serve any meaningful purpose – and may even be counterproductive. In short, there is little benefit in aiming for objectivity when engaging with the field is subjective, human and varied. In the process of ethnography, however, bias is a necessary framing device, one that can be woven into analysis, as it is in this text. The various layers of identity and the presence of subjectivity cannot be somehow removed from the endeavour, a point that will be further developed in due course.

Within ethnographic practice, various methods can be used, with observations and interviews often drawn upon. But even here, within these two categories, there is variety: interviewing can be structured, semi-structured and unstructured. Observing can be formalised within a specific research site (for example, in a workplace setting) or much more casual and ad hoc; in the case of this research, much of the observational data came through opportunistic and even unplanned events, as in the previous field note.[18]

In order to produce rounded and coherent texts, ethnographers describe, explain and translate social processes, characters and important moments captured in the field. During and beyond fieldwork, data are translated into texts; these texts, although complete and independent, remain closely tied to the research methodology that produced them. This brings us to how representation[19] – even the describing of a scene, for example – calls for imagination, creativity and the ability to communicate and be understood, all of which rely on subjective thinking. All representations, and therefore all forms of writing, are subjective; even writing in the hard sciences, whether about an experiment, a procedure or a diagnosis, cannot be produced without the subjective forces that result in unique authorial voices. Ethnographic accounts are crafted constructions that require modes of thought and writing, but are anchored in process and disposition, in which the ethnographer shares and takes part in the life of a culture.[20] Ethnography, then, can value subjectivity and the deep extent to which a researcher can, and often does, influence the shape and scope of the research. Just as importantly, ethnography can be seen as a socially and politically conscious approach, speaking to and from identity.

Not surprisingly, insider ethnographies have covered an array of identity- and marginality-related themes, including sexuality, gender, ethnicity and their intersections.[21] Here, the researcher's identity may be bound closely to the research rationale, process and outcomes. This becomes especially clear in how the researcher is perceived and engaged with by research participants. Furthermore, researcher identity becomes a component influencing the decisions made and the routes taken.[22] Sanghera and Thapar-Björkert's discussion, which makes reference to being (rather than going) 'native', is relevant here.[23] In some cases, those being researched may be 'reluctant and wary about speaking with strangers due to the climate of fear and suspicion'.[24] When it comes to car-related research within Bradford, this reluctance is real, but for two reasons. First, there is still a broader fear- and anxiety-loaded fixation with some ethnic 'Others'; this fixation is manifest in policy and public discourses in which security, crime, 'culture' and 'cohesion' are aligned with Muslims/Islam and minority ethnic groups[25] in general. Linked to this existing narrative, particularly at the local/Bradford level, are storylines that tie in antisocial, problematic and criminal behaviours with ethnicity, class, gender and the car. As a result, conveying an understanding of this context became fundamental in gaining access to, and trust with, participants.

Being claimed

Being an insider researcher can result in the boundaries between the personal and the professional becoming porous; you are a researcher, but you are also one of those being researched.[26] Here, there arise opportunities that help develop an acute sense of integration and involvement with what is encountered, and what initiated the research in the first place. This is more than research, then; this is part of who you think you are, as a social, cultural and political being. Acknowledging this too may have costs and implications, however:

> It does bug me a little.... I'm out there and talking to people about their cars and all that ... trying to convince them that I am genuinely interested in them – and especially what they've got to say about cars. I might see someone, or a car, that looks interesting. Light goes on in my head and I'm now *on* – in recruiting mode. I'll go up to them, offer a *Salaam* and then maybe say something to them about their car.... It's like I'm chatting them up, giving them compliments – and I'm nearly always genuine.... Not chatting them up: this is probably how people who 'groom' operate. So now I'm a car groomer.... Sometimes they even ask me what it's like working at a university. Some of them even say 'Ma sha Allah' [God has willed it; an expression of appreciation/happiness], like they're proud of me which I guess they might be – me being like them, but somehow breaking my way into a middle-class profession.... I wish they didn't claim me because now I'm a role model; now I'm a token, now I am the equivalent of magnolia. But you know what? All that's fine – it's the price of doing business. Problem is, there always comes a point ... where I have to remind them that I am also researching and that I will be writing about this, possibly about what they've got to say.... It does feel odd, forming these relationships ... in a natural and quite organic way, only for it all to be risked by a tape recorder. That's not quite right, either, though: these relationships were not formed naturally or organically; they came to feel like that, but the truth is, they were all predicated by the research. I know. I am being neurotic. If I was a social worker, I'd be calling myself reflective. (Field note, March 2016)

Most of this entry is probably based on a mild habit of being fixated about arguably minor aspects of research as process. However, within the extract, it's clear that first, ethnography can become layered with complexity and impact on the researcher and participants. Indeed, some participants' responding positively to my own biography ("Ma sha Allah") also indicates, as noted in the extract, a sense of ownership and claiming: while I am not their representative, it may be the case that they see me, relatively speaking, as successful and that elicits a sense of 'ethnic', class or even local pride. Conversely, however, this also chimes with the notion that minority ethnic academics are relatively rare, and even when they are present, regardless of their specialism or subject discipline, some can be 'seen as "responsible for race matters"'.[27] This is therefore another dimension of the insider researcher: they are perceived not only as an academic 'expert', but possibly also as an authentic, but credentialised, group representative, or even role model. This is further reinforced because ethnography allows for the professional and the personal to merge comfortably, and at times, unnoticeably:

> Seems I'm always on these days. Everything is data. Even when I'm at home, doing nothing 'ethnographic', along comes *Top Gear* and I start making notes about the cars that the presenters are fawning ... over: it's always one or the other with that show – they start with 'This is a piece of crap' and then, usually Clarkson, growls something like 'But it all makes sense when you press this button...'. And even when I'm on the road, on the way into work or back, usually rush hour, I see all manner of relevant stuff: private plates, tinted glass, custom paint jobs, big exhausts, whatever. But also weirder stuff, things people do when in their cars: people picking their noses, or bouncing around in their seats while listening to music, putting on make up, arguing, laughing, daydreaming. People even cry in their cars. Sometimes, that little metal box seems like the safest place on earth where you can do what you want, be who you want. How much of this stuff do I actually cover? I mean, where does this thing end? (Field note, September 2013)

This segment reflects on the scope of the research, but also shows the lack of a clear boundary between research and non-research moments. Without careful selection, the task of the ethnographer would be impossible. Being open to data is one thing, but this does not mean anything and everything *has* to be situated or explored. Similarly, how long fieldwork should last is a question that has no universally accepted answer. For some, anything from three months to two years could be acceptable.[28] However, for others, ethnographies are never really finished but remain tentative, fluid and in a process of becoming. This seems to be the case here: as noted already, the research started in 2011 and is, depending on opportunities that may arise, ongoing, but the fieldwork is now less intense, added to (through interaction, observation, interview and writing) only when something new, unusual or curiosity-inducing surfaces.

Insider ethnographers may have even more considerations, compromises, costs and benefits compared to researchers operating from more detached, less subjective vantage points. Within ethnography, the personal, political and professional merge: where the research comes from, its operationalisation and what good may come from it are all in the researcher's hands. This does not mean that all these aspects operate immediately or independently of each other. For most ethnographers, the broader approach is learnt, built upon, finessed and developed over time. Like most things in life, the more you do it, the better, and possibly easier, it becomes.

THREE

Communicating cars: television, popular music and everyday life

A salient aim of this chapter is to tune into lived cultural practice, focusing on how mediated and fictional cars are cultural reference points and become meaningful at the level of personal biography. This chapter therefore makes use of various popular cultural reference points (film, television, popular music and childhood play) in which the car is used and represented in specific ways to produce meaning and value, some of which is subsequently fed back into lived cultural practice. At the same time, cultural practice is discussed in relation to advertising and especially commodity fetishism, a system through which we consume objects in ways that reinforce our consumption. In order to add to and develop some of these points, however, it is necessary to discuss the salience of *representation*, particularly in the domain of mass media. Subsequently, how cars are used within hip-hop-oriented popular music and videos is explored. For many working-class youth cultures, hip-hop – regardless of its articulation and aesthetics[1] – features existentially, often cross-referencing and integrating the car, wherein articulations of power, identification and taste flow. Quotations, field notes and deconstruction of popular songs add to the analysis as it develops.

Media, representation and meaning

There is an abundance of academic inquiry attending to the processes within and impacts of mass media in relation to youth subcultures, whether defined according to class, ethnicity, gender or their intersections.[2] Research has also examined the extent to which certain ethnicities, when mediated, become hyper-visible, often couched as a feature within white-majority societies.[3]

Relevant to the many fields of mediated identities is representation, an 'essential part of the process by which meaning is produced and exchanged between members of a culture'.[4] Representation operates at literal and symbolic levels, with the former referring to how objects are described in concrete, rather than abstract, terms: book, car, house – in essence, all these words reference unambiguous, clear and usually shared meanings. Symbolism, however, occurs when one thing stands for, or symbolises, something else. Here, there may be no logical connection between the 'signifier' (a car) and the 'signified' (happiness). Symbolism, therefore, operates as figurative shorthand: a red rose may conjure notions of romantic love; swastikas suggest Nazism and racism as well as, conversely, punk rock. Similarly, a car in an urban setting means one thing; the same car shown by a beach connotes something else. Once a car is bought and consumed, such constructions are shored up or undermined depending on what the owner is aiming to signify. We can, for example, buy into, resist or subvert any symbolism that is presented to us through the subtlety of a number plate, bumper sticker or even more elaborate touches that perhaps aim to make the car unique to us.

While the cars that we consume through mass media are carefully constructed to grab the consumer's attention, the mediated reach is such that the associations within the representational cycle are just as weighty as the object being represented. How cars are interpreted, or read, is contingent on existing associations, often assisted through semiotic signs, or codes. These representations underpinning consumption help explain the ways in which the car is perceived and deployed in 'real life'.

No matter how outlandish the latest *Top Gear* 'adventure', how spectacular the most recent *Transporter* film or how extravagant a popular music video, signification occurs. How cars are framed, even in fictional or mediated texts, is a reflection of actual cultural practice and, conversely, helps cultural practice to evolve. This assertion shares some similarity with the long-standing debate, which extends beyond academic (news) media discourse, around the extent to which mass media reflect or change society, and whether they have the capacity to do either.[5] One way of understanding this is through a feedback loop: mass-mediated cars may be based on actual cultural practice, but their mediated representation may also influence the nature of social interactions. Clearly, the *Fast and Furious* feature films are fictional and 'unrealistic', but they connect with identity within the domains of subcultural car practice, and also in relation to gender, class, ethnicity and, encompassing all these, taste.[6]

Filmic representations are certainly important also, and were referenced frequently among participants. The following extract, while focused on a car that is probably less relevant to most personal histories, nevertheless holds some emotional detail that could apply to many of us:

> The Batmobile in that first Batman film, the one with the Beetlejuice guy in it … that was my first car crush if you like. I used to have dreams about that car.… I must have been about ten when it came out.… I watched that film, I don't know, probably hundreds of times.… It was a big deal back then but for me it was because of the car. I mean, it looked amazing … it looked like something else. Had these big wings on the back … and these massive wheels and it was long and sleek and it was really aggressive looking, with like a big round turbine induction thing on the front; looked mean, you know.… (YK, 36, male, 23 July 2015)

This interview, conducted with a self-confessed car 'fanatic', was one of several in which childhood relationships with and understandings of cars featured as formative. YK illustrates how even fictional cars may help develop what become normative understandings of aesthetics, function and aspiration. This particular incarnation of the Batmobile was located in a dark, gothic and, albeit darkly and comically so, cinematic Gotham City.[7] The Batmobile was spectacular, perhaps 'magical',[8] and signified a range of meanings; loaded with gadgets, it was big, powerful and dark and looked "aggressive", a matter that was probed further:

YK: Cos it looks good; even like proper, production cars, a lot of them, it's about how they stand – what they look like from different angles and all that. Like some cars, they look really aggressive – don't say they don't, because they do.... Audis, Fords, Vauxhalls, Jap cars – not even the sports version ones; a lot of cars, they look strong; just the way they're designed.... In the 1920s and 1930s, you had these great big sports cars – they weren't aerodynamic, but they were ripped; like they had muscles, you know.... But like modern cars, even ordinary cars, nowadays especially, they've become a bit more sharp in design ... they're very solid looking and they look clean and sharp ... maybe because we want a car that looks strong. Maybe people think that's a good thing....

YA: So, and that's what the Batmobile was about, then.

YK: Well, I mean, if you're Batman, then yeah. I mean, anything goes for that guy – he's Bruce Wayne, bloody billionaire and all that.

YA: Not everybody's got money, though. Not everyone's Bruce Wayne.

YK: No one's Bruce Wayne.... You're missing the point, Bro – when I watched that film, I knew it wasn't real.... When you're a kid you think that – I mean, when you're a kid, you believe that you could have that with your car.... You could make your car special like that and that's what'd make you special. You could make it look how you wanted it to look....

YK talked about the toy cars of his childhood, most of which were designed to look powerful and exciting. As he grew older, he had more sophisticated toys, including remote-control stunt cars as well as one toy designed to withstand high-speed collisions. His take on the fictional and toy cars of his childhood especially, however, offers insights into how children may react to, and with, what is encountered through forms of primary and secondary socialisation; play, media and family all help instil within us who we think we are, and part of that involves what we come to see as normative. This is not to say that we grow up believing we can own a Batmobile, but even comparatively exotic sports and prestige cars are depicted as important, status-enhancing and valuable, thus helping to frame value, success and aspiration. In adulthood, while tapping into desires to be seen as distinctive, unique and special, such fictional, out-of-reach and 'magical' cars simultaneously represent the fantastic and the possible.

As will be explored in due course, however, there are some whose relationships with cars are rich, unique and creative, and at times even resist mainstream modes of consumption. While those with insufficient economic capacity may not be able to afford the kinds of cars they may have dreamt of, or even played with, as children, they can still take part in a car culture that is loaded with collaborative, participatory and appreciative practice; car modification scenes, not only in Bradford, are examples of class-cultural creative endeavour, but play out in broader discourse as dangerous, antisocial or even criminal (see Chapters 5 and 7).

Commodity fetishism

Contemporary mass-mediated representations of cars cannot be detached from the real world. Rather than being meaningless incidental props, they hold ideas, values and symbols, referencing the worlds we inhabit, producing a mainstream, normalised and hegemonic embedding of car culture, or 'system of automobility'.[9] Some cars are therefore situated as desirable commodities to be appreciated and privileged and, in various ways, feed into what amounts to 'compulsory consumption'.[10] Here, it is useful to link in with the concept of commodity fetishism operating in a world defined and realised through processes of consumption, thereby involving advertising, mass media and the continual renewal of desire:

LG: It is ridiculous, if you think about it.... Most people do this: they always change their cars because, because why? They don't need to, do they?... But they think buying a car, it's an exciting thing to do and it'll make them happy.... Back when you were younger, I bet you didn't change your car every three years.

YA: Drove them until they died.
LG: Because it was just a car, then.... It's more than a car, now. It's you.... But most people, these days, they do change.... For no reason: just fancy a change.... It's not that – it's the done thing.
YA: Sort of standard practice.
LG: Standard practice now. And they don't just go like-for-like.... No, they'll upgrade.... It has to be something better as in comparison to what they're driving now.... Like start off with a standard A3 then jump to an S Line A3. Then S Line A3 to, I dunno, a Mercedes Benz, and then three years later, Mercedes to a newer Mercedes. It never ends, does it? (LG, 30, male, 17 February 2019)

Commodity fetishism, developed by Marx in *Capital*,[11] refers in part to a sense of 'collective amnesia', alluding to how consumers may have little appreciation or understanding of the processes and costs contributing to an object's production.[12] This in turn helps produce alienation within ourselves, between us and the things we make or labour over.[13] In the realm of the things we make and consume, however, when defined by intrinsic use value, a produced object remains ordinary. A table, for example, requires wood to be chopped, sawn, treated and otherwise laboured over in its manufacture before being sold and subsequently used for what it is. As a result, 'the table continues to be that common, every-day thing, wood. But, so soon as it steps forth as a commodity, it is changed into something transcendent'. Here, commodities are imbued with 'metaphysical subtleties and theological niceties', replete with qualities beyond themselves: a table is not only a table; it is now a commodity that can be exchanged and valued extrinsically, from beyond itself, and can include references to quality, design and taste as well as age or 'vintage'. More importantly, commodities become removed from their conditions of production, particularly labour, 'the expenditure of human brain, nerves, muscles'.[14]

Within capitalism, then, the human processes within the production of commodities are diminished, or even eradicated. We therefore make a fetish of commodities, seeing them as simply financial entities, ends unto themselves, without recognising labour's role in their creation. Because our belief and investment lies in the power and centrality of commodities, and thus capitalism, we become alienated from each other and our labour. In order to maintain this, we continue to consume. Commodity fetishism operates ideologically, keeping us locked into a system in which those who endure exploitation also collude in its creation and maintenance. Because of our faith in the *value* (which is not the same thing as 'price') of commodities, our understanding of the world becomes increasingly economic, not human, in orientation.

Manufactured goods have their own processes of production and distribution within capitalism: labour, raw materials and so on result in a final net cost to the producer. At this point, exchange value (what a commodity *seems* to be worth) overpowers use value (what an object *is* worth in terms of economic cost and utility). Perceiving commodities for what they are, not how they *become*, therefore, replicates in all social relations so that, ultimately, we weigh and value each other's worth through the universal currency of exchange within capitalism: money. This is 'fetishism' because we buy into and co-create a system of belief in which some commodities are prioritised over others; thus results a hierarchy of value. Adam Smith's example of a diamond being worth more than fresh water is helpful here;[15] a diamond, aside from being hard, has no intrinsic value in terms of its usefulness, other than the uses we have made for it, which in turn have made it highly valuable. Of course, diamonds are supposedly rare, but rarity alone does not explain value. Water, however, is not valuable, but only when it is in abundance. Diamonds, however, became valuable through marketing élan and innovation: they are valuable because we believe they are valuable, and that is because we are told as much. Their value, therefore, is linked with a symbolic and representational worth that transcends their use value:

> Value, therefore, does not stalk about with a label describing what it is. It is value, rather, that converts every product into a social hieroglyphic. Later on, we try to decipher the hieroglyphic, to get behind

> the secret of our own social products; for to stamp an object of utility as a value, is just as much a social product as language.[16]

Exchange value in particular can be explained when desire, happiness and enjoyment[17] are present in the realm of advertising, an important component of and within capitalism. Here, we see fun, or happiness associated with the consumption of commodities. Happiness is aspirational but, ultimately, doomed to remain unrealised and beyond us, no matter how much, or what, we consume:

> The Nike brand, for example, promises all sorts of amazing experiences and enjoyments when one buys a pair of one of their latest trainers. Yet, once bought, we realize that we cannot jump quite as high as 'Air Jordan' or play golf as skillfully as Tiger Woods. The symbolic regime of the Other is thus always lacking, which, however, does not prevent us from desiring and believing in it.[18]

Commodity fetishism also refers to particular attributes being loaded onto commodities, extending their value beyond concrete worth, or actual monetary price. Somehow, like the diamond, some commodities become over-valued. There are other vantage points from which the same social phenomena are explained; for example, Veblen examines the conspicuous consumption of 'status symbols', or rare 'positional' goods that enhance 'social status'.[19] Consumption, then, is not due to neat economic, arguably rational, formulae being in play. Rather, commodities help enhance our presentation of self[20] in ways that go beyond their 'prop' utility, and can further tap into manifestations of taste (see Chapter 4).

When it comes to cars and other forms of motorised personal transport, they are couched as either 'magical' or 'mundane',[21] or sometimes both; they are represented as extraordinary or ordinary objects worth having. In advertising, this works by stimulating a cycle of persuasion for commodities among consumers. This involves advertisers showing us that we need a certain commodity in order to become happy, complete or better, or merely to satisfy some amorphous sense of *desire*; we know we need something to feel more fulfilled, and maybe a big screen TV will do it. We may literally buy into the premise of the advert through enacting *consumption*, but we soon find there is still a void. Our lives are not noticeably better: we do not have more friends because we are chewing a certain gum; a new car has not brought bliss. We end up lapsing into a phase of *disillusionment*, which is temporarily resolved through a *renewed desire* to consume a different commodity. The stages of desire, consumption, disillusionment and renewed desire continually revive themselves, and thus keep us invested in capitalism.[22]

Alongside these aspects of commodity fetishism, there is also an element of superstition whereby the objects we consume somehow make us a bit more special: using a certain brand means something to us and often to others, who may notice and interpret our consumption, thereby interpreting us. This is one way of seeing superstition operating within commodity fetishism; something supernatural, illogical and not even necessarily coherent happens before, during and after a commodity is even temporarily consumed:

Drove a Bentley today.... Drove it and I wish I hadn't.... I'm no petrol head – I say that all the time – but that thing showed me something else, something about myself that I'm not sure I really knew before.... When you slide (*Slide*? When do I ever say 'slide'?) behind the steering wheel of a car like that, you realise it's more than a car, even though, ultimately, you know it's still just a car.... Sitting in the thing feels special. Different. Starting it up and then driving the thing makes you feel special. Different. Better, somehow. More.... And I felt ... big. I hate to say it, but I felt important. That's how it made me feel; like things didn't get much better than this. I only drove it; not like I bought it. I couldn't even afford to pay the insurance on that thing, but for those brief minutes ... it felt like I was in control – and I'm not just talking about the car. (Field note, 26 April 2014)

This extract, while picking up the thrill of driving such a car, also makes explicit reference to something that transcended the immediacy of emotion. However, nothing of material consequence had changed, yet simply driving this car temporarily altered a sense of self: the car did elicit a sense of power and control. Again, this was not even a 'test' drive, but rather an opportunity presented by a participant (a motor trader), who thought his interviewer might benefit from the experience. Despite the ownership of this car not being remotely possible, behaviours nevertheless tuned into a frequency in which both driver and car communicated with, and beyond, each other. 'Superstition', therefore, seeps into the realm of signification; ownership of a Bentley would probably denote relative wealth and arguably power, at least in strict economic terms. However, the same connection between individual and object may also imply a certain taste, through *connoting* an appreciation of design, motoring heritage, speed, handling and luxury. All of this adds to an individual's identity, even though possible connotative inferences are not based on any corroborating evidence whatsoever, but instead rely on the presence of consumer and object, ready to be rehearsed and read. Such cars therefore produce overwhelming information that usually leads to a narrow range of interpretations (see Chapters 6 and 7).

Cars in the frame

When traditional television is scanned for car-related programming, there is an abundance of content, varying in niche, style and purpose. Masculinity, however, runs through car-related media output, with shows such as *Monster Garage* and others representing 'a nostalgic desire for traditional masculine identities'.[23] Similarly, regardless of changes in personnel, *Top Gear* remains a programme that celebrates speed, power and design, and in so doing speaks from and possibly to a particular male psyche.

Several car shows are syndicated and broadcast all over the world, and even those that are no longer in production remain accessible online: episodes of *The Garage*, *For the Love of Cars*, *Britain's Worst Driver*, *Barely Legal Drivers*, *Fastest Car*, *Fifth Gear*,

Where to, Britain?, *Top Gear* and *The Grand Tour* are not too difficult to locate. Given the volume of such output, the car provides an opportunity for TV producers to populate schedules, most of which are already brimming with programming that helps keep viewers distracted and content.[24] Within the mix of programming, quasi-documentaries employ the 'makeover' angle (*Chop Shop: London Garage*, *Overhaulin'*, *Fast n' Loud*); others demonstrate how cars can be bought and sold for profit (*Wheeler Dealers*, *Flipping Bangers*, *Chasing Classic Cars*); while some help 'save' or restore cars, and sometimes their owners, through the benevolence of the shows' producers, who decide to repair and/or recreate a previously decrepit vehicle (*Classic Car Rescue*, *Pimp My Ride*).

Chop Shop: London Garage

Many of those interviewed, particularly males, were familiar with the now defunct *Chop Shop: London Garage*, featuring designer/fabricator 'Leepu' Nizamuddin Awlia and Bernie Fineman, reputedly a mechanic for the Kray Twins in his younger days. *Chop Shop* initially ran for two seasons (2007–08) on the Discovery Channel, with cars being so radically modified from their original donor vehicles that they became virtually unrecognisable. Many males consume such programming, but females also engaged, in a different way, with motoring media:

> I'll watch like *Top Gear*, but that's because it's funny.... Jeremy Clarkson, I didn't really like him, but he was sort of funny. But the new presenters, they're different and they're better.... No women on it and I'd have thought they'd have done that this time. They have that lady German racing driver on it, though, so I suppose that's good – you know, she's a wicked driver and she's ruthless, isn't she? My brother watches anything and everything.... I don't go out of my way to watch stuff about cars. Too busy doing other stuff! (AT, 19, female, 23 March 2018)

Chop Shop demonstrates, in very stark ways, how different elements within a mass, largely male, audience may react to what they are seeing. Many segments from this show are available online, most of which have user comments. Comments from one episode segment include: 'you don't do that to an [sic] BMW! Idiots!'; 'Shitty designs. Lacks creativity and originality'; and 'it WAS very nice till they got their hands on it. now it looks like an indian joke that only indians understand'. There are, however, a small number of more positive reviews: 'love the show, top stuff'; 'Nice work :-)'; and 'chop shop aceally [sic] makes BMW cars look nice'.[25]

Among the noise of user and viewer comments, some reference race or nation but many appear offended, often referencing a lack of taste, creativity or general worthiness, with some lamenting the destruction of the original object. For this category of comment, commitment to original design purity seems significant, but more importantly, such commentary is located through class-based appreciations of taste and creativity,[26] a point reinforced by DC, for example:

> They made this little monster that ran on bio [biodiesel] and that looked really bad. But they did a Saab, a Beemer, Golf and those were good. Different – out there, a bit. Like you get done up cars, but not like that.... Mate: I'd love one of those cars – the Golf; didn't even look like a Golf in the end. (DC, 23, male, 5 August 2013)

Those who consider themselves to be working class (in economic terms) were appreciative of *Chop Shop*'s endeavours, whereas those who were of professional, economically successful backgrounds (ostensibly, perhaps, middle class), were less favourable in their reviews. Compare DC's view with that of AP, a 40-year-old, self-employed businessman who drives an unadulterated, modern BMW saloon:

> I do watch, only now and then. Not regular viewer you might say. But you see, what I don't like in this is the way they ruin these cars. Okay, some are already ruined and so on, so why not? *But dekho na, changee pahlee gadee, yaar* – and look what they do – *uss kee thabayee karnay kee kohee fahidaa nahee* [but look, perfectly good car, mate – and they

> destroy it for no benefit]. Look at it: it doesn't look nice. (AP, 40, male, 24 October 2014)

AP went on to bridge the gap between media content and what he saw on the roads of Bradford, adding, "You see young men, they like to do this way. They look like joke, no? I don't like this what they do. No value left and who will drive this thing? *Bkwaass*: rubbish."

These distinctions in taste also operate through practice, with middle-class car owners tending not to modify cars, whereas, subject to economic capacity, working-class owners may improve or enhance their vehicles. Recognising its opposite, each class position engages in a performance of self through devaluing the other, and this too is a significant element in the construction and maintenance of identity, not just in relation to cars (see Chapter 4).

Top Gear

While shows like *Chop Shop* may not have a universally positive following, *Top Gear* has mainstream success and appeal. Originally a consumer-oriented review show, *Top Gear* ran from 1977 until 2001, with features on technology, fuel economy and motorsport, but, as the series progressed, reviewed cars that a mainstream audience were likely to buy. In the original *Top Gear*, cars took primacy over the personality of the presenters. Certainly into the 1980s, this was a less dramatic and arguably more helpful programme aimed at educating and informing, rather than entertaining its audiences through presenter adventures, escapades and hyperbole, as well as the occasional racist utterance.[27] Operating in a different media context, the show was relaunched in 2002, departing from arguably dry and factual material that was unlikely to stimulate appeal beyond a marginal motoring-interest audience.

A typical episode of the relaunched *Top Gear* is not overwhelmed by the presence of everyday cars, but often features expensive and usually fast vehicles (including supercars, hypercars and top-of-the-range performance cars), despite the fact that such cars make up a small proportion of car sales even globally. Occasionally, the presenters undertake challenges: racing budget supercars to the North Pole; constructing amphibious cars; making limousines; and so on. Once the presenters and their vehicles are in place, the hilarity ensues, with all manner of japes and pranks, some less puerile than others. *Top Gear* is not, therefore, a show that consistently provides guidance, information or even useful insights into ordinary motoring. However, such shows do provide a platform on which some cars and some behaviours are privileged over others. Although rarely do the presenters explicitly promote dangerous, let alone illegal driving, the challenges and adventures weave into the fabric of the show a celebration of horsepower, handling and speed. Indeed, cars are tested mainly under these categories, with limited commentary on the cost of the vehicles – for the majority of the audience, these cars are, at best, perhaps aspiration:

FI: Most lads I know, and lasses actually, they do watch *Top Gear*.... It is, it is good – they do have some serious cars, don't they?
YA: Anything that you would own?
FI: If I had the money, course I would.... Realistically, let's be honest, no chance!
YA: So what's good about it? Why's it appealing?
FI: It's well made, exciting and it's funny.... It's not real so it's like, I dunno, meant to be entertaining.
YA: Well, yes, it's called factual programming.
FI: It might be, but it's not realistic enough. I'll watch it and then with mates or whatever say *did you watch it*, but you do that when you watch *Game of Thrones*, you get me?
YA: Oh, right: see what you mean.
FI: And all, not all – most cars they have [on *Top Gear*], they are sort of rare aren't they?
YA: And they're expensive.
FI: Yeah, but they test them on a track, drive as if they've nicked them, and no one else would ever do that, would they? That's what I mean.
YA: Because it's for entertainment, right?

FI: I suppose so, yeah. But to be truthful, I prefer the *Pimp My Ride*, *English Garage*, *Chop Shop* kind of show. Get more out of them.

YA: Because they're more real?

FI: Yeah, they are, even though it's still only TV. (FI, 21, male, 23 July 2017)

FI, a car enthusiast and amateur/hobbyist mechanic, offers useful insight into levels of media literacy, and the footings upon which successful programming operates: *Top Gear* blends the 'factual' with entertainment, resulting in output that has a strong sense of identity and reach. With creative use of editing, sound mixing and voiceover, viewers are channelled speed, emotion and pleasure seamlessly. Consequently, as with fictional and non-factual programming, viewers are prepared to 'suspend disbelief'. Shows like *Chop Shop*, however, are equally important, though less successful, due to their niche thematic scope. However, in the case of *Chop Shop*, the capacity to "get more out of them" (design and problem-solving instances) appeals to viewers with more practical interests.

Much of the television output relating to cars, therefore, is based principally on being able to maintain audience interest and viewing through offering spectacular, rather than ordinary, motoring narratives. In many cases, the cars we see through such media are beyond our reach, either because they are very expensive or because they have been restored, enhanced or modified to such a level that they are truly unique. This does not, of course, mean that segments of audiences necessarily ape these mediated, quasi-factual representations of cars and car culture in their own lives. However, through such media output, we certainly gain insights into what is possible, and in some cases, we may respond with our own interpretations and practices with our cars, and on the roads.

The hip-hop connection

During the latter part of the 20th century, most luxury, exotic and prestige cars remained within the domain of elite social classes and, occasionally, celebrities, overnight millionaires and captains of industry. This is no longer the case, and it is therefore worth exploring how and why the mainstreaming of elite cars might have happened. This following field note covers some of this through reflecting on bumping into an old acquaintance in a supermarket car park:

Soon enough, we start talking cars – everyone has a view when it comes to cars; it's the sociological gift that just keeps on giving:

'These young ones these days, don't know they're born, thinking they're all that, driving around in cars on HP, hiring them out … driving cars that their dads buy them, not even insured … different when we were kids … we were stuck with our dads' battered old Jap estates….'

He may be right about that, generally speaking – I mean, the first car I drove when I passed my test was my dad's – an old Datsun 140J; yellow, except for the blue passenger side wing and the rust on the driver's door. But that was a different time, and a different context – socially, economically and culturally. He tells me he didn't even dare dream of having anything that was out of his reach. Some bits of his rant, it's not a million miles away from the 'Four Yorkshiremen' sketch.

'Everything that we knew that was impossible, for youngsters today, for them it is possible. Kids these days, they're deluded. They live in bubbles…. When we were kids, we didn't think we'd be like superstars or millionaires or driving around in fifty grand cars but this lot, they do. They actually do.'

Usually, people blame themselves; we, as parents, we did a bad job of raising our kids; we didn't discipline them firmly enough, or we were too keen to be their friends or we just messed it all up by giving them what they wanted; too many burgers and not enough salads; too much Playstation and not enough homework. But, not this guy. No, for him, it's one thing:

'Hip-hop: you seen the videos – half-naked women … big cars with the big alloys, all that bling and drugs and thug life…. Our youngsters, there's the role models they see. That's what they see so they go after it.'

I make a face that tells him I'm not convinced.

'It is. You've seen the videos – rappers driving customised Rollers and Bentleys and Porsches and…. Once upon a time, like only royalty drove them sorts of cars. This lot, they think, if rappers can own them, anyone can.' (Field note, 8 August 2016)

The range of music videos in which the car appears as status symbol, adornment, or object of mystique and desire grows on a daily basis. Older participants cited this as a potent channel through which identities are formed and framed by images, and ideals, of masculinity and femininity. Here, especially younger consumers were perceived as less able, or less willing, to make distinctions between fantasy and reality. Therefore, they were more prone to integrating lifestyle messages and images into their own renderings of identity; clothing, language and attitude were mirroring content encountered in film, advertising, digital social networks and especially song. Miller, however, challenges this: 'Rather than seeing consumers as the merely passive end point of economic activity, I argue that they actively transform the world. They too see both the negative and positive consequences of consumption and have their own critiques.'[28]

For NP, and many others in the sample who had modified their cars in minor or major ways, critique is in and on their cars:

YA: So what sort of stuff have you had done?
NP: Nothing big, you know no massive things but subtle; I like, like little subtle touches.
YA: Be honest, I couldn't even tell.
NP: That's right, you can't because it's subtle.... Badges and that, dechromed; decatted – obviously can't see that; interior and so far, remap.
YA: Okay. Like you said, subtle. Question is, why?
NP: ... It's like if you move into a new house, you'll change things – carpets, furniture, wallpaper and everything. It's like that. You make it yours. You put your stamp on it.... Why isn't it important? We do it with our homes so cars, why not? (NP, 25, male, 12 June 2017)

This using and appropriating of artefacts, often resulting in new meaning, is a vital component within the study of car culture, particularly, though not exclusively, at subcultural levels. Indeed, even in the now apparently passé, 'over-determined' 'subculture theory' moment,[29] elements of subculture are appropriated, occasionally accompanied and aided by processes of sanitisation (marketing) by traditional mainstreams within capitalism, often with little or no resistance.

Some of the lived cultural practices evident in Bradford, and no doubt many other cities, are associated with diffuse, wide-ranging and ever-evolving hip-hop culture, which, over at least four decades or so, has influenced material and non-material popular culture, globally and locally.[30] Indeed, what started out as a counter-hegemonic, working-class African American (sub)culture now influences popular music (including its production), art, dress, language and even the poetics of mainstream political discourse.[31]

Alongside distinctiveness developed through national and ethnic cultural contexts and practices, hip-hop has grown to such an extent that it is no longer only subcultural, or only mainstream. Commercially successful hip-hop today may be defined principally by practices and modalities of creativity that neglect the politics of race into which it was born, but in the 1970s, black bodies, voices and lives really did not matter – and this is not just a comment on the current prevalence of hashtags and the uptake of social networks as catalysts for social change. Hip-hop evolved as a response to a broad social experience that was defined through an interrelated economic, political and cultural marginalisation of blackness.[32] As a popular cultural idea, process and product, hip-hop is defined by contradiction and fluidity, and therefore maintains commercial, creative and political orientations simultaneously; for every Sean Combs/P. Diddy, there is, hopefully, at least one Chuck D.

Hip-hop may have enabled more confident, assertive and positive expressions of blackness, but black popular culture continues to be built on a repository of moments where definitions and perceptions are tied to racist readings of black identity. Despite 'progress' and debates about the possibility of a post-racial society,[33] African Americans continue to be disproportionately criminalised and institutionalised.[34] As a systemic, institutional feature of racialised societies, this can be seen in those mass media that serve to inform and entertain,[35] with output remaining particularly racist in relation to news media also.[36]

Like working-class car cultures, hip-hop culture is built on a range of arguably postmodern but subcultural processes of appropriation, excorporation and bricolage.[37] In hip-hop, we see this in the production of music (turntablism, sampling, backspinning and scratching), in dress (sportswear as fashionwear) and in language, elements of which transition from marginality to mainstream and vice versa. With car culture, we see similar patterns and shapes: alloy wheels, designed for Porsche models, find themselves on Mark 2 VW Golfs; exhaust systems being de- and reconstructed in order to create new and distinctive notes; and, of course, parts from other cars being either copied or simply fitted to cars for which they were not originally designed.

When artefacts are taken from mainstream culture and used in ways for which they were not initially intended,[38] conversations and tensions involving taste and cultural appropriation come to the fore. This is not surprising, given the extent to which ethnicity, class and popular culture are interconnected. Drawing on the work of Bourdieu, specifically in relation to class and power, Fiske notes, 'We understand proletarian culture to be a form of popular culture – that produced by a people subordinated by class in a capitalist society'.[39] Here, claims of authenticity and the ownership of products and ideas are inherently political in their premise. Class, race and taste swirl to form a helix in which appropriated artefacts are read with particular meaning and value:

> The heavy winter boots as year-round attire flowed out of their use by crack dealers clocking on corners. In the tradition of appropriation that is integral to the scene, Timberland boots – high-quality footwear – worn by folks in New England and the Midwest for decades – suddenly became official urban style.[40]

Here, George refers to a Timberland boot, sales of which increased due partly to increased exposure through hip-hop. If the brand was not lyrically referenced in the songs, Timberlands were worn in accompanying music videos. However, hip-hop artists carried Timberland into their creativity because the footwear was worn by black urban youth, and thus held an air of street authenticity and credibility. But these urban youths were themselves appropriating a boot in order to produce fashion. In this example, a particular object with a specific market becomes appropriated by a new type of consumer, whose mode of consumption is radically different to that which preceded it. In turn, this subcultural appropriation of a mainstream product becomes further appropriated by artists, who then, perhaps inadvertently, 're-mainstream' the product, with the newer mode of consumption becoming as normative as the one that was originally favoured.

By the early 1990s, other mainstream, but often niche or 'designer' brands had been appropriated by hip-hop artists.[41] The associational power of the new modality of consumption may have been a threat to Timberland's brand identity and reputation, which, of course, was built on a consumer base wherein its products were associated with particular values and principles. Timberland's contemporary marketing materials suggest consumers are capable of buying into whichever series of associations exist, whether transmitted by lived cultural practice or projected through marketing campaigns. A construction worker, a shooting and hunting hobbyist and a hip-hop fan may all own the same style of boot, but consume it in a way that resonates with their social class, cultural habitus and status.[42]

There are probably thousands of songs, and indeed 'compositions',[43] that could be included in this chapter. The car features in popular music stretching back to the early days of recorded rock 'n' roll.[44] Some are frequently cited, within mainstream media,[45] as significant for whatever reason, whereas others have been explored by scholars. Rosenbaum and Prinsky, for example, discuss in part 'Little Red Corvette' by Prince, a song that they interpret as a metaphor for the female body.[46] Meanwhile, Portelli's richly layered text exploring Bruce Springsteen's music offers insights around the car, class and gender.[47] Brodsky's work, however, includes various lists, one of which is 'The 100 Greatest Car Songs', compiled on the bases of popularity, subject matter and whether automotive references appeared in the lyrics, 'as DJ Cup [the list compiler] claims that composers who have grease under their fingernails generally write a better car song'.[48] Even here, in the process of ranking songs about cars, judgements about worthiness become linked to notions of authenticity, with the songwriter's car credentials factoring into the evaluation.

There are other popular music genres where the car is also present (including rock, country and blues), but given its dominance and popularity,[49] it seems appropriate to focus on the ways in which the car is used within hip-hop music culture; particularly in relation to 'performance' (song lyrics and especially their accompanying music videos). This section, therefore, unpicks four songs, two originating from the US and two from the UK.

'German Whip'

One of the music videos accompanying the song 'German Whip' has, at the time of writing, close to 11.5 million views on youtube.com.[50] Released in 2013, the song inspired a number of parodies and remixes, and a special recording in which the actor Hugh Jackman performs with some of the original artists.[51] 'German Whip' is something close to a (UK hip-hop) music 'standard'. Given the scope of this text, it is neither necessary nor possible to offer an in-depth qualification of what Bramwell calls 'UK' hip-hop.[52] However, it is sufficient to note that popular musical genres are now, more than ever, hybrid, fluid and reliant on other traditions and forms. As such, such genres are subject to interpretation and claims of ownership. 'German Whip' is no different, in that it sits within the (sub)genre of 'grime', itself a formation that has been influenced by hip-hop and reggae. The song's lyrics outline the prestige associated with German-manufactured cars as well as what such cars can symbolise for usually male, urban youth in mundane, normative and everyday contexts. 'Whip' has an interesting, although arguably contentious, origin, including, for example, the usage of the word during early phases of automobility; the whip controlled horse-drawn carriages, but the steering wheel controlled the car – the word 'whip', apparently, became analogous with the steering wheel. Through whatever means, however, the synonym was then revitalised in the 1990s, when 'whip' came to stand for, specifically, prestige-model Mercedes Benz cars.[53] Today, however, 'whip' refers to any prestige, exotic or expensive car.

The song itself has three rhyming verses, bridged with a repeated chorus/hook section. The music video opens with Meridian Dan walking down a street, carrying a small fuel container. He opens the fuel flap of his car, a Ford Ka hatchback, pours in the fuel and then tries, but fails, to start the car. Playback begins: Meridian Dan leans back in the driver's seat, sighs and covers his eyes in frustration. We are transported into his daydream, where the 'German Whip' is regaled. Meridian Dan is now behind the wheel of a high-end, AMG Mercedes Benz coupe. He raps as he drives; there is some intercutting with other scenes (inner-city, urban settings), but the car is visible in much of this segment. The second verse is performed by Big H, also shown driving the same car. The third verse, performed by JME, begins once we are in the second half of the video, when all three artists are located in an innocuous urban car park setting, performing in front of two equally impressive and status-affirming cars: a BMW X6 and an Audi RS8.

Throughout, the visuals seem appropriate and connected with the song's subject matter. However, the lyrical content and the visuals can be located within the prism of representation,[54] in which economic success, wealth and, of course, power are signified. Read more carefully, those scenes that show the artists, and the cars, in what appear to be inner-city spaces may produce juxtaposition, or mismatch, between car and location: expensive cars in economically 'deprived'-looking neighbourhoods may seem out of place. This interpretation, however, is only coherent if the video is read without the benefit of local, insider and existential connections; if such videos are read as incoherent, then they are read by those who inhabit different cultural spaces. There is of course a further, complementary aspect of disjointedness, in that such cars are being driven and celebrated by young black males. In stark economic terms, what we see and what we hear should not fit together, even though young black men driving expensive cars is not unusual in such settings. However, such identities are usually read in distinctive ways that rely on normative, ideologically grounded and contingent expectations of race.

Within the song, however, these issues are ignored. Instead, the verses and lyrics contain detail connecting the car with identity, particularly masculinity and wealth, as well as symbolic and concrete manifestations of power, explicitly referencing respect, money and speed.[55] Perhaps curiously, the lyrics do not reference law enforcement, or how policing disproportionately impacts minority ethnic communities, particularly younger males.[56] While this may not necessarily be the first reaction from audiences, it becomes highly relevant once a particular 'parody' version of the song is stumbled upon.[57] Unlike the original, this version adds the dimensions of race and criminality explicitly, and throughout, with lyrics[58] and the performance within the video laced with satirical humour, adding yet more depth and potency to the song's overarching themes.

The parody opens with a clamour of frustrated voices, all of which seem to be resisting police interest. The chorus, like the rest of the song, is delivered by the performers taking on the identity of police officers who make various statements about black men, race, racism and criminality. This is no celebration of the car, but a sketch in which the pitfalls of 'driving while black' are cemented.[59] Throughout the remainder of the song, the lyrics are delivered with pace, common to the genre of UK hip-hop/grime, but the tone mocks, caricaturing law enforcement. The visuals show the performers not only dressed as police officers but also, depending on their own ethnic heritage, in either 'black' or 'white' face, and this too raises other questions about how power, in and out of uniform, continues to present itself, especially in relation to the perception and policing of ethnic minorities.

The video features a number of cars, some German, some Italian, but they are not overbearing in their presence, as the majority of the visuals frame the performers, occasionally with 'suspects' or in roles that enhance and reinforce the song's themes. The claims within the song are clear: the lived experience of minority ethnic identity, behind the wheel or not, is connected with the power, legacy and continuing prevalence of race, and its impact through behaviours, beliefs and consequences of normative racism. With lyrics referencing police brutality and 'black criminality', the song constitutes a clear critique of race as ideology and practice. The song ends with a brief disclaimer, in a voice that is more austere and reserved, sounding 'respectable' and reasonable, saluting young black police officers and good police work. While this may be a rejoinder to the broader message, the mocking note of the delivery further underscores the experience of racial discrimination.

'Officer'

Similar themes are raised in the US originated 'Officer' (1992) by The Pharcyde.[60] Given the original release date of this song, it is possible to glean some insights into how hip-hop has changed in terms of focal points within lyrical and visual content, with particular reference to how the car subsequently became positioned ideologically and aspirationally. In the late 1980s and early 1990s, cars rarely featured as 'aspirational' objects within the evolving lexicon of hip-hop visual-musical culture. Coolio's 'Fantastic Voyage' (1994), LL Cool J's 'Illegal Search' (1990), 'Sobb Story' (1991) by Leaders of the New School and Public Enemy's 'You're Gonna Get Yours' (1987) all feature the car, driving and racism. By the mid-1990s, and certainly into the 2000s, these themes had been supplanted by the car as a highly visible, potent and vital symbol within some genres of hip-hop. Even when economic success was not being extolled lyrically, the car was present.[61]

'Officer' begins with a short, light-hearted introduction and then moves into four verses, with a chorus appearing after the second and final verses. In the first verse, performed by Fatlip, the protagonist receives a letter stating his driving licence has been suspended. Regardless, he drives to school, picking up friends in a dirty-looking (it is blue, but looks grey) car without licence, insurance or registration. During the next two verses, delivered by Bootie Brown and Imani, respectively, the lyrics reveal the anxiety of driving with risk, reinforced by the chorus, which asks "Mr Officer" not to pull the car over. In the second verse, without explicit references to race, policing or criminality, the lyrics create a sense of anticipation where alternatives to driving are rehearsed: bus, foot or bike. Any underlying concern escalates in the final verse, when a clear, perceptual and existential link between ethnicity and criminality is made: four young black men, in a car, driving slowly, are unlikely to be seen in a positive way, with the possible outcome of being subject to harassment from the police.

This fear is realised between the third and fourth verses, where the occupants stop and converse with a female; the conversation is cut short when the police appear on the scene. After a short chase, during which the lyrics dwell on the immediacy of the moment as well as the ramifications of being caught, the chorus is repeated. This is followed by the remarks of the police officer on the scene, spelling out the consequences of driving without a licence and noting various driving and traffic violations, with occasional rebuttals from those in the car.

'Officer' develops a story-like narrative involving events and consequences, but what does not explicitly feature in its lyrical content is also important. 'Officer' references the risk of being stopped by police, but the underlying theme is that of racism's connections with not only law enforcement but also the criminal justice system in America. The counter, of course, is that the occupants *were* breaking the law; their car *was* unroadworthy and, as indicated toward the end, none of the drivers had a licence. However, the subtext covers the risks black drivers are presented with, even if they are legal, a theme that is negotiated in academic research[62] and in films such as *Crash* (2004) and *Green Book* (2018). One of the key, but subtle, almost throwaway moments in the song references the existential threat and risk of police interest, and specifically harassment.

According to critical race theorists, the strategic and operationalised orientations of race are at the heart of any analysis of racial inequality in particular, and multi-ethnic societies in general.[63] As a result, it is white supremacy, rather than racism, that elicits racial discrimination, and, furthermore, it is the weight of race – as a pure, arguably uncomplicated concept – that has the greatest impact, despite variations in a person's experience depending on class, gender, age and so on. To develop this, white supremacism is no longer the sole domain of far-right nationalist, usually racist, hate groups, but seeps into the running of mainstream society in subtle and not-so-subtle ways. This can be seen, for example, in political and mass-mediated discourses in which racial identity features. This white supremacy also operates in more everyday contexts and is noticeable, for example, when leaders offer solutions on immigration and immigrants, or when we encounter spikes in the enduring, and arguably normative, presence of racism in sport, education and employment. 'Officer' shows white supremacy as latent, beneath the surface but nevertheless present and potent, being subtly referenced in lyrics and the song's broader themes, which are no doubt anchored in lived experience. 'Officer', while merely a text, illustrates what it is to be black, young and male, especially in those multi-ethnic spaces where racism is present and pernicious.

'#1 Stunna'

'#1 Stunna' (2000) by Big Tymer$, featuring Lil Wayne and Juvenile, is, by comparison, a completely different text in terms of its thematic scope, and especially how the car is located.[64] Comprising four verses, each broken with a chorus/hook delivered by Lac, Lil Wayne and Baby, the song begins with a short 'intro' in which Baby claims he cannot be out-stunted, referencing driving prowess and risk-taking, connecting with perceptions of and behaviours associated with merely listening to hip-hop.[65] Baby proceeds to deliver the first verse, densely populated with references to consumption and power; expensive cars, driving prowess, jewellery, socialising, and sexual appetite and potency all feature. There are further connections with agency and control, with authenticity and belonging also present. These themes, along with mention of other commodities that confer status even further (private planes, car upgrades, a house by the water), are repeated in the remaining verses. Indeed, as the song progresses there is an escalation of the claims being made around sex especially, along with physical strength and wealth, all of which are signified through the centrality of cars.

The video accompanying the song references economic success, status and conspicuous consumption, adding further depth and life to the lyrics. The first 20 seconds or so is dominated by cars, being driven, stood by or otherwise showcased. Throughout, particularly expensive and/or exotic cars (Rolls-Royce, Lamborghini, Mercedes, Jaguar, Ferrari and other makes) are shown. In between these car moments, rappers are performing, but there are also scenes in which storied situations play out: jewellery shopping, attending a barbecue, buying wheels, playing cards for money. Together, the lyrical and visual content point to what things can be purchased and to other, less concrete and quantifiable, materialisations of power. Taken with many similar texts,[66] this offers insights into how the car features as one element within broader debates of what may appear to be excessive consumption, but which has bound within it a thread of individual agency in which liberation is closely aligned with economic signifiers. Money, jewellery, cars and control (possibly even the social dominance that accompanies wealth[67]) are all present in such videos. While open to interpretation, and in line with Miller's view, such texts can be read critically:

> The videos are the videos, aren't they? I don't even watch them to be fair. Listen to the tunes, that's the main thing.... When you do see the videos, they're a laugh – I don't take them seriously. I doubt anyone does.... Because they're mental ... everything about them, the lifestyle they show, the money, the cars, the women or should I say *bitches* – that's *bitchez* with a zed [laughs] ... so I can't see how anyone takes the videos seriously. (US, 32, male, 23 October 2018)

The inclusion of three well-known African American comedians in the video – Steve Harvey, Cedric the Entertainer and D.L. Hughley – may suggest '#1 Stunna' is meant to be read ironically; as a pastiche of essentialised and racialised tropes that remain prevalent in the representation of black identities,[68] especially those that hinge on sexuality, crime and irresponsibility.[69] However, given the sheer quantity of such output, even in the early 2000s, a more realistic, though less nuanced, approach would be to take such texts more literally. For artists such as Talib Kweli, whose style and politics appear to sit at odds with those invested in excessive consumption,

> mainstream rappers suffer from the "Grand illusion…" articulated by Pharoahe Monch. One consequence of the delusion that popular/mainstream artists suffer from is that their lyrics and songs often grapple with reality in ways that allow them to celebrate conspicuous materiality without any conscious understanding of how human commodification in American Slavery is the predicate for the capital accumulation and material success in America that they seem to so readily and wantonly celebrate.[70]

Furthermore, content that references 'gold chains' operates literally and metaphorically, and 'puts into bold and powerful relief an inherent irony of celebrated materialism in popular hip-hop music'.[71] Exploring whether the lyrics in '#1 Stunna' are meant to be taken seriously, literally or as metaphor may be interesting, and tangentially relevant, but the song remains a popular cultural text that resonates with its audiences and, in some ways, has become another mainstream cultural reference point.

Show and hype

The way in which the car is used within genres of hip-hop – through being referenced in either lyrics or videos, and often both – has within it variation and evolution. Since the early 2000s, hip-hop's use of cars consistently points to economic success as an ideal. This has enabled artists to curate their biographies with status, power and signifiers of what constitutes 'taste'. And this is not middle-class taste; nor is it arrived at through a middle-class habitus. What we see, however, is an assertive, confident and rational mode of consumption, one that is further underscored by the modalities of hip-hop wherein taking, reusing, reintegrating and reinventing is done without anxiety or fear. This may be a somewhat sentimental or romanticised point of analysis, but given the history of African Americans, wherein the ownership and commodification of human beings was central to what is often cited as an extreme moment in capitalism, hip-hop draws out existential, and metaphoric, reclamations of power.

While audiences may appreciate texts with irony, or at least critically, there nevertheless is a relationship between mediated representations of consumer objects and our understandings of their role, form and function in everyday life. This takes us back to the view that hip-hop is perceived to be negatively influencing younger generations:

> you see all these cars – Bentleys and Ferraris and ... it's all, sort of bollocks. Don't get me wrong, they're nice cars and they show big houses and all half-naked birds and this and that, but it's all an act ... about show and hype and what you show, not what you actually are. But you know a lot of people, they see it and seeing is believing. To me, they think they can do that and be like that.... They're like playing at gangsters, and they'll be wearing knock-off clothes, fake jewellery, driving around in their mum's 1.4 Golf, that she's got on disability, but badging it up like an R32. For what? It's all show. (KM, 35, male, 19 November 2017)

KM's comment helps us connect the dots between mediated African American hip-hop culture and what can be encountered on the streets and roads of a northern, British, multi-ethnic city. However, this kind of disposition toward high-end cars is further facilitated through economic and cultural mainstreaming. In Bradford, as is the case in many cities, elite car hire outlets are thriving, often attracting customers willing to pay thousands to hire a car for a wedding, birthday or other special occasion. Changes in consumption have been aided significantly through mediated discourses on 'improving' our homes, minds and bodies; the car is by no means excluded from this list.

There are deeper levels of connection, however, between hip-hop, cars and multi-ethnic cities in the UK. The active consumption of US hip-hop speaks to the prevalence of hip-hop throughout the world. A further layer of connection lies with the widespread production of hip-hop, and hip-hop-related genres, in cities such as Bradford, Birmingham and Nottingham, as well as parts of London; there are countless examples of such content on youtube.com, with 'views' ranging from the hundreds of thousands to the millions. There are growing, vibrant and innovative scenes that produce musical formations, appreciated by and connecting with audiences in highly meaningful ways. Although the lyrical content varies, one element within these songs is the desire to be recognised and valued. From depictions of gangster lifestyles wherein violence, criminality and power are clearly present,[72] to more banal, and at times unusually creative and amusing, comments about a city's food culture,[73] there is an insistence that articulates real, lived, caricatured or aspirational notions of identity. Present throughout the majority of this creative production is the car, either in and of itself a marker of ambition or success,[74] or an appendage serving the purpose of reinforcing gangster personae.[75]

For those who are involved in especially 'modifier' scenes, creativity, labour, taste and identity are integral to the car's physical shape, and the meaning that flows from it. For those whose engagement with their cars is less noticeable, there are also elements of identity being read and reacted to through widely held understandings of what particular cars signify. These themes are therefore traversed in the following chapters, and subsequently situated within the realms of class, culture and taste – as well as, later, incivility, criminality and danger.

FOUR

Consuming cars: class, ethnicity and taste

This chapter covers distinct modes of car cultural consumption with particular reference to class and ethnicity. Subcultural car scenes, layered with creativity, emotion and taste, are actively present in the city and are discussed against this context. However, intersecting with taste and forms of social and economic capital, attention is also paid to middle-class car cultural practice. Throughout, any manifestation of class remains influential, but rather than being fixed, its performance is fluid and ambiguous. Similarly, rooted in these class formations is taste, best understood when memory, history and identity slip and slide over each other, producing contingent, subjective and varied meanings. With that in mind, an outline of habitus is offered wherein taste, its realisation and its constructions are visible through the car. To begin with, however, it is useful to spend some time on minority ethnic car consumption in Bradford. Here, the ways in which taste, as a corollary of class, continues to evolve in relation to the car hinges on Bradfordian-Pakistani car cultural practice over the last 50 years or so.

In seeking to understand why there appears to be a lively growth in car-related consumption in Bradford, asking how it is economically maintained is reasonable. As documented elsewhere, some Pakistani-heritage residents are now in the position of having levels of disposable income that have led to growth in conspicuous consumption.[1] Declining levels of remittances and increasing levels of education and entrepreneurship suggest an economic middle class is becoming, if not already, established. In effect, an overlooked form of 'integration' enables such consumption to take place. Car-buying practice is therefore framed by wider modes of consumption within which choice is a dominant feature. TA offers a model of rationalisation that helps make coherent what appear to be disproportionate investments in cars:

> For our lot, cars aren't a problem.... We can afford them because we don't spend money getting pissed, going clubbing and all that.... Plus the young ones, they get a job, they buy a flash car if they want – parents don't charge rent and things like that, so it's not as hard as you might think. (TA, 43, male, 1 April 2015)

Again, there is also a strong element of rationality driving cultural and economic practice; not spending money on some lifestyle habits opens up other opportunities. Through the majority of the sample there was a similar echo around available spending choices, but these were tacitly couched within ethnic- and faith-based identity; for most Muslims, generally speaking, drinking alcohol is simply non-negotiable. At the same time, among working-class Pakistanis, there is still a tendency to financially support their children, even when they are married, and this too, once again, has an impact on the amount of income available to spend on cars, dining, travel and home improvement. Although not central to the discussion here, the economic and familial support infrastructures enable a distinctive type of integration that is usually overlooked or ignored in especially political and media discourse.

Denying taste

It is not the purpose of this text to explore why the salience of class seems to be absent from especially British public discourse, but its economic and cultural facets are clearly at play in the forming and rehearsing of identity, particularly in relation to the car. The following extensive, but abridged, field note touches on some of this:

A colleague asks me if I've caught a radio programme called *Women Talking About Cars* or something[2].... She found it fascinating; how women experience and live with cars, and that's different to how men experience and live with theirs.

'Yeah, I start. Hmm. Didn't really like it. I mean–'

'Oh? I only heard the one last night, with Lynda La Plante, and it was very interesting.... A woman presents it, and there are women who talk about their cars.... There was one with Jennifer Saunders. That was good.'

I heard that one, too: Jennifer Saunders' dad got a CBE for something, apparently.... I know that most of the stuff related to cars is very male; produced and fronted by blokey types who are there to talk to other blokey types so yes, the endeavour to rebalance that male skewed world is necessary.... But it's not serious and it's not real and that's the point: it's not meant to be. Anything more real and grounded is not attractive, or appealing enough. Truth is, if you're making programmes, celebrities can help you stand out. Radio 4, this middle-class, respectable institution, is offering a narrow, possibly elitist and marginalising narrative by validating the behaviours of the celebs, as funny or ironic or something equally human. The celebs can comfortably regale and amuse their audiences about the irony of taking their driving test in a Ferrari (something La Plante apparently did), or a story – told and received with humour – of buying a dangerously repaired car (and being advised to sell on such a 'potential deathtrap'), as well as owning a ... 6.7 litre Rolls-Royce Corniche. Not for a second do notions of responsibility, privilege, risk or danger come into play. It's alright for these people to do what's ordinarily tagged as deviant, dangerous, irresponsible or antisocial, but no, for this lot, it's okay because they come equipped: celebrity and class status elevates and inoculates their stories against critique. What they do with cars, regardless of the detail, is unequivocally unproblematic. The same respect and appreciation is not afforded to younger, especially working-class, drivers. I've talked to them and they have funny stories, and stories in which their love for their cars comes through clearly but you don't get to hear them on Radio 4, or anywhere else for that matter. (Field notes, 13 December 2018)

Written almost immediately after the event, the extract relates to how car culture is expressed in broader, mainstream media such as the *Top Gear* series, or output aimed at arguably more discerning audiences. Such programming represents an object in relation to the identities that produce or consume this type of programming; it presents a sanitised, stripped down and appropriately refined, and limited, rendering of car culture, including how and why the car is used, lived with and appreciated. The approach found in these mainstream outputs is not particularly, if at all, interested in bringing working-class car cultures to the fore. Indeed, when working-class identities and cars are present, media outputs often combine the object (the car) and the subject (the driver) to form a recipe for disaster: criminal, antisocial, dangerous and so on. Why this is the case is in part linked with how mass media operate. Arguably a simple, but not necessarily simplistic, aphorism tells us that 'bad news sells'. While media can and do influence how we think, the manufacture of media content is also subject to social norms, values and a broad, morally derived consensus on what constitutes good and bad. Media outputs, therefore, depend on a feedback loop between what exists and what should exist. And here, some class cultures become invalidated through hyper-visiblity or, conversely, through their absence.

The force of habitus

Widely held as a high point in understanding the nature of class, Bourdieu's *Distinction: a Social Critique of the Judgment of Taste* brings into focus class position and how it is practised and thus maintained as a systemic feature within capitalism.[3] Bourdieu examined various constituents that result in a deeper understanding of one, usually taken-for-granted, seemingly natural feature of human individuality – taste – and the conditions, forces and agents that feature in its nature, development and impact. Underpinning his argument is the view that class position, in mere economic terms, is not enough to understand the process of class reproduction: 'Social class is not defined solely by a position in the relations of production, but by the class habitus which is "normally" (i.e., with a high statistical probability) associated with that position.'[4]

Habitus refers to how, due to class position, and therefore levels of educational, social and cultural capital, we come to hold certain habits, skills and attributes. Here, we are connected with social and institutional arenas – education, religion and employment, as well as more mundane 'fields' – through which we reproduce our dispositions.[5] We may find ourselves experiencing different levels of power, or efficacy, depending on the field we are in; an individual may become very wealthy, but without the necessary elite cultural capital, for example knowledge or experience of elite social etiquette, the performance of elite class identity is partial. Central to our experience of field and disposition is the presence and force of habitus, influencing how we speak, behave, dress, reproduce and consume – and how we develop 'taste'. Habitus runs subconsciously through our relationships with education, leisure, food, art and the world of work. We internalise these elements of culture to such an extent that they seem natural. As a result, 'the schemes of the habitus, the primary forms of classification, owe their specific efficacy to the fact that they function below the level of consciousness and language, beyond the reach of introspective scrutiny or control by the will'.[6]

Because class operates at both structural and individual levels, so too does everything that flows from it. Habitus, therefore, influences how we make sense of and relate to the wider social world; even readings of ourselves, as well as those around and beyond us, come into relief through the habitus that is bound with our class position. In Bourdieu's analysis, the general nature of habitus is not unique to us as individuals because we share various markers of identity with others, and it is through these social, cultural and economic zones that habitus is transmitted, en masse, thereby reproducing social structures, including understandings and experiences of class itself.

Through this elaboration of social structures, Bourdieu defines and situates types of 'taste' within one of three zones, 'which roughly correspond to educational levels and social classes': 'legitimate', 'middle-brow' and 'popular' tastes; these he exemplifies with instances of art or creative production corresponding to each zone. 'Popular' taste, although not exclusively aligned with working-class position, tends toward

> the choice of works of so-called 'light' music or classical music devalued by popularization … and especially songs totally devoid of artistic ambition or pretension.… [It] is most frequent among the working classes and varies in inverse ratio to educational capital (which explains why it is slightly more common among industrial and commercial employers or even senior executives than among primary teachers and cultural intermediaries).[7]

Although these same descriptions may not hold entirely today, some popular music arguably aligns closely with Bourdieu's notion of that which is 'devoid of artistic ambition or pretension'. Of course, there are strong counters – that popular music is more than this, being creative, commercial and even political[8] – but in Bourdieu's work, this categorisation serves the purpose of demonstrating his point: that some products, practices, preferences and tendencies correspond with class position. Similarly, taste is relational and often 'the practical affirmation of an inevitable difference', inasmuch as tastes 'are asserted purely negatively, by the refusal of other tastes', resulting in 'disgust provoked by horror or visceral intolerance ("sick-making") of the tastes of others'.[9] This is reinforced by PF, a teacher, who associates what he perceives to be a decline in civility with subcultural car aesthetics. Here, however, taste is a key element of his cultural repertoire:

> The pupils I teach – should say try to teach, teenagers.… I'm not exaggerating. I sometimes think they're brought up to be wild and inconsiderate.… They're like that in school and they get worse when they finish.… I see them driving around in their cars.… Loud, bright, tacky. Crass.… Tasteless. Crap. (PF, 32, male, 3 June 2016)

Taste, therefore, is not a simple construct, and although there is extensive, and more recent, writing on the subject,[10] Bourdieu's work remains convincing, despite the fact that 'class' is today occasionally offered as a historical, no longer socially relevant or determining force in contemporary societies. This is not surprising given that taste, like class, is itself ideologically grounded, and 'owes its plausibility and its efficacy to the fact that, like all the ideological strategies generated in the everyday class struggle, it naturalizes real differences, converting differences in the mode of acquisition of culture into differences of nature'.[11]

Culture, ideology, attitude and especially taste are all framed, to varying extents, by the spaces we occupy, which in turn have an influence on the opportunities and life chances that open up to us – and this includes work, education and even partnering.[12] In relation to taste specifically, broader sociocultural contexts become crucial in enabling 'tastes to function as markers of "class"'.[13] Within the location of habitus, and class identity, taste is an important feature to explore when assessing how and why some cars are preferred over others. However, it is worth bearing in mind that taste and economic position are near symbiotic in their relationship: if one element falls out of line with the other (middle-class taste but working-class economic position), then compromise or dissonance may occur.

'Ethnic' taste

Miller offers useful and cogent examination of some contemporary popular commodities, and the tastes and communities by which they are favoured, in Trinidad.[14] For example, distinctive meanings are laid upon types of cola drink ('red' or 'black') and which ethnic groups are likely to consume them. Indo-Trinidadians, whose history is defined partly through migration and indentured labour, appear to have a distinctive taste compared with Afro-Trinidadians, whose heritage has links with slavery:

> The red drink is the quintessential sweet drink in as much as it is considered by consumers to be the drink highest in sugar content. The Indian population is generally assumed to be particularly fond of sugar and sweet products. This in turn is supposed to relate to their entry into Trinidad largely as indentured labourers in the sugar cane fields. They are also thought to have a high rate of diabetes, which folk

> wisdom claims to be a result of their over-indulgence of these preferences.[15]

Taste may be connected to the nature of migration routes, but is also susceptible to being read and made sense of through folk or scientific types of wisdom in which 'ethnic taste' is made coherent and applied. Modes and patterns of consumption, memory, biography and history therefore interplay to construct contemporary and coherent ethnic identity narratives: who they are, what they like and do, and why.

For British minority ethnic individuals in the 1960s, many of whom were still in the process of becoming settlers, acquiring a car, or a van, was neither economically viable nor worthwhile in terms of utility. Migrants of the 1950s and 1960s were principally economic in their orientation, earning and spending as efficiently as possible in order to commit remittances to their homelands. Of course, those with specific forms of social and cultural capital (where speaking and writing the English language helped elevate status, for example) could perhaps consider the viability of a long-term, secure and comfortable future. Indeed, in some inner-city areas where ethnic minorities were settling, relevant infrastructure blossomed, supporting and maintaining an ethnically appropriate economic, social and cultural milieu. At this point, however, car ownership among Bradford's Pakistanis, even in relation to the wider population for whom car ownership was not a given, remained limited.

A decade later, Pakistani Bradfordians marked their transition from migrants to settlers through home and then car ownership. However, most drivers were male, with working-class economic position (many still worked in the textile industry, even if they had professional status in their country of origin). The majority of this first generation usually bought small- to medium-sized saloons, estates and hatchbacks, with a growing preference for Japanese cars (Datsun and Toyota). Of course, given the established presence of European- and American-owned car manufacturers in the UK, Vauxhalls, Austins and Fords, among others, were also owned. Most cars were bought second-hand, and this too is an important strand that informs present practices. Indeed, the business of selling cars has similarly grown rapidly over at least the last 20 years, with a significant proportion of research participants actively buying and selling used cars on a part-time, 'side-hustle' basis. In the 1970s and 1980s, however, retailing cars was largely the preserve of dealerships, small and large, and established sole traders. A small amount of second-hand car stock was also purchased through small but growing informal networks: by the 1980s, everyone's dad knew someone who knew something about cars. Buyers sought out those who had developed their car cultural capital, comprising necessary knowledge (which cars were good/reliable/economical or sold well), skills (haggling/valuing) and trade networks (auctions, repair garages, and dealerships disposing of old or traded-in stock).

In the 1980s, with a growing young Pakistani-heritage population, the number of drivers increased. Taking driving lessons, passing the driving test and then accessing a car became a normative aspect of young male adulthood in general. There were, however, exceptions:

> My sister were one of the first girls to drive in Bradford, you know that?… In those days, it was a really bad thing. I'm not joking. People would come up to my dad in the shop and say, you know, 'oh, it's really bad, your daughter's driving' and that. And my dad, he'd tell them to, you know, mind their own business sort of thing. But that's what it was like in those days. You'll remember yourself: hardly any women – Asian, Pakistani, women driving – when we started … and not that many white women, really, compared to now. (SR, 39, male, 1 September 2011)

Car ownership positively influenced a family's cultural and economic capital, was liberating, and held symbolic and concrete forms of power.[16] Cars reduced dependence on public transport and car-owning friends, relatives and neighbours. Cars, therefore, became increasingly vital in the case of births, deaths and marriages, especially if the distance to be travelled stretched beyond the local.[17]

Subsequent British-born generations have been educated and socialised within both Pakistani and British cultures, producing 'hybridised' identities[18] marked by the evolution of cultural practice and taste in music, fashion, food and cars. As a result, brand preference broadened: Ford, Vauxhall, BMW, Rover, Fiat and others appealed to British-born Pakistanis. With this expansion in brand taste, a shift in car type preference emerged. Unlike their parents, young drivers in the 1980s and 1990s favoured style and aesthetics over functionality and efficiency, with two- and three-door coupes and hatchbacks becoming more appealing to younger driver cohorts. This following interview segment references this transition:

FB: So let me see, this would have been eighties, maybe late seventies and you'd see a few – not a lot – of these cars floating around.... There weren't many at all, really.... I was only little – five, six, summat like that but I remember there were two that were local and one that was in Heaton I believe.

YA: Right. I know which ones you're talking about: they're the three I'm talking about – a red one–

FB: Dirty red–

YA: Yeah, a black one.

FB: Big alloys, I remember.

YA: Yeah – vinyl roof. And there was a blue one.

FB: Vinyl roof, as well.... The blue one was the best one, though.

YA: It was the prettiest – nice colour, white wheels.

FB: The black one, that was jacked up at the back. Not as nice as the blue one.

YA: The red one was a bit–

FB: Rough. Looked rough. But you know what, those were like the first of sort of our generation – of people born here – who tried to do their own thing.... Matter of fact, I remember talking to a friend of mine, and he was telling me how his dad played hell with him when he bought his first car.... Obviously, his dad was thinking he'll get a nice family car, but no, he gets a Capri–

YA: Two doors–

FB: What good's that to anyone?

YA: But things were changing.
FB: Things were changing at that time especially; Jap cars were common, everyone knows that – bread and butter cars but what this new lot wanted, that was different wasn't it? Your dad's driving around in a, I dunno, a 120Y, a Carina, Corolla or something and he's happy because–
YA: Does the job.
FB: For him, the dads it does, but not for their sons – they want something better than that. That's when these Celicas, Capris and then later, you had your coupe Corollas and Nissans coming in. (FB, 46, male, 10 April 2016)

By the 1980s, when a second generation had matured and started to drive, a 'disproportionate investment' in the car, found among marginalised African Americans in the US,[19] was evident here also. At this point, for Bradford's Pakistanis, the car became an object imbued with strong public visibility, connoting status and, because of the distinctiveness in tastes between them and their parents, a form of cultural integration. Even at this point,

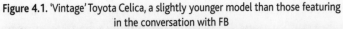

Figure 4.1. 'Vintage' Toyota Celica, a slightly younger model than those featuring in the conversation with FB

British-born minority ethnic identities were rehearsed through new modes of consumption. Being caught 'between two cultures'[20] may have resulted in some sense of confusion, of being neither wholly one thing nor another, but these hybrid and still racialised identities nevertheless went on to remain citizens and raise families of their own. At this point, and although not dominated by the kinds of cars we see today, the roads were becoming more diverse and loaded with traffic, in turn providing more opportunity for race to be read and reacted to. This, however, operated beyond the basis of physical encounters with ethnic others, and was transmitted through the work of imagination, stereotype and what became normative wisdom. Like Miller's cola drinks analysis, the circularity of meaning was so complete that even the unattended, undriven presence of Toyotas, Nissans and other Japanese models signified Pakistani-heritage drivers.

AE86 Corolla: a study in crossover

Although subject to high-profile safety issues between 2009 and 2011,[21] Toyota continues to signify reliability along with efficiency and economy. Over the last two decades, however, Corollas made by Toyota in the 1980s have developed a distinct set of connotations that become meaningful when age, ethnicity and class intersect to produce taste, reputation and value. In turn, we find distinctive modes of consumption wherein existing cultural objects are appropriated and reinvented to stand for values and meanings beyond, and sometimes in opposition to, those the original manufacturer intended. This element of the discussion enables us to integrate quite recent developments and shifts in consumption at the level of subcultural car practice in which some older, but unusual, Japanese cars are prominently appreciated.

In the early 1980s, large manufacturers began production of their own 'hot hatches'. Most notable, and groundbreaking, was Volkswagen's Golf GTi, but Ford responded with XR variants of their Escort, Sierra and even Fiesta. Vauxhall, similarly, made GTE versions of their Astra and SRi Cavalier, and also collaborated with Lotus on their high-performance Carlton.

Renault, Peugeot, Citroen, Fiat and even Skoda all saw the market for relatively fast, but practical and affordable cars. Such cars from this era are today designated vintage, collectible and often given the prefix 'classic', seemingly appreciating in value to such an extent that many are worth more now, used, than they were when brand new.

Toyota, meanwhile, produced two 'GTI' Corollas: a rear-wheel drive three-door fastback coupe (the 'AE86'), and a front-wheel drive three-door hatchback (the 'AE82').[22] Both models used the same engine, but each had its own aesthetic and structural upgrades. These versions of the Corolla have today become emblematic for car enthusiasts in general. Not many AE86/82 Corollas remain in the UK. Although rarity gives objects a premium, collectible value, these cars hold particular resonance especially for younger Bradfordian-Pakistani drivers and enthusiasts, particularly those who appreciate subcultural vantage points. Speaking in 2012, AS illustrated this point:

> I know lads who've been all the way to Scotland looking for one.... And not runners, neither. To look at them, they look like they're scrap but they'll pay strong money for them; at one time, you could pay a couple of grand for a non-runner.... So they ferry them down the M1, stick them in a garage and then throw money at them: strip it and rebuild the whole thing from scratch sometimes. (AS, 45, male, 23 April 2012)

Figure 4.2. Toyota Corolla, AE86

Among car journalists, the AE86 has developed a 'driver's car' identity. The lack of driving aids enables the owner to drive, especially at speed, in a focused, close, attached and responsive manner. With a reputation for being fun, lively and exciting when driven to the edge – the combination of limited but raw power and rear-wheel drive – AE86s are also known to be unforgiving:

> It was a bit wet, nothing major – just rain. So, in first, foot down, clutch out and that's it – game over. Back end's all over the place, spins and kerbs passenger side. Us lot in the car, heads hitting the roof, the windows, shouting and screaming. Nearly wrote it off – back wheel, big ding-crack in it – knackered; wishbone – knackered; leg, hub – knackered. Taught me to be a bit more careful, I tell you that. Tasty cars; you got to know what you're doing. (IZ, 42, male, 26 June 2015)

By the early 1980s, most mainstream car producers (excluding BMW and Mercedes Benz) had all but completely switched from rear- to front-wheel drive orientation. This offered advantages: more leg room, and with the weight of the engine and transmission over the front drive shafts, higher levels of grip and traction could be yielded in comparison to rear-wheel drive cars. In wet conditions, rear-wheel drive cars were more likely to skid than their front-wheel drive counterparts, a point reinforced by IZ. Front-wheel drive cars, therefore, had benefits that most drivers, certainly in Northern European winters, would appreciate.

Drift

Over the last two decades or so, the rear-wheel drive car's greater propensity to skid (when compared to front-wheel drive cars) has been subverted and appropriated to become an important, and high-profile, aspect within car-based subculture and beyond. Although ostensibly originating from car scenes in Japan, 'drifting'[23] has become a performative, competitive art form, finding its way into mainstream culture. Within relevant car subcultures, a repertoire and knowledge base around cars that are known as 'drift-machines' has evolved:

> Quite a few, really – Japanese cars, Supras, GTRs, Corollas but German cars are being known for it as well now.... No, not Audis – front-wheel drive but saying that, there is a video someone sent me showing a modified Audi drifting like a devil.... I've thought about it but it's something you've got to be really into.... Mine, it can drift, but not like the way the professionals drift.... Alright, yeah, you can do doughnuts and handbrake turns and go sideways for a bit, but not how they do it.... You see them on YouTube, especially in Europe, Japan also – which is where it started, really. Those guys, and some them ladies as well, they know – they know exactly what the car's doing and they can control it.... You can't just jump in a car and do like them.... Like with me, it's the car that can do it but the driver, me, he needs to go on some training! (RA, 31, male, 14 June 2017)

The AE86 sits in localised, subculturally grounded contexts, but some elements of its reputation and value have fed back into mainstream car culture with references in cinema,[24] television,[25] computer gaming[26] and music videos, while the language and discourse of drifting has also made its way into wider motoring media. Toyota also capitalised on the cultural value of the AE86 with the launch, in 2012, of the GT86, by appropriating '86' into the name of the new model, and also by incorporating the new car's credentials and packaging with the older car's reputation and engineering simplicity. The AE86's heritage and pedigree, therefore, helps connect the old and established with the new.

Performance and a car's drifting 'nature' rely on the interplay between physics, engineering and the driver. This may reference the experience of speed, danger and skill, but it is the car's *capacity* to outperform and out-drift other cars that is just as, if not more, important:

> I go to meets and stuff like that, and you see them all there, in their Scoobys and all that, just ripping them.... I spend

> too much time and too much money to be arsing about, killing off tyres and knackering the engine – I seen one lad do it at this car meet. Showing off, burnouts, handbrake turns, doughnuts, really giving it some – loud as anything. And then, TOK – something's fucked. I thought, you know what, serves him right. Idiot, man. (CB, 34, male, 4 November 2013)

Owning such cars does not necessarily mean driving styles and behaviours correspond with their capabilities – cars have the potential to be driven at speed and even dangerously, but this can be realised only through the agentic presence and competence of the driver. For CB, however, this car in particular also said something about himself that could be read by those who encountered him and his car:

> I look after it, don't bring it out when it's wet – I won't let it see the rain. I know it, I know this car inside out, every inch. I've had some things done to it, so it's not standard; nowhere near.... It's a one off. Different.... You get it, you know, pull up at lights and give you the look: I smile and ignore it. I'm not into racing at lights but if I were, then, you know, they'd lose [laughs].

When questions around motivations for owning such cars were asked, several others responded with similar views. Again, identity is both performed and read through cars with particular signification and meaning. When it comes to rare and older cars, a shared cultural capital is also present.

Bright, loud and so antisocial

Like Warren and Gibson's respondents, who had a central role in the production and development of their own customised cars,[27] modified car owners in Bradford are committed. However, many will source cars previously subject to processes of individuation wherein taste, preferences and innovative practice have shared resonance and buy-in. Notwithstanding this sense of 'completeness' at the point of purchase, creativity often continues, occasionally with further modifications and maintenance:

> You never stop sort of doing stuff to it. Like mine, it had some nice wheels on when I bought it. Not standard but nice split rims: 19 inch with low profile tires. Nothing wrong with them but I fancied some nicer ones, ones that would make it stand out even more. So I bought some.... put them on and it looks pretty mean, now. I got a few other things I need to do to it but I've already spent a lot so it'll have to wait. (AA, 30, male, 4 November 2011)

Much of this aligns with 'blue collar', 'vernacular' creativity, a system and process that depends on 'its own skills, networks, circuits, and spaces of production'.[28] Here, car customisation is couched as work and conveyed through song, image, film, social activity and oral tradition. Supporting infrastructures evolve and become key components of local economies; in Bradford, there are custom paint shops, car valet and detailing specialists, and boutique customisers, all linked, in essence, to the presence of a varied, vibrant and tangibly rich car scene.

While some parts of the 'modified car' scene in Bradford involve younger, Pakistani-heritage males,[29] the appeal is not shared by *all* young, Pakistani-heritage Bradfordian males, nor is it a passion exclusive to *only* the young or *only* those of Pakistani heritage. Indeed, during the course of this research, visits to 'car meets' were distinctly diverse in terms of the ethnicity, locale, gender and age of attendees:

MAA: We do get all sorts, really – it's meant to be like that.... Young people, older people – your age people–
BT: And even older–
MAA: We get women, as well – look around – some of the best cars here are owned by women.
BT: White people are here as well–
MAA: Not as much as Asian, Pakistani people–
BT: Yeah, but this is Bradford so that's who comes.
MAA: Like if we went to a city that had mostly white people – and we have done – it's the other way around.

YA: So you do that, though, right? Any issues, any bother, hassle?

MAA: No, well I've never had trouble when I've gone to an out-of-town meet.

BT: Not like that, not like racist trouble like that–

MAA: It's the cars, you get what I'm saying? That's what people come to see and show. (MAA, 21 and BT, 20, males, 7 May 2017)

For some who consider themselves to be more educated, more successful and more professional (in terms of employment or, indeed, disposition), drivers of modified or 'loud' cars can symbolise and encapsulate ethnic differentiation in terms that are viewed negatively by wider society. In turn, the behaviours corresponding to such cars and their drivers connote a lack of integration, and possibly even resistance to and defiance of middle-class values and taste:

> We're all free to do what we want, within reason, you might say but some things lie beyond the pale.... These cars you mention, they're not how you might say attractive, they're not interesting in the way, erm, a design classic might be. They look, and sorry for putting it like this, chavvy.... But they are so vulgar.... Bright, loud and so antisocial, really antisocial to my mind. They should be illegal because some of them are very loud, they are very disrupting.... You hear them at all hours, and I just think, I wish I could live somewhere else where this doesn't happen. (WJ, 43, female, 15 June 2017)

Modified cars may well be a means of expressing identity and voice, but for some, this voice says the wrong thing. Yet again, therefore, questions of taste along with class, habitus and cultural practice are relevant but operate at structural and individual levels. For example, in some countries, culture and the creative industries are used 'as new sources of employment and investment', and as 'hip' sectors around which place-making campaigns can be generated. However, 'custom-car work remains either stigmatised by conservative commentators ... or ignored by policy makers and civic leaders who fail to register it as legitimate vernacular industry'.[30] In Bradford, there have been attempts to revitalise the city's economy through formal regeneration (in particular, a new shopping centre and various state-funded financial grants to businesses), complemented by efforts to support and foster the growth of 'traditional' arts culture (the city has a national media museum and various festivals throughout the year). In addition, Bradford hosts a 'Classic Car Show', but it is reasonable to assert that this is not closely, if at all, aligned with the kinds of spectacular, unusual and creatively reinvented vehicles that are to be seen in some parts of the city.

At present, there is significant activity, created and developing without the support of authorised, formal infrastructure, be that facilitated through law enforcement, local government or the city's established 'culture industry'. Partly, there are public perceptions whereby particular types of cars and driving behaviours become linked: 'loud' cars = unruly behaviours. Similarly, modified cars often elicit adverse reactions that are neither neutral nor natural, but instead come from class-based definitions of good and bad taste. Such readings result in selective renderings of class. This links in with the premise of the Culture Studies discipline, which sought to demonstrate that working-class cultures did have substance, were valuable and were just as rich as those cultures that had been privileged as the only types of culture worth celebrating.[31] Although it has been over half a century since these invalidations were debunked by cultural theorists and, indeed, artists, some manifestations of working-class culture are still deemed deficient, and thus excluded, marginalised or rendered deviant and problematic. It remains perfectly possible for those with relevant social and cultural capital to appropriate elements of car modification in producing art, but the same does not apply to those who more wholly inhabit the very same milieu that is always open to interpretation, and exploitation.[32] For Skeggs, middle-class groups, with their corresponding levels of power, can and do appropriate those elements of a subordinate culture that are appealing, and subject to being propertised, a process depending on the existence of middle-class entitlement and working-class exclusion.[33] Subordinate groups, given their lack of power, cannot similarly propertise aspects of middle-class culture and instead appropriate, resist, or in some cases consume, but by doing so, they end up devaluing middle-class culture to such an extent that it is no longer defined as a middle-class artefact. This is arguably the case with some clothing brands (Burberry, for example), and appears to be the case with some cars, especially those that are modified, or enhanced and self-evidently go beyond function. As Warren and Gibson note,

> readings of such cars and their scenes is often infused with classist and parochial assumptions about what constitutes creativity (O'Connor, 2009); in whom such creativity resides (Barnes et al, 2006); and from where the creative class must be recruited in order to bolster chances of creative reinvention.[34]

As things stand, the vitality and creativity finessed through cars and their users seems destined to languish as a testing feature of an overlooked English, minority ethnic, working-class culture in which creativity is critically active. Rather than being acknowledged, let alone celebrated, aspects of this culture are policed and rehearsed as inherently bound to the restless nature of toxic, at times nihilistic, ethnic minority masculinities.

Gangster cars

Sitting alongside the car subculture discussed in the previous section is a similarly distinctive and ostensibly contradictory layer of car cultural practice. Here, it is not working-class identities inhabiting this mode of arguably rational but conspicuous consumption, but those who, at least in economic terms, occupy middle-class positions. However, given the broader idea wherein race operates and influences the readings of ethnic identities, even those who are comparatively privileged are also subjected to stereotype and racialised sentiment:

Done a few interviews this last couple of weeks. Trying to focus on one thing or another, but we end up drifting into wherever the conversation takes us. Nearly had an argument in one. She drove a nice car (Merc four-wheel drive thing), worked for a 'big firm' – I think she called it a 'proper company'. She lives near XXXX, couple of kids, husband works as well. I did ask her about social class – and she said she was probably middle class, but her parents were more working class. That seems to happen quite a bit.... I asked her about what she thought about some of the expensive cars in and around Bradford.

'Obvious, isn't it: everyone knows where the money comes from.'

'Yeah, the bank, right?'

'Oh come on, you know as well as I do that it's all drug money.'

'I don't know that. I mean–'

'It has to be. What else explains it?'

'So, you're a drug dealer?' I try softening the impact with a smile but it doesn't work.

'Me?'

I mean, it was an obvious thing to say, right? She's driving a car that's worth at least 30k easy. If she bought/leased it new, then it's worth even more.

'How can you say I'm a drug dealer?'

I guess she figured I was being obtuse – I was, but these sorts of judgements about the nefarious funding of expensive cars, I'm not always sure people actually believe them.

'I understand what you're saying,' she says, sighing: 'But it is a problem that we, as a community, need to face up to.'

Heard that one before, as well. (Field note, 21 June 2017)

Similar views connecting object with criminalised identity surfaced more than occasionally. While the dynamics within conversations varied, the 'expensive car = drug dealer' equation was not unusual, and was grounded in a set of consistent, rational and relational experiences: the necessary components to produce a particular resolution. Explaining expensive cars driven by Pakistani-heritage drivers in 'deprived' neighbourhoods is a phenomenon that uses imagination, generalisation and the availability of supporting tropes, stereotypes and even conventional modes of accepted wisdom to build an outcome. Some ethnic minority males underachieve educationally; the same groups associate and identify with mediated lifestyles in which excessive consumption is celebrated. On top of that, drug dealing is supposedly one of the few career paths available, and apparently attractive to these individuals. Together, these elements help situate and embed expectations of and explanations for what is encountered on the road.

Figure 4.3. Small selection of quite expensive, but fairly common cars

Money to spend

When it comes to more down-to-earth and affordable cars, taste is a powerful factor in interpreting and rehearsing identity. Even in fictional representations, the articulation of taste is at play. The yellow three-wheeled Reliant Regal, as featured in the television series *Only Fools and Horses*, seems to correspond with a caricatured British (London East End/Cockney) working-class identity. Meanwhile, the Volvo P1800 in *The Saint* series of the 1960s, or any of the cars used in the James Bond franchise, all speak to the more refined, serious and 'tasteful' types who own and drive those cars in particular, and further function as props through which characters become more coherently developed and meaningful.

It is unlikely that James Bond would own a well-used, yellow, three-wheeled minivan, but Del Boy Trotter – one of the characters in *Only Fools and Horses* – would probably own an elite or high-end car if he could afford it; indeed, when the Trotters become millionaires, Del Boy is gifted a Rolls-Royce. And this too is noteworthy, because while the Trotters rise above their working-class position in strict economic terms, their cultural capital remains more or less the same, which, indeed, is heavily influenced by a lifetime's worth of working-class habitus. Del Boy also moves into a mansion. Although wealthy – nouveau riche – he lacks the cultural and social graces befitting those traditionally associated with mansions, expensive cars and the 'finer things in life', which, again, are usually reserved for those with a more complete and rounded experience of elite class position. Herein reside the intersections with taste and economic capital: an individual's economic status and class can change, but the cultural appearance of their class identity – 'taste' – is more difficult to adopt, or revise. The best that Del Boy can do is access, own and consume the objects associated with a corresponding class position. Without a repertoire of class-bound knowledge and experience – the relevant and corresponding cultural capital – he can only attempt, and fail, to pass as authentically middle class in his performances. Transition from one class to another, therefore, is rendered challenging because our individual, but shared, sense of habitus makes the business of movement between class categories difficult, and it may take generations to realise, if desired in the first place.

Taste, therefore, cannot be understood unless it is anchored in history, migration, and, of course, cultural, economic and sociopolitical forms of power. The present buying preferences among British-born Bradfordian Pakistanis generally favour German-manufactured cars, but this preference is not unusual, given the broader increasing popularity of German brands over several years: the Volkswagen Golf, for example, was the second most popular car to be registered in 2018. Overall, the UK market share is dominated by Ford, followed by Vauxhall, then Volkswagen, BMW and Audi.[35] Communities, even in general, are therefore not fixed, but instead subject to intersecting levels and modes of structural changes that begin with economic position and end with manifestations of taste. FS, an established car trader, explains some of these changes based on his car retailing experience:

> You can't go wrong with your Audis, VWs and BMs – Mercedes, they're okay but not as good sellers as the others.... But yeah, your German cars, they've become more and more popular since I'd say about 20 years now. Before, people were buying them but not as much.... People have money to spend now – in our dads' days, not everyone had a car and if they did, it was say a Toyota or a Nissan – Datsun should I say. We're not rich-rich if you get where I'm coming from, but a lot of us can afford decent cars and look around, see what people are driving.... Everyone wants them [German cars] because they're good cars – reliable, look nice and they have build quality reputation. They're more expensive compared to your say Fords and your Vauxhalls, Renaults and what have you but they're worth it.... People still buy Jap cars because they might have that old-school mentality that they're the best value but more and more go for your A3s, 3 Series, Golfs and that kind of thing.... Unless you buy a lemon, they don't give you any trouble and that's what people want as well. (FS, 48, male, 22 November 2018)

Once it has been given the opportunity to be seen through its cultural operations, such as taste, which in turn influence the nature of consumption, class becomes a more meaningful concept, one that does not work individually, but combines with other elements of identity – in this case ethnicity in particular – to reveal its impact. The nature, form and consequence of class, notably explored in a range of settings that are by default rightly significant – education, employment, crime – are all acutely, but quietly, apparent through the car and its drivers. In the following chapter, some of this is covered in more depth, under the themes of car-related work and leisure.

FIVE

Car work: production, consumption and modification

In this chapter, car culture is framed as a two-way process of production and consumption. Here, particular tastes become concrete through aural, visual and performance-enhancing modifications. Furthermore, everyday practice is located against the context of existing and evolving infrastructural dynamics, thereby resisting normative and racialised modalities featuring ethnicity, class and culture. These issues are, therefore, examined through illustrative examples of car-related employment and leisure activities, as well as Bradford and its demographics. To begin with, however, some discussion of broader car-buying data is a useful backdrop against which more specific issues can be set.

Changing up

According to UK census data (2011), close to 75 per cent of households had access to at least one car or van, with 42.6 per cent of households having access to more than one vehicle.[1] Lansley uses the UK's Driver and Vehicle Licensing Agency's (DVLA) database of car model registrations in ascertaining socio-economic characteristics (occupational categories) based on ownership of ten distinct car types, with data further segmented according to the geographical distribution of cars. Unsurprisingly, small 'city' cars are more likely to be found in cities; larger vehicles are more prevalent in both rural and suburban settings. 'Higher managerial' occupations are linked with access to prestige, sports, sports utility vehicle (SUV) and luxury cars, while those who have never worked or are long-term unemployed favour large family cars. Especially relevant to places like Bradford, with notable levels of self-employment and entrepreneurship, small employers and 'own account workers' are most likely to drive SUVs.[2]

An individual's socio-economic position influences the choice of car, as Lansley indeed acknowledges, but 'the value of cars varies considerably'.[3] Those with less economic power (unemployed) may be more likely to own large family cars, but we do not really know how much these are worth, or which brands and models are preferred. Given that the average age of all cars and vans in 2018 was 8.2 years,[4] we cannot pinpoint who is more likely to own older or newer cars. Furthermore, having access to something is not the same as owning. Ownership also varies – some cars are owned outright, some are in the process of being owned through hire purchase or loan arrangements, with some cars later dis-owned, or repossessed. Associations between economic status and car preference are evident, but there is a much more revealing storyline beneath the veneer of statistically derived data, including how and why, rather than which, cars are bought.

The subject of car acquisition may seem simple because, as with any other consumer object, all that it requires is demand (with necessary consumer capital) and supply. Unfortunately, however, the prevalence of race and racism can disrupt the pragmatism of production, distribution and consumption. This can be seen elsewhere, for example in housing: estate agents, as gatekeepers with vested economic interests, help ensure particular neighbourhoods remain mono-ethnic and therefore desirable.[5] With the car, however, something else, but no less noteworthy, has happened.

Writing in the 1990s, US researchers found that new car dealers tended to offer white males better deals than they did to females and black and minority ethnic buyers.[6] Motivations for this form of direct discrimination hinged on two, not altogether mutually exclusive, factors. In part, it may have been simple prejudice or racial and gendered forms of bias ('dealer animus'). However, race and gender were proxy clues about buyers' reservation price: some markers of identity carried enough weight to help dealers estimate how much different customers would pay for the same car. While it is not within the remit of this book to suggest the same 'dealer animus' has ever existed in the UK, there are examples where something similar may have been in operation:

> So you gotta remember this is back in the day, like 1980s.... Even in those days, it was rare for us lot to buy new; we all bought second-hand.... Anyway, anyway, we turn up and er, no Asians in there ... a few customers, a few workers, but no Asians. My dad goes up to one of these fellers, and says, you know, *I wanna buy a Carina....* Nothing. No smile, no, you know, *have a seat, let me show you around....* At the time, there were an offer or something, might have been interest-free credit or a part-exchange deal.... Dad didn't qualify, you know. He was working, steady income, had cash for a deposit. But no, you know, *yeah, you can buy the car, but it'll cost you more than it would John or Fred or whoever* ... wasn't said like that, you know, but that's what was going on.... His money, same colour as everyone's else but I remember him saying to me: *it's this thing* [pinches skin on top of his hand], *never forget that they'll always see that.* (SG, 42, male, 11 March 2017)

For SG, this experience was defined as racist, whether structural or personal. This may have been an isolated incident, but others in the sample also referred to being treated differently in comparison to white customers, not only in car-related contexts, but in everyday life also. Alongside such incidents, however, are some structural and systemic channels through which racial discrimination appears to flow. Car insurance, for example, was often mentioned in the context of Bradfordians having a reputation for generating expensive premiums due to their apparent underwriting, actuarial, risk. Added to this, there was a belief among some participants that insurance companies tended to offer more expensive premiums to those with non-European names, a point supported by Phillips and Webber, who 'estimate that insurers are imposing an "ethnic penalty" on motorists who live in areas of high ethnic minorities which can vary from £50 per annum to £458'.[7] While the 'penalty' is financial, being verbally and physically abused as well as subject to 'stop and search' procedures is not uncommon either.[8]

As shown in the previous chapter, how cars are bought and sold among Bradford's Pakistanis has been informed by responses to the impacts of economic position and ethnic identity, specifically leading to the development of support mechanisms and the acquisition of skills and knowledge networks. As a result, there are buoyant and innovative levels of car-related business. Within this, car traders or dealers are varied in their approaches. Some in the sample appreciated cars on the bases of design, engineering, comfort and performance, and as objects of desire, capable of evoking emotion and feeling:

> I've had some cars and they've been everything. Look the part. Feel like a million dollars.... Not, obviously, worth that much, but nice, rare cars that have a bit more to them.... Oh man. Just even looking at them, you get excited; *lailaanh* falling out [drooling/salivating], I swear! Some cars, they do that to you. (CG, 26, male, 13 March 2017)

For many who earned their living through car-related work, however, a much more pragmatic orientation was an unsurprising element of their approach:

> The main thing in this game is moving them on at profit. That's what I have to do to make money.... I never have a car and think, *yeah, I could have that for myself.* What's point? Dead money. You lose out. I need to make money. Some cars drop [depreciate] in no time so best get shot as soon as you can. (YI, 28, male, 21 March 2017)

YI went on to explain elements of his strategy, which covered his knowledge of the market and particular issues that signalled significant risk (condition of bodywork, mileage). Tying into LG's view regarding the practice of changing cars for no rational reason, YI was also appreciative of the vibrant levels of demand he encountered: "In Bradford, there's a lot [of people] selling cars but a lot want cars as well; more and more people passing [the driving test] and don't forget, a lot like changing up."

Something special: bespoke

Some traders, however, did more than merely buy and then sell a car. Through modifications and enhancements, they developed 'bespoke', boutique-type businesses. Here, traders adapted and refined higher-end, evidently attractive, in-demand and marketable cars. In some cases, modifications were merely cosmetic: what ended up *looking* like a performance hatchback (for example, an Audi S3) was actually a basic model (1.6 Audi A3); a 'plastic rocket'.[9]

IP and his brother operated from home, with their spacious back yard sporting a total of 15 cars. Unlike YI, however, they tended to focus on sports, prestige and upmarket SUVs: during one visit, their stock included Range Rovers, BMWs, Audis (S3 and S4) and a Bentley Flying Spur. For this business, however, there were additional considerations before, during and after the buying stages. Identifying a vehicle involved knowledge about the market and customisability, and required access to specialists in completing the 'project'. As IP's description in the following extract suggests, motivation beyond profit is significant:

Figure 5.1. Basic model Audi A3, with visual modifications indicating a sports variant

> It started its life as a standard Range Rover Sport HSE. Basically, the car got stripped down to bare metal. Then he [IP's brother] painted it to his own colour. Land Rover never did them in this colour; this is like BMW M3 Estoril Blue. So it's bespoke, then, isn't it?… He gets a buzz out of it – you know, going to the garage and seeing it changing. (IP, 23, male, 17 January 2013)

In most cases, the strategy involved buying vehicles cheaply, possibly with scratches and scuffs. Once bought, cars were repainted, often in custom (non-factory) shades, or in some cases 'wrapped', a process involving covering the body panels with a semi-adhesive, semi-permanent vinyl-type veneer. The internal cabin could be upgraded, through enhancements to door cards, in-car entertainment (ICE) and seating. In addition, cars could be 'remapped', a means through which the vehicle's electronic control unit is enhanced according to the owner's preferences: more economy, more acceleration, more top-end speed, or a combination of these and other features. Enhancement increases

Figure 5.2. One of IP's bespoke Range Rovers

the price, but these cars become more marketable because they are made 'bespoke'.

This kind of approach is not solely aligned with an economic outcome (profit), but also functions through labour, creativity and pleasure, elements that complement the pursuit of profit. Such businesses have very little profile within mainstream car narratives, and especially fail to be recognised as worthwhile endeavours. The process of recreating cars elicits satisfaction, and this too is largely absent from public discourses especially. Even at a project's inception, creative intelligence and flair visualises an end product:

> Some cars are like, they can make you feel, like, *wow, that's something special*.... Like with me, it's here and there – random stuff, here and there nice exhaust, wheels, coilovers but it's not proper – [not] a professional way to do it.... The people who can do that, they are clever ... good ideas and it is like a work of art. For me it is anyway. (KA, 21, male, 14 July 2014)

Once projects are completed, more pleasure is gained on the road. Here, however, they are no longer merely cars; they are a version of the car/driver hybrid,[10] a fusion object that would not exist without the intersections of vision, labour, capital and aesthetic sensibility that offer new and unique performances of identity. Selling these projects and making profit also yields pleasure. The human involvement before this end point does not neatly fit with the processes more usually aligned with modern capitalism. If, as with commodity fetishism, we are detached from objects we make and consume, then this approach to production points to social and economic relations that are far from disconnected. Indeed, several car businesses seemed to be a counterpoint to the now-traditional, largely economically oriented, modes of production and consumption. Despite their work being valued through money, this was by no means the most prominent driver of social relations:

> I started over ten years ago, doing this. First few I did, I made a loss or broke even probably.... I've never made a

> loss on a car since then.... People know my work – they see the quality and the finish of my work and they know it's worth what I ask. A lot of time, these jobs take time and it's not easy work. Not everyone can do this.... It's skilled work and getting good at it, that costs time and money as well.... My buyers, they know how good I am and they don't have no qualms or issues about my prices. I know my price is expensive, but I have to pay myself what I think I'm worth, and what I'm worth is because the work, you understand? (KV, 33, male, 23 September 2018)

KV and his customers see labour as something that is to be appreciated and valued not only through monetary exchange; his references to quality, time and skill provide a sense of that which is beyond *price*: a more rounded appreciation of labour. Despite the rampant casualisation of work, the growth of the gig economy and the devaluing of labour that are woven into the very fabric of a contemporary capitalism that aims to maximise profits through increasing efficiencies, KV's approach may seem quaint, old-fashioned and small-scale, but nevertheless it exists, and businesses like his are thriving. Arguably, this mode of capitalism functions only because of a very specific 'market', with particular, specialised forces of demand and supply at play, but regardless, it does demonstrate a further, and significant, layer within the workings of a car culture. Indeed, there were several similar operators whose expertise, reputation and car biographies not only enabled a steady demand for their skills, but also enhanced their sense of job satisfaction, which, again, seems to be absent from more widespread experiences of contemporary work.[11]

Glad we came

Car subcultures are made coherent and enacted through 'car talk', as well as shared knowledge and passion and, in some cases, through car ownership. Through car talk emerge legitimacy, behavioural expectations, and definitions of in-group membership: owning a modified or interesting car may be enough to elicit in-group belonging, but 'car talk' cements this membership. The converse is also true: membership may be present but only partial if, for example, car talk is done in the absence of an appropriate car. Moreover,

> around each specialist or classic type of car a whole world develops with its own form of specialist knowledge and publications, practices and argot, which seek to explore and define the details of car anatomy, 'look', styling, image and ride. A world which offers the pleasures of common knowledge and distinctive classifications, which work with shared embodied habitus and membership, through car talk as much as driving.[12]

In advertising, we understand a system of language and symbolism that 'packages' particular cars for particular buyers, often defined by their purchasing power, class position, status and lifestyle aspirations. Why someone buys a sports car and not a multi-purpose vehicle, given that they may cost the same, hinges on 'consumer choice', but also because, in essence, different cars have their own symbolic meaning and value, and this extends to smaller, more localised and marginal car subcultures. Initially for the purpose of research,[13] several 'car meets' were attended, mostly in and around Bradford. The following abridged extract, from a not very active blog set up in 2015, explains what a car meet is, what happens and the variety of people, and cars, in attendance:

> These are fairly informal, relaxed and interesting events through which car enthusiasts of all backgrounds congregate with their vehicles. A lot of admiring, a fair bit of showing off and a reasonable amount of noise is to be expected.... Well, not noise, but music.... Within an hour the car park was fairly close to full.... People from all over Bradford and beyond – Huddersfield, Keighley, Leeds, Birstall and other parts of West Yorkshire. Different ages, varied ethnic backgrounds, a couple of pensioners ... and all with their takes on what their cars could and

should look like.… Some of the cars were barely changed (a Bentley, a few high end Mercs, Audis, Beemers…) but others had been modified with any and all of the following: looks, performance, sound, ride, comfort, handling. Taste and identity figured heavily throughout the whole thing – even when I asked some of the owners why they did what they did, their responses were layered with enthusiasm and appreciation of something that held part of themselves. Within each and every one of those cars, there is creativity and even art. Yes, that's right: for

Figure 5.3. Scenes from a car meet (7 May 2017)

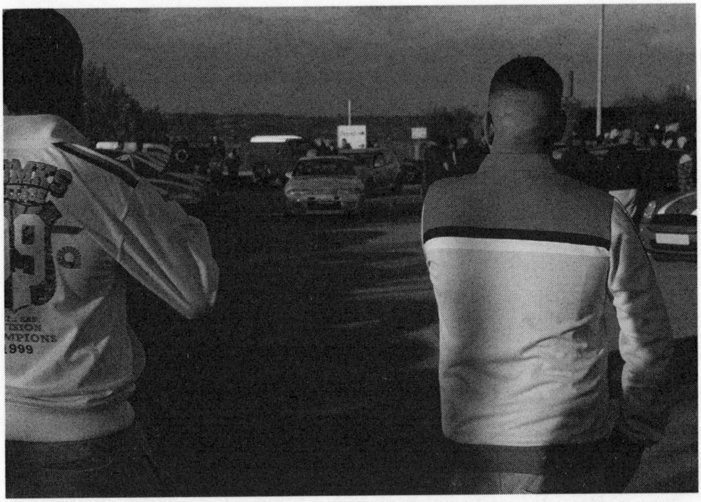

> some of those people, and even though they might not recognise or name it as such, their cars are more than mere objects of fundamental and utilitarian function.[14]

Occasionally, the organisers would 'have words' with individuals about their antisocial driving behaviour: doughnutting, rapid and noisy bursts of acceleration, and forms of showboating. However, something unusual occurred in relation to the thesis that some British Muslim communities tend to self-segregate, principally motivated by reasons that sit at odds with notions of Britishness, belonging and integration. At the start of these meets, ethnic demarcation was evident, with white-heritage and Pakistani-heritage visitors occupying their own spaces. However, once the car park started filling up, people started fanning out and engaging with cars and users outside their original territories. While there may have been some initial trepidation about engaging with the unfamiliar (for both ethnic groups), this subsided to form a moving mass of car enthusiasts. Central to enabling negotiations of space was an appreciation of cars. These observations were raised with one organiser:

> I tell you what it is, yeah – we invite everyone.... There are other clubs like ours that we go to their meets. Leeds, Castleford, erm ... last one I went to was in Birstall – Batley end. So they know me and I go their's and I say to them, *come to ours.* And some of them, you know, they come out with it.... *Look, we know* you're *all right but Bradford, not sure about that....* Because for them, what they know is, you know, is what they get told even though they might not never have been.... *It's a dangerous place ... Pakis and Muslims ...* that's what some of they [sic] tell me.... But once they're here, you know, they're all right. They see it for themselves and they say to me ... *good meet that, mate – you know, glad we came. Not like we thought it'd be* kind of thing. (MAA, 21, male, 21 June 2016)

It is necessary to note that these car meets, of questionable legal status, were organised without any approval from the owners of the spaces where they often took place (supermarket car parks, for example), and, indeed, were usually subject to police interest. In some cases, meets were 'shut down' by the police, but occasionally, officers would wander around, engaging with car owners and even admiring some of the vehicles. However, as a result of the risk of being shut down, some organisers demonstrated innovation and resilience through using their own networks and contacts. For example, meets were also arranged on private land with the agreement, and sometimes encouragement, of the land owners.

Mediated representations of young people's behaviour with and around cars further reinforce youth moral panics. Primed through class bias, such antisocial, irresponsible and often illegal behaviours[15] become expectations, grounded in the cyclical nature of myth-making, scapegoating and deviancy amplification. Unsurprisingly, mainstream readings of working-class car culture deny this as creative and artistic cultural endeavour. As a result, definitions of what constitutes worthwhile and worthy culture are restricted to narrower, elite and middle-class sensibilities and tastes. Deeper understandings of such working-class car cultures challenge forms of mass, dominant culture, itself contingent on both elite and popular aspects of hegemonic control. Because of the homogenising impact and reach of mass culture, 'authentic' folk culture is unlikely to gain traction. Despite this, mass-produced objects hold the potential to be transformed:

> The creativity of popular culture lies not in the production of commodities, so much as in the productive use of industrial commodities. The art of the people is the art of 'making do.' The culture of everyday life lies in the creative, discriminating use of the resources that capitalism provides.[16]

Cars can be finessed, reinvented or overhauled to such an extent that they hold meanings that sit at odds with whatever they stand for when originally produced. Some of these meanings are organic and grow over time through mainstream usage, becoming further enhanced by the circularity of reputation. Others change through interventions informed by taste, but enacted through agency and capital, adding to notions of consumption.

The cost of doing business

In this section, divergent tastes, as well as practices and dispositions toward cars that are owned or worked upon, are revealed through field notes, interview transcripts and small, descriptive passages relating to specific examples encountered in the research. The first of these is based principally on observations, undertaken over many and continuing visits, to one of several garages in the city. Other examples use interview data, covering changes to the contemporary car culture in Bradford as well as offering insight into modes and features of consumption as practice and idea.

AS has been in the car repair/service sector since leaving school.... The garage works on pretty much anything, from what I can tell – standard, anonymous and plain vehicles, quite a few taxi/minicab drivers come in with glum expressions, but there are also rather more specialist cars; the usual, high-end Audis, BMWs and even I saw a Lamborghini on one of his ramps a while ago. On top of that, the garage does have a few people coming with cars that have been or are being modified.

While hanging around, I chat with all sorts of car owners. Usually, I manage to pass as someone who maybe knows a little something about cars – I know what a spark plug does, I think; what blue smoke from the exhaust indicates, and what a creamy oil filler cap signifies. Most of this I've learnt informally, but some of it, I pick up in these sorts of places.

Some customers don't really want to be here; this visit to the garage, short or long, will no doubt burn a hole in their pocket. They don't resent their cars, but they don't have affection for them in the way some do. Taxi drivers, for obvious reasons, see their cars as money makers and while off the road, they don't earn. Younger drivers, though, they like to talk about their rides: how long they've had it, what's been done, what it's like. A few even give personalities to these things, with adjectives, metaphors, similes and alliterations in flow:

'Tasty.'

'Naughty.'

'Fast as fuck.'

'Like shit off a shovel.'

'Handles like it's on rails.'

'Sticks to the road like glue.'

Then come the comparisons, decisions and mistakes:

'It'll eat an M3 for breakfast.'

'Thinking of getting it remapped.'

'Lowering it, it's absolutely ruined the ride.'

AS tells me stories, occasionally epic, most small and precise:

'Dry as a bone. No wonder it's fucking knackered.'

'Been back to me three times with the same problem.'

'The guy who owns this car, he treats it better than his wife.'

If anyone can fix it, AS can. While not exactly revered, he does have a certain power, maybe even charisma. After all, something broken comes to him and he makes it better – this is not magic and neither is it rocket science, but it does require processes of elimination in order to diagnose, and other forms of intervention, in order to remedy. For over three decades, AS has been doing this. Thousands of cars later, he must be the closest thing to a car whisperer that you can get. (Field note, 2012–present)

A number of similar garages were visited during fieldwork, with most having an understandable interest in maintaining the viability and longevity of their business. HK's garage is situated in purpose-built premises, with several ramps, a number of mechanics, and walls adorned with cabinets and shelves holding signs, spare parts, cans of engine oil, lubricants and tools of the trade. The following abridged and edited interview segment illustrates some of the main features of HK's business, his approach and his motivations:

> We've been grafting since we were kids and my dad was in this game for decades and then he passed it on to us.... We have good turnover, get through 19–20 cars a day on the ramps.... We used to be smaller, but we couldn't handle it – too many, too-too many and we were turning customers away.... If you're right with your customers they'll always

> come back. We don't try to er, do our customers by ripping them off.... We spend a lot as well but that's the cost of doing business. Updates to software might be £1,500. With every new car there'll be dealer-only tools and they're expensive as well.... That's the only way you can do some jobs on some cars.... The trouble is Asians still don't want to pay for it – Pakistanis don't want to pay for it, so they always want it cheap and give you headache.... The more they pay for their car, the more expensive their running costs and repairs. Older cars, cheaper cars, don't have that problem ... but those don't usually fuss, they pay whatever we say.... People who drive these big cars, they're the ones who give you headache. (HK, 31, male, 2 February 2019)

HK was not the only mechanic who expressed dissatisfaction with how some customers failed to appreciate his capital expenditure. His mention of Asians/Pakistanis not willing to pay full price is not about ethnicity per se, but rather operates in conjunction with expressions of status, specifically with high-end or expensive cars. Cars that require less technological input are more likely to be owned by the less affluent, but yield less 'headache'. This aspect of consumer behaviour was not pursued in any meaningful manner, but the veneer of whatever an expensive car signifies does not necessarily correlate with the corresponding economic capacity, or willingness, to pay for its maintenance.

No more bangers

This following conversation covers a range of themes, including new modes of consumption influenced by technology, and how young driver behaviours are rehearsed not only across ethnic and class groupings, but also intergenerationally. KH, now a property landlord but formerly a taxi driver, has a fondness for cars, previously owning cheap 'bangers' as well as expensive, and usually fast, vehicles. He lives in an affluent Bradford suburb, but was born and brought up in Girlington, an inner-city neighbourhood, often located within the rhetorical terrain of social and economic decline:

KH: There's no difference between now and when we were younger because we were doing the same things. The only difference is – what's different is – the cars. The cars they're making now, they're much faster and they've been given to these drivers who can't drive them. The cars we drove … they weren't so quick like they are now. When I passed my test, I bought a banger – most of my friends, that's what we did; pass your test, boom, buy a banger for a couple of hundred quid. Why? Because that's all we could afford. Didn't care what it was, but it was probably a banger – Datsuns in those days, really, sometimes Toyotas, Carinas and that.

YA: Mine was a Honda, but yeah, it was a banger.

KH: Still, a banger. A few people, just a few mind, all right, they had you know, nice cars.… My brother, he had a Rover. One of my mates, he had a Granada, you know … but even them, they weren't even 200 brake horsepower, I bet. Don't forget, the car that changed everything was the Cavalier … SRi 130 Cavalier, that changed everything.… They were everywhere and you know what, they were fast. They – were – fast.

YA: Yeah, so, there *were* fast cars back then, then.

KH: Not really, only people who could afford them bought them. I had one by 25, 26 – but that's because I started doing taxi. I needed a car: SRi – done and dusted. (KH, 50, male, 1 November 2018)

For KH, contemporary car driving is relational; he would be no different, he argues, if he was young today. He cites his own earlier experiences of car ownership and driving as being contingent on economic capacity; in his youth, cars had to be affordable and even if they were barely functional, that was enough. Due to changes in technologies, modern cars are de facto 'better' in most ways: economy, reliability and performance.

Figure 5.4. 1980s Vauxhall Cavalier, SRi variant saloon

He also mentions the rise of the hot hatch, in particular one model that was not only 'fast' but also practical, affordable, reliable and thus popular: the Mark 2 Vauxhall Cavalier, SRi 130:

> Like now, that's what they're all designed for now. Every car now is fast compared to what we had. And we had to learn how to drive those old cars – those bangers we had – and that driving made us better drivers. Now you have A3s, Mercedes B Class and other very quick cars and these young drivers who don't have driving experience and that's what the difference is. By the time we got something a bit quick, a bit decent, we'd been driving for years so we built up that experience. Now they pass and a year later, they're in a GTI and they're tearing around – which is what we would have done. But because there were fewer cars and the cars weren't that fast, it was safer.

It was through the pitfalls and challenges of owning and driving a 'banger' that driving prowess, for his generation of drivers, was honed. Not quite a rite of passage, but certainly this appeared to be a retrospectively valued experience among a number of older drivers in the sample. The availability of faster cars today, in conjunction with the economic position that enables consumption, leads to greater likelihoods of risk and danger, especially if younger, less experienced drivers are "tearing around". The driving and car-owning preferences of contemporary younger drivers, however, are subject to a shift in habitus. The social, cultural and economic position in turn forms a distinction in taste:

KH: This is part of us, now. I got kids and I know what they want. My daughter, when she passes her test she'll want a car. I turn up with what you and I would call, you know, a decent little car … a one litre Micra, Yaris, something similar. I did that? She'll probably be upset with me.… I know she will because A, she doesn't want a Japanese car and B, she wants something, you know, a bit funky, something with a bit of summat to it.

YA: Why not a Japanese car?

KH: Because that's not them. That was *us*, and it was really more our dads and uncles, but now, our age people: look at what we drive now. We don't drive Jap cars, either. For us, it's BMW, Mercedes, Audi: *zindabaad* [long live]. Our youngsters, they want what their friends have, what they think are, you know, cars worth having.

Central to KH's explanation is the idea of social, economic and cultural change – that younger contemporary generations are affluent and have greater agentic power in comparison with their parents in their youth, and that this enables a departure in the choices available to them. In order to more fully explore some of the points raised by KH, the next example, relying heavily on an interview transcript segment, cross-references some of the themes and details explored in this section.

Too Asian

In 2012, some six years before the interview with KH, ZA was driving a seven-year-old Toyota Yaris, a car she had bought with the guidance of her father. The car was cheap and reliable; an ideal first car. ZA could later upgrade to a 'better' car that she would afford to run, and especially insure. When asked what sort of car ZA would like to later own, she was less interested in the kinds of car her father's generation appreciated:

ZA: Corollas, Auris, Yaris and all that – they're just too Asian. Pakistani, more than Asian.... Like the Japanese are like that but even like some others that aren't Japanese as well. You know, like BMs, VWs, Audis and all that – our lot, we drive everything now but there's some cars that only we will drive and those are some of the Japanese ones. Like I never see a white person driving in an old Corolla. They might have like a new, a brand new Auris or Yaris or that Hybrid one or something like that, but you hardly ever see white people driving older Japanese cars.

YA: So what do they drive instead, then?

ZA: White people? Well, depends on sort of how rich they are, I suppose. For poorer people, it'll be like Fords and Vauxhalls. They're more common and so are Citroens and Peugeots and Renaults. If you're poorer and white, you'll drive one of them cars but poorer and Asian, you might be driving something Japanese.... Doesn't matter if you're rich, you'll buy whatever you like, whatever takes your fancy. Doesn't matter what colour you are then. But I noticed that our lot are more into posher, nicer cars – bigger, expensive, showy cars. X5s, Q7s and Mercedes and even sports cars as well, our people buy a lot of, I think.

YA. So, what sort of car are you getting next?

ZA: Something sportier and slicker than what I've got. A Leon ... Golf, obviously.... Because it's the best car for what it is. Everyone says good things about them: white people and Asians. It's a car that everyone can like because it's classy, I think. Not posh, but it's got a bit of style to it and obviously, it's got a really good reputation and everything like that.... Obviously I'd like to have the best one, the R32 – the Mark 5 – but I could never afford that. (ZA, 22, female, 17 January 2012)

By 2018, ZA had changed cars several times. After the Yaris, she upgraded to a Ford Focus, followed by a Volkswagen Golf and later a five-year-old Audi A3. Like others, ZA references ethnicity and class as shaping distinctions in the production of taste, but also suggests that ideas around 'ethnic taste' can invariably tie in with prevailing stereotypes, but remain concrete, though perhaps benign in their reach and potency. Another female, DW, had overlapping views with those of ZA:

YA: So, what are you driving?
DW: Citroen. C1.... Pathetic.... It is. One litre. It hasn't even got four cylinders.... I thought it had something wrong with it when I got it....
YA: So, you don't like it, though.
DW: It's alright, as a car. But, how can I say, it's not my top car.
YA: What is?
DW: Too many. I like my German cars. I like Subarus.
YA: Mitzys?
DW: Yeah. But Subarus are better. But I'd like a Q7, at some point.... That is *whooh* something else. (DW, 22, female, 11 September 2018)

Seven years prior to this interview, another female was asked what kind of car she would buy. MK mentioned German models, in particular an S3 Audi, but this preference was offset, to some extent, by their cost and their reputation as 'boy racer cars'. When asked about owning a Japanese car, her reaction referenced taste, class, ethnicity and identity even in general: "Never a Yaris or a Nissan Micra. They're like TP cars.[17] In Bradford you can get away with it because there's a lot of Asians." Here the relationship between place and identity surfaced: in Bradford, Japanese cars are common and therefore unremarkable; as a result, the driver is one of many other, arguably anonymised, drivers of Japanese cars. When subsequently asked if her choice was restricted to (older) Japanese cars, she maintained that

> I'd rather not drive! It's about your identity: you can't be driving a crap car like that. It's not about them being beneath you, but you have to have something more

> acceptable. If you can't afford it, then take a taxi or use public transport! (MK, 22, female, 20 November 2011)

For MK, then, some cars represent not exactly negative or problematic images, but they undervalue the identity, and status, of the driver. In other interviews, this theme was pursued based on an existing knowledge and experience of car-buying in the city over the last five decades or so, and similarly fed into Miller's discussion of Trinidadian taste in soft drinks, with participants feeling confident in identifying cars that were typically 'white' or 'Asian'.

Not fitting the profile

Our impressions of cars and their owners are based on some degree of coherent sense-making processes within particular social and cultural contexts. These are populated with narratives, in turn informed through the embedding of stereotypes and tropes. While some of us might believe we are enlightened enough to be immune from these elements of perception, the following extract indicates otherwise:

I'm picking someone up from their work and waiting in my car, doing nothing much. I see a white Subaru Legacy estate crawl past me. It's a late nineties model but it's in very good nick. More than that, it looks like someone's spent a lot of money on customising/modifying it.... I should get out and introduce myself to the driver and tell him about my interest and research in cars and car culture.... I imagine he's some young kid, maybe early twenties, all tracky bottoms and Rockport boots, tramlines in his hair and a bit of bling on his hands. Not a thug, but probably sees himself as a bit bad arse, him having such a bad arse ride. I get out of my car and start to walk over, rehearsing an introduction, apologising for intruding on his time, but then stop and stare. The driver's door of the Subaru opens and out steps a figure in black. For a second I can't believe what I'm seeing. It's a woman in a burkha and she opens the boot and pulls out a pram. This doesn't seem right. A woman? Never mind a woman, a Sister? She does not fit the profile and I tell myself it's not her car, but her brother's or her husband's. There is no other explanation. (Field note, 21 June 2012)

Upon encountering a break or disruption in normative, culturally and economically bound scripts, alternative answers are sought. In the previous extract, a rather distinctive car is noticed, and generates associations and sense-making processes that explain the car (what it looks like and what it signifies) and the person who is expected to be driving it (obviously male, probably young, possibly working class, definitely interested in cars). Our confidence in stereotypes is such that any deviation requires further components that help sustain them. In this case, once a female is seen and acknowledged as the driver, this is made coherent through additional scaffolding: it's not *her* car, but a male's (her husband, brother or similar). The actual owner of this car remains a mystery, but that is not really the point: what is significant is the work we do when trying to make sense of what we see and how that, as a series of processes, enables the perpetuation of stereotypes, and their creation also.

From the research participants, stereotypes[18] about cars and their drivers became regular: Audi drivers as aggressive; Mini drivers as invariably female; Range Rover drivers as 'gangster'; Ford drivers as dull; BMW drivers as risk takers; and various cars (high-specification Subarus, Mitsubishis, Vauxhalls, Seats, VWs and Hondas, for example) being designated typical 'boy racer' cars. Very expensive cars were also, unsurprisingly, signifiers of economic success, but often there was a caveat relating to criminality. Given that Bradford has a varied socio-economic profile, understanding the bases for such assertions is not difficult. Even in general, 'young men in the inner cities are seen as urban interlopers, agents of street crime and violence'. Such representations are one-sided: 'While these men *appear* spectacularly in news reports purporting to represent "gang yobbery", "football hooliganism" or "race riots", they almost never speak: they are seen but not heard.'[19]

Youth and especially race are rehearsed through the prisms of threat and danger, enabling partial and incomplete readings of identities to take shape. Added to this, interactions are interpreted through the immediacy of the moment, its setting and the positionality of those being read and those doing the reading. If an expensive car is being driven in a middle-class neighbourhood by a white, male, middle-aged driver, we are likely to view the driver as successful and wealthy; at this point, the matter is closed. Compare this to the same car being driven in an inner-city neighbourhood, by a young, black male, dressed in designer finery, playing, at volume, 'German Whip'. Here, the reading may not be clear or easy, but in fact may end up bringing together race, space and identity: expensive car + inner city + young black male = successful (dubiously so).

Spare cash

The performance of identity is subject to motivations of those who own and drive cars, as well as those who encounter them. This following example resonates with the development of grounded skills and how these are acquired, often through networks and experimentation. It also shows identity working through the car, enacting taste, leisure and creativity.

AB had owned his Mark 5 Volkswagen Golf for two years at the time of interview (2011), when he was 28. AB had a soft spot for Golfs, and since that initial interview has owned a Mark 6, as well as a Mark 4. Before 2011, he owned Subaru Imprezzas, an Audi, a BMW and a few other Golf GTis, all of which had been, in one way or another, modified. AB is more than just an owner, or even an enthusiast. Not a trained mechanic, AB does much of the work (other than respraying) himself. His knowledge and skill set has been developed through friends and contacts in the motor industry and, more recently, through scouring internet forums or videos on youtube.com, especially when diagnosing faults.

AB is meticulous in his pre-purchase research, in order to ensure the car he buys is "the right one": he checks its condition, how it "looks" and whether there are any risks. Once it is bought, he undertakes a long-term series of enhancements, in some cases repairs, starting with the necessary, before moving on to elements that align with his own creative vision. On the Mark 5 Golf, for example, modification included uprated

19-inch alloy wheels, a lowered suspension, a custom exhaust, sway bars, a K&N air filter, Alpine audio equipment, uprated/tinted rear light clusters and an engine control unit 'remap'. Such work has a cost, but,

> I don't spend much on anything else much anyway. It's just sort of spare cash if you know what I mean. I work pretty hard and I don't drink, don't smoke or anything like that. I do shop around for bits when I need them. Like the alloys, I got them from XXXX Accessories on XXXX Road. I know the guy who owns it and he sorted me out. (AB, 28, male, 3 March 2011)

AB acknowledged his car was worth not much more than the price of an unadulterated model. Here, financial outlay enacts leisure and channels creativity, as opposed to producing profit. AB, however, made no claim about artistic endeavour; at best, there was among several such modifiers a modest acknowledgement that this *could* be seen as artistic. This may reference a broader point around the force of habitus and class disposition wherein working-class identity is so devalued that creativity is rarely acknowledged, even internally, among those who occupy the culture itself. In AB's case, the object is created in class-bound conditions through which habitus is given physical and psychological form. Here, it is the broader force and reach of class as idea and practice that influences internal and external renderings of identity. Those who are loaded with higher forms of social and cultural capital are able to have their creations accepted as creative, artistic, interesting or valuable, whereas for those of a similar class-cultural location to AB, any value is recognisable only by others, in the main, like themselves.

The wow factor

The final example comes from a male businessman, SJ, who in 2013 had upgraded to a fairly new and reasonably high-specification Range Rover. Other than a private registration plate and number, SJ's car was factory specification. SJ, however, did not see himself as particularly interested in cars, but once the interview started to flow, his views indicated a fairly in-depth understanding of how cars can be perceived, and what such perceptions can reveal, accurately or not, about their drivers. When asked about his previous cars, he mentioned what each meant to him:

> The first one was a BMW 7 Series so that's the biggest you can get.... It gave that impression of style and sophistication.... The latest car, which is the Range Rover, which is like a four-by-four type of a car, is the best car I've had so far. And the reason for that is that it does give all the right messages to the people. I know it has an image of a gangster car but when you're not a gangster and you're doing business and you're working hard, it gives you that feeling of driving a big car because you deserve it and because you've earned it.... It really does roar.... It gives you the power, the height, the looks, it gives you the wow factor and people notice you. I found that none of those cars did that, whether it was the 7 Series or the A8, it just wasn't big enough. This car's big enough to get noticed. It's a car you can't miss. It stands out. (SJ, 36, male, 19 July 2012)

Size, power, taste ("style and sophistication") and presence, as well as the mediation of identity ("messages") form part of SJ's motivation underpinning the value and virtue of such a car, rationalised as positive business and self-image decisions. While this is not a specific matter of concern for SJ, he was nevertheless one of many respondents who referenced Bradford's car scene as highly positive, occasionally substantiated with an endorsement: "Even Jeremy Clarkson said if you want to see nice cars, go to Bradford." The existence of this statement by the presenter[20] is not the point; the fact that it is used, however, indicates a degree of confidence in and appreciation of the city even in general. As SJ stated, "We've got this reputation out there of being quite out of the ordinary. That doesn't worry me. That's something we should be proud of. We're actually good at being different."

This is developed in the next chapter, through discussing how cars yield emotional responses from others. Road rage, for example, sits within existing understandings of particular spaces and of how some drivers are framed as less competent than others. This broader framing therefore feeds into how widely held views about behaviours are assigned to specific minority ethnic identities.

Throughout this chapter, class has remained a salient marker of identity through which car-related practice can be seen. However, class is not the sole contributor to the variety of themes, issues and car-related practices that have been explored. From car enhancement to car repair and retailing, class, along with age, gender and ethnicity, intercedes to produce a myriad of possibility, which is then realised, read and reacted to. Within subcultural car scenes in particular, there is a consistent, robust and highly visible presence wherein elements of taste, aesthetics and preference are constituted through appreciations from within these groupings. Despite the risks to modifiers of being labelled problematic, the existence of modified cars may also form resistance to mainstream and more conventional sensibilities around what a car does, how it looks and who drives it. At the same time, it is noticeable but unsurprising that car cultural practice continues to evolve, drawing on the interplays between identity, taste and consumption.

SIX

Social psychology, cars and multi-ethnic spaces

This chapter introduces additional social psychological insights into the understanding of the dynamic whereby cars and identities intersect within mono- and multi-ethnic spaces. Here, the car and what it signifies – who is likely to drive what, where and how – enables insider and collective group affiliation on the one hand, and moments of intergroup tension on the other.[1] The car and roads further enable individuals to claim ownership, superiority and confidence, often channelled through emotions and behaviours that without the car would be deemed rude, uncivil, aggressive, or otherwise inappropriate and unwelcome. At the same time, cars can be places in which we can be and express ourselves: we can sing, laugh, shout, cry. On the flip side, a car can be a sanctuary of sorts in which we make moments of calm and quiet, helping us to switch off, relax, reflect and think:

> We find it familiar to consider objects as useful or aesthetic, as necessities or as vain indulgences. We are on less familiar ground when we consider objects as companions to our emotional lives or as provocations to thought.[2]

Memories are made with people, but our lives are punctuated with the fleeting or recurring presence of toys, pictures and other things that seem to hold value and meaning beyond their utility or purpose. Alongside a capacity to elicit emotion, objects colour the stories we construct around particular events and moments. Donath, for example, anchors her mother's 1964 Ford Falcon with an identity of its own, and, perhaps more noticeably, what the car meant to her once she became its keeper:

> Everyone wanted to go for a ride in the Falcon, even though it had no air-conditioning in the summer, iffy heat in the winter, and the sort of doubtful brakes and steering that kept it in the right-hand slow traffic lane. The blue paint was faded, the fenders were rusty, but the car had style. No matter how dully mundane I felt, in the Falcon I was the Driver of that Cool Car.[3]

Cars also function as provocations, with drivers experiencing or even enacting instances of road rage and anger-induced outbursts, some of which reveal insights beyond the merely interpersonal.[4] This chapter, therefore, also forms a bridge to the following chapter, in that it sheds more light on how the car is used in the perpetuation of racialisation and racism.

Road rage and racist hostility

For several participants, busier roads are a fact of modern, busier life, and in the rush to be somewhere else, moments of despair, anger or hostility can surface. For some males, however, part of their experience – as either being subject to or subjecting others to rage – was voiced mostly through the recognition of (in)competence:

> You see, there's people on the road – I don't know how they passed.... I've been driving a long time. I know how to drive but people don't. They don't know how to use roundabouts, what right of way is, anything like that.... Even today – just now on my way here. Get to a roundabout, three-way roundabout.... And there's two other cars just parked there – waiting, for what? *Give way to the right, you idiots!* Neither of them are budging, so you know what, I just go through. Now they *can't* drive, I *can* drive but for me to not get late – which could have happened, you know, could have waited all day at this rate, I'm thinking – I have to break the highway code because

> the bird to my right isn't moving, and the one to her right, she's not moving either.... And I know it sounds sexist, but some of them, they can't – they don't know, I don't know what it is, but they can't drive. My own wife – she's been passed nearly 20 years, and I won't – I will not sit in her car if she's driving. Either I drive or, you know what I mean, we go in my car.... Because she winds me up – number of – number of near misses I've had when she's driving. I said *you know what, forget it – I'm not getting in with you. Bad for my health*. Heart attack material, you know what I mean? (PS, 47, male, taxi driver, 14 May 2014)

Even talking about road rage seemed to provoke in PS a genuine form of anxiety: shaking his head, sighing, trying not to get too impassioned about this arguably banal element of driving life. Other males, however, were less invested in the impact of any incompetent driving they encountered, regardless of any noticeable markers of identity. For example, the following type of comment was not unusual:

> There is some appalling driving in Bradford but it's everywhere, really.... It's a fact of life isn't it? You get used to it.... My wife, when she drives, she gets really angry and starts swearing and horning at people; she'll even reach across and horn if I'm driving! She's a different person in a car.... But, you know, it's not worth getting upset about, is it? (PF, 32, male, 3 June 2016)

Going back to PS, however, two mechanistic elements were at the heart of his view – and again, they were co-relational, rather than discreet and operating in isolation. Driver incompetence, in general, was an issue that caused him discomfort, and this was given a more tangible, reproducible cogency through relating bad driving with female drivers in particular: for whatever reason, for him females were less likely to be competent drivers, with competency being defined by his standards. Females, therefore, constituted a certain type of driver. Feeding into this, another male also referenced roads as gendered spaces:

> Women, when they're driving, it's not the same for them.... I know this, right, didn't always know this, but if you sit with a woman who's driving, you'll notice she has to do other things that we, as men, don't.... I got banned a few years ago, right.... So I'd be cadging lifts everywhere.... In the end, I just, you know what, buy her a car ... buy missus car, problem solved.... She's ferrying me around and then I see how it's different for women drivers. They get a different drive to men.... So, let's say she were dropping me off at work – eight miles away in Keighley. She'd get bother – people overtaking her, jumping in front of her, giving her abuse even – shouting and horning and all that.... She drives careful, doesn't speed but she can drive, an all right driver. Not just saying it – probably better than me. Safer than me. She got no points: I got banned. Who's better driver?... Horning, swearing, flashing, tailgating – you name it, they do it.... But they do it to women more than with men.... Because they're women and they think they can. (RI, 31, male, 6 November 2013)

Added to this, as one female driver put it:

> It's men who feel inadequate, I'd say. They see us women and young girls, driving nice cars and they upset themselves.... You have the young lads, because you have a nice car and they want to impress their mates or it's some precious mid-life crisis man who thinks his life's more important than yours and you shouldn't be on the road. It happens to me more out of town.... When I travel, I get some road rage ... most times white people, most times men.... Rage, it's about frustration and more of a man thing. I don't get angry like them ... I just laugh it off. (GA, 36, female, 16 March 2017)

While it is not a deeply developed line of inquiry in this book, there is little doubt that the road is a gendered space, in relation not only to how gender in a car is read externally, but also to how cars signify – either by design (and marketing) or through particular symbols, flashes of creativity or other cues – driver identity: colours, stickers and private registration numbers can signify gender, class, politics and even that most personal element of biography, our name. When it comes to emotional outbursts on the road, however, the force of normative, underlying patriarchy can and does qualify some responses. This is not to say, however, that road rage in Bradford is particularly sexist or misogynistic in nature, but rather that gender is one marker of identity used to inscribe difference, and in this case, render judgements of competence.

Road rage is a mechanism in which driver ego surfaces through reliance on the offended person's claims and definitions of competence. Driving, therefore, is performative even though, fundamentally, it involves a set of technical, mechanistically learnt skills, aiming to ensure all drivers have the same baseline competence. Whereas expressive, and sometimes dramatic, elements of driving skill are regularly amplified in films, in everyday life such actions are rightly deemed dangerous. However, beyond danger, a further break from usual conventions of civility is experienced when a driver, *not the car*, is 'cut up' or overtaken, which constitutes a personal insult. If we are subject to this, we might shrug it off, but, if the person who has committed the act happens to be of a particular 'type', then the instance is no longer unique, or specific to that single event. Instead, it is emblematic of and pathological to 'them'. And the 'them' could be 'old fogeys', 'drug dealers', 'chavs', 'white van men', 'women drivers', 'Pakis' or, indeed, 'Muslims'. CM and her husband, JS, recalled a distressing instance in which not only her gender, but also her ethnicity and the car she was driving, seemed to provoke a worrying reaction:

CM: This driver, he pulled up in the next lane at the traffic lights and it was a right-turn lane, so I thought, *well, he's turning right....*

JS: Like you would.

CM: Yes, so, the lights change and I set off and he's, you know, still next to me. I thought, *what's this idiot doing?* I slowed down, thinking *let him overtake me*, but he doesn't. So I speed up. Now he speeds up. And now, he's right next to me ... almost touching my car. So

I braked a bit and he brakes as well. *My God! What's wrong with this* … [sighs].
JS: Should have pulled over, called 999.
CM: You weren't there and you're not thinking when it's happening.
JS: True.
CM: I'm not joking, but he was like that for nearly a mile until I accelerated away from him. I parked up and called the police. He drives past, slowly, and his windows are down … shouting, swearing, name calling.… (CM, 41, female, and JS, 42, male, 14 March 2016)

CM's husband offered his own interpretation of the reading and impact of the incident, and subsequently its cause. For him, this event was provoked not specifically by his wife's presence, but what she represented:

JS: I thought, like you would, that she's pissed someone off but–
CM: Excuse me!
JS: And she's not, you know, she's not a bad driver at all – you can't be to survive on these roads these days.…
YA: So, what happened? I mean, what do you think it was about?
CM: He's got a theory, haven't you?
JS: I know exactly what happened: guarantee this is what it was. It wasn't road rage, it was road racism! This happened soon after the solider was murdered a few years ago.… And she, you know, obviously a Muslim woman – headscarf on, driving a nice car – not a flash car, but, it's nice.…
CM: I had a BMW at the time.
JS: Right in XXXXX – a white area.
CM: Awful around there.
JS: And you know, you think things might have changed, but no, the test is: when something bad happens, how do people react? And that's how they react: harass people, and worse.

CM: I didn't do anything to him.
JS: Obviously, it had nothing to do with you, but for that guy, it had *everything* to do with you.

Such instances may be isolated and rare, but in social psychological terms, they become intergroup, rather than interpersonal, encounters.[5] Any responses directed to the driver in question are nevertheless framed by the perception of the group, the category membership of the driver. And it is through this that stereotypes come to life: 'they' are all the same, at least potentially. On the road, this not only translates to interethnic tension, whereby wholesale Muslim identity can be inscribed from above onto individuals, as with CM, but is also specifically utilised in the domain of car consumption and driving. Swanton's work, albeit not explicitly situated within the field of intergroup dynamics, does illustrate the performance and utility of racism through the car. For example, one of his interviewees mentions a moment when road rage was a result of underlying (driving and arguably ethnic) prejudices:

> And I am the world's worst. I really do give 'em some, 'Paki'!… I don't find … Asian drivers particularly good.… And they are so discourteous. Really discourteous.… I came to an emergency stop once down this busy road and this man, he was parked and I was doing 40 mile an hour down here, so he did a U-turn in front of me. And I rammed on horn and as he's gonna up the other way, I remember shouting through the window: 'I hope Allah makes you impotent.'[6]

Here, race and racism are provoked into life by the driving of someone else; a single instance results in a quite peculiar, almost incoherent and bizarre outburst. But the quote reveals a tendency to stereotype Asian drivers as incompetent or not 'particularly good'. Words like 'Paki' are therefore ready to be deployed in the context of anger, but are given further justification through definitions of group behaviour. Here, race and racism are simply waiting to become operationalised in the form of racist language.

However, because such utility suggests it is always available, the significance of race as an ideological, structured and embedded concept cannot be underplayed. What these sorts of examples illustrate is that without the ideological apparatus of race – woven into discourses of biological, cultural and increasingly intellectual inferiority, superiority and supremacy, racism would not work.

Sound and fury, aurality and outrage

Alongside the appeal of owning and driving cars, the act of driving weaves in physical, emotional and psychological activity. Indeed, owning and driving a car produces emotion-rich responses,[7] but the performative elements of driving are worth exploring also. This can be stripped down to two distinct elements: the driver's performance within the car, and how those outside the car perceive that performance. Here, the aesthetics and aurality of car culture are significant and particularly connect with modified vehicles. Modified cars, as well as motorcycles and quad bikes, have a visual and aural texture: they can be seen and especially heard, either in the form of pounding music or via custom exhaust systems.

Vehicular loudness is not an arbitrary, neutral or vacuous aspect of car design. Even among mainstream manufacturers, how a car sounds is an important feature of its identity and appeal. In some models, for example, Volkswagen fitted a 'Soundaktor', a device designed, apparently, to amplify or enhance engine sound.[8] In more localised contexts, loudness enables identities to be performed and acknowledged: even if the sound produces a form of taste-induced 'disgust',[9] it is still recognition. When asked about the appeal of loudness, specifically in relation to his car's audio system, ZD replied, at least initially, in somewhat reserved terms:

YA: So your system, seems a lot's going on there.
ZD: Yeah, it's right now. Took me time to get it how it is.
YA: Money?
ZD: A bit [laughs].
YA: I won't ask how much, then. But it's loud, though.
ZD: It's not that loud, not always.

YA: I could hear you a mile off. It's loud.

ZD: That wasn't loud. To you it might be loud, but not for me. (ZD, 20, male, 6 August 2016)

Figure 6.1. Selection of louder than usual 'big bore' exhaust tailpipes

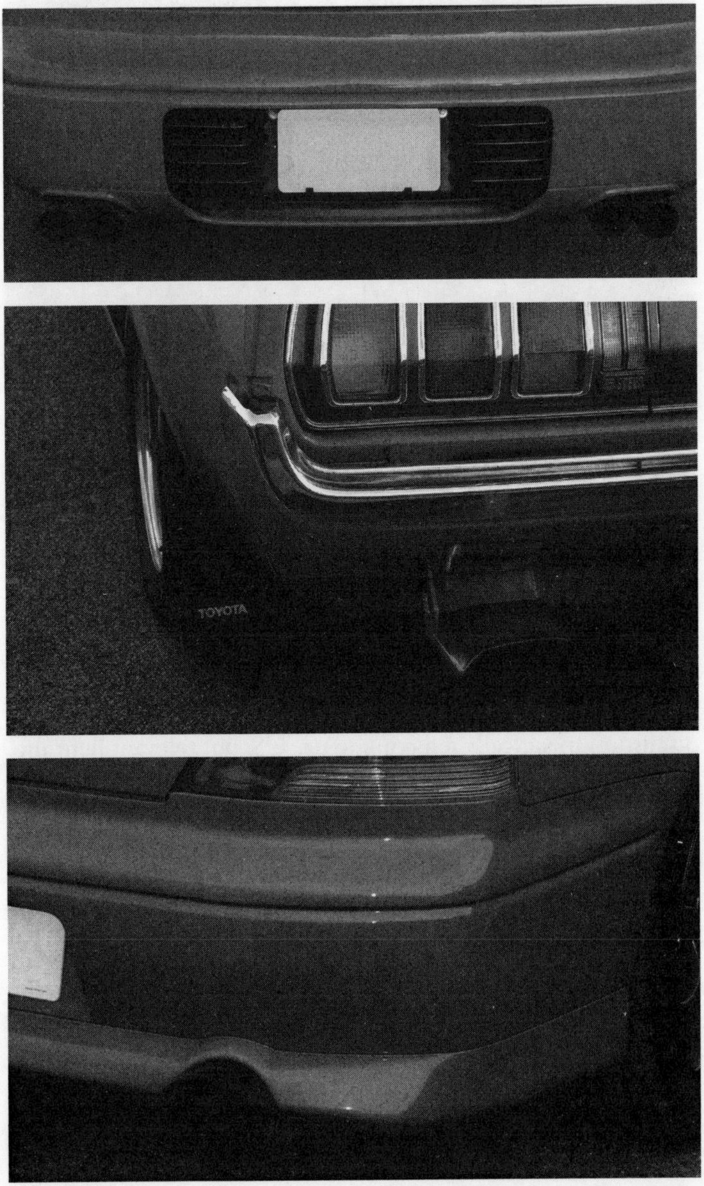

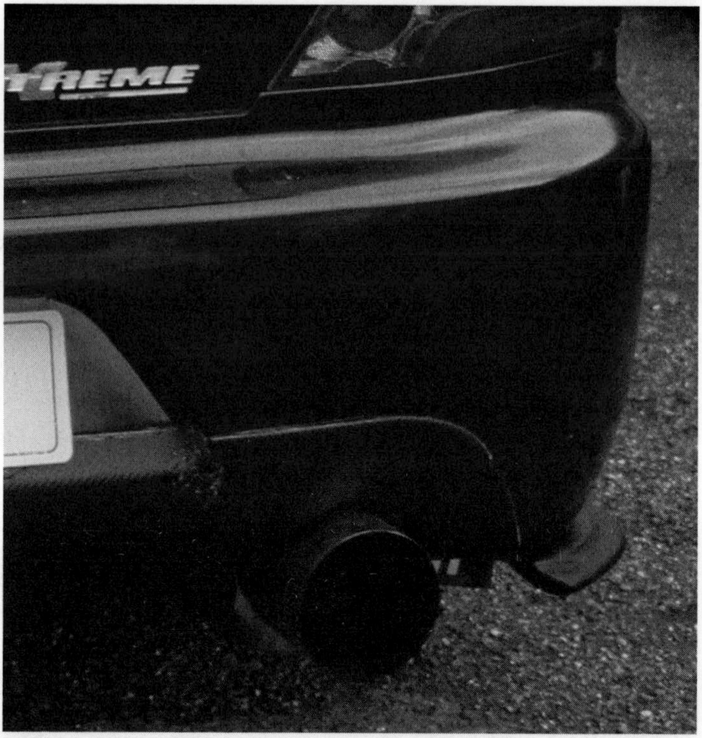

Like several others, ZD invested thought, time and money in his car's audio system: with the array of speakers, the head unit, and the additional amplification, wiring and fuse arrangements, the car seemed like an appendage for the sound system. In a discussion specifically referring to the US, but relevant here also, Crawford notes, 'For those within the car stereo culture, it is a hobby and a passion, with some spending thousands'.[10] This clearly ties in with ZD's practice, which also involves a subjective appreciation of sound quality:

ZD: It's not just loud, it's clear sound and all the speakers, how I've got it set up, it sounds good. You'll be hearing the sounds at different levels and channels. So–

YA: So, it's an experience? More of an experience?

ZD: Yeah. What I was saying was it's not just having it, like loud music.

Figure 6.2. Bass speaker array fitted to a 1995 Toyota Starlet Turbo

Expensive and usually loud sound systems, playing quite specific musical genres, offer opportunities in which identity and taste are rehearsed publicly, but are often received without enthusiasm or appreciation. Indeed, loudness can yield usually subtle, micro manifestations of intergroup hostility. Most casual observers, or listeners, may simply interpret unworthy music being played at unnecessarily high volume as antisocial behaviour. For the curators of these moving sound exhibitions, it is the quality of the sound that enhances the experience. At a later point in ZD's interview, how other people reacted when they heard his car's music was given space for response:

ZD: Sometimes, people be standing and staring, you're driving and you know what they'll be thinking.... You know: *why's he playing that music so loud for?!...* They think whatever they think. I don't worry about them, why they bothering about me for?

YA: Because you're loud. Your music's loud.

ZD: Free country, though.

YA: [laughs]

ZD: I'm not doing anything illegal, though, am I? I'm not hurting no one so, whatever, big deal.... Don't really care, like I said. My car, nothing to do with them.

ZD's responses could be read as a disregard for the needs, values and expectations of others, but his responses can also be placed within notions of freedom, individuation and agency. For him, his car is primarily a private-sphere domain, even though its presence seeps out to become public, visible and heard. A few minutes later in the interview, however, things took a slightly different turn when his family, particularly his father, who was also born and brought up in the UK, became relevant:

ZD: My dad? He doesn't like it.... Like you said, it's loud, isn't it? To him it's like being disrespectful – doesn't want neighbours to be complaining him. Doesn't like it because it looks bad....

YA: What would happen, worse case, if you did it outside your home?

ZD: I wouldn't.... I don't think he'd kick me out, but he'd make me sell my gear [car audio system]. Yeah, he would do that 'cos he's said it when I first started it.

There is, therefore, a line that even the likes of ZD aren't prepared to cross. Whether or not ZD is referring to the complementing concepts of *izzat* (respect) and *behsti* (shame) is not the point, but what appears relevant is deference to parental authority, and to some extent, those cultural values and practices that resonate and connect with his own sense of identity; and this is not just the hybrid notion of British-Pakistani, but also involves being a son, a male, and demonstrating to his father at least that he is, or can be, 'responsible', 'sensible' and 'mature'. Furthermore, as ZD still lives with his parents, his music system is at least indirectly supported because he does not have the economic burdens of living separately. The reactions to the aurality of his car, meanwhile, do become significant when heard on his own patch, a point that reinforces a certain amount of respect and appreciation of his home and territory, despite his behaviour being influenced by the expectations of his father. When the topic of conversation drifted into discussion of law enforcement, this too reflected the need to adapt behaviour:

ZD: If you see them [police], then turn it down. That's all you can do.... You know – everyone knows ... police, they think we're all dealing, around here especially.... Most think it. You can tell when they stop you, how they be talking to you, how they get hard and clever with you.
YA: Some are all right.
ZD: For you they are. You're older and you're a professor so you're all right. You, you're not a drug dealer.
YA: But neither are you.
ZD: Yeah but thats not what they think. I'm telling you, my friends and that, they're getting stopped regular and same thing tossing car, checking it out, wasting time.
YA: Because they're young and Pakistani,right?
ZD: Course. What else?

Like The Pharcyde's 'Officer', ZD's comments referenced a pragmatic and existential risk of police attention; this is not a fear, but he is aware of the risk of being stopped, questioned and searched, a risk that is heightened because of how his car looks and sounds, where it is, and the fact that he is not white.

While there is pleasure in creating and modifying cars, the process is completed once the car, and by extension the owner's presence, is noticed on roads, in motion or not. It is here that a new set of reactions and emotions are generated. For some, witnessing spectacular or somehow special cars can evoke an appreciation of taste or flair, or even nostalgia if a car is old or deemed 'vintage'. For others, however, the loudness – visual and aural – and how cars are driven, especially when ethnicity, class and gender are present, produce reactions allowing narratives to develop in which cars and driving become acutely problematic.

Cruising

This brings us, then, to the overlapping element of car cultural practice that deepens contemporary understanding of cars and their users. 'Cruising' involves an almost aimless, unnecessary (other than having the benefit of killing time) journeying, and, significantly, using cars as shared, social spaces. Cruising requires access to a car – any car – and two or more occupants; the more unusual the car, the more chances there are of being noticed. Largely a group and male endeavour, cruising is not, however, a new way of socialising, nor is it peculiar to Bradford, or even Britain.[11] What cruising does, from the outside looking in, is give the car and its occupants visibility and profile. Across the sample, reference was routinely made to cruising, which was couched as either a valuable or a damaging social practice:

> Boys in, cruise around a bit, grab a bite to eat, cruise some more. Something to do. (MAA, 21, male, 21 June 2016)
>
> It's not just driving around. You catch up, flex out, talk about stuff. (KA, 21, male, 14 July 2014)
>
> We used to cruise a lot ... but we stopped because we grew out of it. I got married.... More important things to do. (CG, 26, male, 13 March 2017)
>
> It's like when people go to the pub, they talk and do things. It's like that. (DC, 23, male, 5 August 2013)
>
> I just think, haven't you got anything better to do? Get a job! (GA, 36, female, 16 March 2017)

While cruising can be a sedate endeavour without speed or risk, the practice becomes noticeably taxing through screeching tires, screaming engines and 'big bore' exhausts. Adding to the cacophony of noise, all of which is witnessed and experienced by other road users, is loud music. The result, which can go beyond mere annoyance, is not surprising:

> They have no shame, no sense. It's such a bad example they set. What other people gonna think when they see it like that? They think ... white people they gonna think, *well, that's what they are all like – they are idiots* and that kind of thing.... In summer it's even worser. Heat gets to them or something, must be that! The bikes ones, motorbikes and the quad bikes, they are crazy and they look like kids. Racing around like the roads are bloody racing courses. Someone gonna get hurt.... They don't think, they don't think like you and I think.... I don't know what they think but they don't look at how this is making our whole community look bad because it is very dangerous what they do.... White people, they do it like that as well but for us, we already targeted and in a spotlight so it's worse for us. (RT, 34, male, 20 November 2017)

For RT, the presence of young men riding quad bikes in particular is challenging due to the danger it can present, but also because it gives further substance to how British Pakistanis especially are profiled; it becomes yet another 'behaviour' that is amplified, stereotyped and weaponised. Against this view, however, AR outlined a more complex process:

> I know it's a problem. But you have to understand, it's a buzz ... exciting's not the word. Power's there: acceleration, can't describe it.... Loud, it is loud, but there power's there and that's what you have to watch out for.... I'm not saying it's difficult, but it's not easy – you can't hop on and away you go.... Takes skill, a bit of bottle and a bit of luck.... But yeah, I try not to do like stupid manoeuvres any more like some do ... you learn, don't you? (AR, 29, male, 20 January 2013)

The experience of driving quickly – and, yes, irresponsibly – may enable the testing of skill and courage, through taking risks or attempting illegal or otherwise unsafe manoeuvres. The experience is further heightened, for the driver and the 'audience', by the noise made, even without modifications in the case of quad bikes. Across especially older members of the sample, there was a greater tendency to locate such driving behaviours negatively, as indicated by RT. However, those who also happened to be partial to such driving in the past located this as something close to youthful exuberance, rebellion or even naivety:

> Wouldn't dream of it now. As a youth, you don't know, do you? You think you do, but you know nothing, really. Older people tell you not to but you still do stupid stuff.... I say that now, because I'm telling my son, he should know for himself, but you know, *don't mess around ... it's dangerous out there*. Anyway, even if you wanted to, you can't now: roads are nothing like they used to be. There are cameras everywhere – everyone's got phones and now, that's all you need and you're feeding police information whenever you like.... If I were young now, knowing what I know now, I wouldn't do the stuff I did do. No way. (AS, 45, male, 23 April 2012)

Like AS, KJ was more reserved in his approach to cars and the road, and also mentioned a greater likelihood of non-white drivers to be read as problematic, even if they drove cars that were not loud or modified or, in other situations, those that were not even remotely distinctive:

> You know yourself how it is when you're out and about on the road.... Say for example you're just going about your day, your business, you're minding your own business and then someone will give you grief on the road.... Used to happen a lot when I was more on the road, like more than I am now, when I was younger – drove a lot when I was younger, because you know, that's what you do.... But yeah, like I says, it happens, I think it happens because it's sort of normal.... What I mean by that is that if you're Asian, you get a lot of shit and always it's for no reason.... Not all the time, but you notice it, don't you? (KJ, 38, male, 14 June 2018)

When probed further, like others, KJ referenced the background noise of how people like him – of minority ethnic and visibly Muslim (KJ has a beard) heritage – are more than occasionally read and reacted to. That is, the broader discourse around Muslims in the West surfaces even during banal, everyday moments, when the ordinary becomes spectacular but not so unusual.

Internalising negative reputation

The car, through its symbolism and capacity to signify meaning, helps establish normative race- and class-based readings of minority ethnic identity. For Gilroy, however, the direction of flow is not one-way: when African Americans consume prestige or expensive (white) cars, this challenges and resists prevailing racial – and racist – hierarchies, but conversely, maintains them at the same time.[12] The presence of minority ethnicity on its own is not enough, however, to produce these reactions. Indeed, even young white males are also problematised within the realm of 'chav' behaviour, especially when a particular kind of car is loaded into the scene. The nature of the car and where it is, when combined with ethnicity and especially class, produces and reinforces very particular, often simplistic and stereotype-based pathologies, referencing not only behaviour, but also biographies in which upbringing, civility and morality are first recognised as present, and then actively responded to in usually denigrating terms.

The coding of race, however, is not simply a matter of being labelled externally, but operates even among Bradfordian Pakistanis internally. This is evident in the following field note, built on an encounter that took place in a 'back street' garage:

> I meet this one guy, quite randomly, while at a garage – kind of a back street garage, where the price is cheap and the turnaround quick. Decent guy who runs the joint, though.... Anyway, one of his punters strikes up a conversation and it ends up being more of a rant than anything else. He's going on about 'Pakis' – he's Pakistani, too, but

doesn't seem to mind using that word. And he keeps talking about 'them', like he's not including himself....

'Them lot, all they do is make life hard for themselves. You know, if they're not dealing drugs, they're doing terrorism and grooming.'

The garage owner gives him the usual kind of rebuttal that you give: 'Not all of us.'

The guy interrupts and does the thing that white people used to do years ago:

'No, no: not you. You're alright – people like us, we're not the problem. It's the others.'

So then he starts going on about how this city is doomed; that Bradford is one of worst places you could live because 'them Pakis' make it so difficult; there's always bad news when it comes to Bradford, and it nearly always involves 'Pakis'. I nod, not because I agree ... but because I want him to keep going.... In the hope of getting more, I say 'Tell me about it. They don't integrate, do they?'

The garage owner suppresses a smile and turns away. The ranter, now refuelled, continues. The garage man is now actively ignoring him but I stay engaged, maybe because I'm bored or just curious about how far and wide this guy will go. Eventually, after a smaller rant about 'them Eastern Europeans' and 'checkos', he's more or less spent. I hang around a bit more, waiting for him to leave. The moment he drives off, the garage man looks at me, shakes his head and, with a smile, swears at me. I shrug my shoulders:

'Couldn't help myself.' (Field note, December 2018)

Demonstrating some degree of mischief-making, the field note also shows the extent to which established stereotypes around ethnicity have taken root. In the vignette, the 'ranter' is not entirely unusual in his views, but sees himself as not one of 'them', but rather one of 'us'; whether wider society sees past his skin tone and therefore agrees with his self-image is not entirely relevant. However, this kind of interaction does show the extent to which those being oppressed take ownership of and invest in the very same narratives that demonise them. This is especially relevant when behaviours are locked firmly into accounts that essentialise young, especially[13] male and minority ethnic, identities as bad or antisocial and drivers of questionable legal status: without a licence, showing a lack of civility on the road, without adequate (or any) insurance or, indeed, without any right to drive in the first place.

Place, as already noted, is a cogent variable in how interpersonal communications and interethnic relations develop when the car visibly signifies identity. One way of interpreting the presence of 'loud' or otherwise hyper-visible cars is that they constitute a practice of resistance that goes beyond the symbolic. In some neighbourhoods, the kinds of cars that feature as deficient are owned invariably by young, Pakistani-heritage males who can recognise, but reject, their status as racialised and inferior.

Knowing your spaces

The salience of territory, particularly the idea that some zones are reputedly safe and others less so, adds a further layer into which class- and race-based discriminations can be given licence to operate. Although the focus here is on Bradford, it is worth bearing in mind that many multi-ethnic cities share similar features. Back, for example, mentions Lewis' experience of everyday journeys in and around London areas through an extant knowledge of (un)safe spaces for a young black woman. For Lewis, and for many involved in this research, such grounded knowledge becomes embedded as a normative feature of contemporary life.[14] For example, quite a few participants reflected on their forays into neighbourhoods that had a known 'race' reputation – racist or not racist, safe or unsafe, white or not white:

MAA: Some places … you know what you're gonna get. It's not a guarantee, but I know they're not the safest places … for someone looking like me. But you don't expect that in, like Ilkley, Hebden Bridge and Harrogate and that.

YA: Really? Even Hebden Bridge?

MAA: You what? I hate going up there. It's probably one of the worst places to drive, you know. If it wasn't for having to go there for work, I'd steer clear of it, well clear, I'm telling you. (MAA, 21, male, 21 June 2016)

MAA, who works as a delivery driver, mentioned neighbourhoods in Bradford, all characterised by the likelihood of facing racism; these, broadly speaking, are defined by social housing estates, white working-class populations and a fairly well-established reputation (certainly among Pakistani-heritage communities) for being particularly unsafe, or at the very least risky enough to warrant caution. However, even before he had ever driven into any of those areas, he already had an awareness of the possibilities – some form of racial abuse, aggression or reaction based on his identity could be predicted; the fact that he wears a beard also increases the likelihood of an adverse reaction. But not so with the more affluent and more middle-class parts of Yorkshire to which he referred, where his mere presence behind the wheel of a van may elicit negative, often explicitly racist, responses. Of course, it is perfectly possible either that he is a terrible driver or, generally speaking, that people have a profound dislike for the 'white van man'. If either or both of these were the case, however, it is unlikely that the abuse would be of a racial nature:

> Sometimes they wind the window down and start shouting shit.... Usual stuff: Paki, Paki wanker, Muzzy terrorist, that kind of shit.... Maybe once or twice a week, out of town especially.... In Bradford it's not often at all, really. Very rare in Bradford. I think people are used to us, here. Or ... they know they can't get away with that here.

In some circumstances, driving behaviour is not even necessary to provoke offence. Even static, the car resonates with performative potential, which in turn can be recycled and read as a means of presentation of self, a central element in how identity is projected and received. As noted already, the car can express individuality or even assert membership of a specific group, and this is not only the case with subcultural in-groups, such as car modifiers, but also surfaces during sporting and political events, in which flags appear on homes, on social media and on cars. Indeed, during international football tournaments, cars bearing flags not only denote investment in the event itself, but also, for some Pakistani-heritage taxi drivers in particular, become a shortcut that demonstrates national belonging and pride:

> Yeah, yeah, I do it. We all do it – World Cup, European Championships and whatnot: stick the flags on the back and you're done, jobs a goodun, Yunis.... No, I don't think any of us really care – come on, it's England and everyone knows, even those who don't follow football, that England ... they always blob.... No, they're there for the punters, innit, really – they see little flags on your car, get in and think, *oh yeah*, you know, *he's a good lad – might be a terrorist* [laughs], *but he's got an England flag, so fair dos to the lad.* (WH, 45, male, 14 November 2015)

Alongside the spaces occupied through car modification, the tinting of windows – not especially favoured by any one ethnic group – is worth mentioning. Like wearing sunglasses, tinted windows help 'create a characteristic emotional tone' that changes the interpersonal dynamics between those in front of and those behind the blacked-out glass:

> The result in both cases is to create an aura of mystery rooted in a practical problem of interpretation: the reading of whether and where attentions may be directed becomes a unique problem for the person not sporting shades.... Because the person in shades does not as readily give off indications of his or her disposition but is presumably unimpaired in detecting the direction of others' gazes, an emotionally provocative potential for an asymmetrical uncertainty is built into street transactions.[15]

This 'asymmetrical uncertainty' results in a power differential during on-road interactions especially, with those behind the tinted windows being able to see without being seen. While tinted windows can elicit stereotypical expectations of affluent, political or celebrity classes, in some parts of Bradford, more accessible associations are drug dealer or gangster, 'wannabe' or otherwise. Without anything being said or done, other than being present but unseen, the groundwork for interpretation and reaction is laid, and thus elicits recognition of symbolic threat.[16]

Threat is one possible outcome of encounters on the road, but does not necessarily mean a concrete or physical (violent) reaction will result. Instead, threat can be experienced as something that subverts or undermines 'our' values and cultural practices: tinted windows suggest something is being hidden, and we tend to hide the things we do not want others to see. This is not the same as privacy, but rather helps the imagining of something illicit. With the car being both private and public, such hiding in plain sight may well lead to suspicion. Similarly, attitudes toward tinted windows may also be rooted in British class consciousness; tinted windows were the preserve, almost, of elites or the very affluent, and therefore were relatively rare. Although today 'privacy glass' features as standard equipment for some car manufacturers, it is the interplay of variables that produces readings of identity: place, car and, in the case of tinted windows, assumed driver. Regardless, tinted windows, arguably insignificant within the discourse of motorised mobilities, nevertheless offer opportunity in which meanings are produced, and further heighten intergroup sensitivities.

As noted elsewhere, young Pakistani men are subject to being read as partaking in problematic scenes and issues: drugs, crime, policing, no-go areas, religious radicalisation and racially motivated sexual predation.[17] The depth and range of these readings form a dominant storyline in which they are a threat, risk and danger. As a consequence, they are not blank canvases, but instead already hold meanings, associations and expectations: underachiever in education and work, thus likely to deal or use drugs; or intellectually and morally vulnerable, and therefore susceptible to being groomed into radicalisation; and if not that, then frustrated, or stupid, enough to riot; and, of course, there is also his unhealthy sexuality, a by-product of religious conventions around gender and sexual norms. All this noise cannot be ignored and, indeed, is active even in banal discourse. As a result, perceptions are primed through existing narratives, and subsequent readings are therefore biased, or at best incomplete. In relation to cars, young Pakistani men are not *merely* drivers in the way that white drivers are *merely* drivers; whiteness still holds a neutral, centred position. As implied by Swanton, being abused by a white driver, for other white drivers, holds no racial element. The incompetence of minority ethnic drivers can reconfigure specific utterances and insults: 'wanker' becomes 'Paki wanker'; 'dickhead' becomes 'Muzzy dickhead'; or, indeed, the effective and simple 'Paki!' may suffice.[18]

Intergroup relations and behaviours can generate a sense of 'realistic' threat,[19] in that an out-group, an 'other' or a 'they' are jeopardising something 'real': a risk to life, for example. However, this operates in tandem with 'symbolic' threat whereby the in-group's culture, way of life or existence is in peril because, for example, previously unique access to high-end cars has opened up, or because these 'others' are infecting and polluting the national or ethnic culture. Behaviour becomes pathologically tied with ethnicity, but the reverse is also true in that ethnicity explains behaviours. This repertoire of knowledge and sense-making is embedded deeply, and normatively, enough that it can be called upon and enacted as and when the need arises.

Understanding the fabric and texture of emotional content on the road can be usefully couched within the more general insights of in- and out-group dynamics. The car on its own is an empty signifier, but becomes replete with meanings, associations and imagery once located in a social context. In the next chapter, some of the themes raised thus far are inserted into specific domains of crime, criminality and danger. Again, the variable of race informs and drives debates that, as is far too often the case, serve to marginalise and all but silence those who are designated as key actors and, often, perpetrators.

SEVEN

Fun-loving criminal: speed, danger and race

This chapter tackles various contemporary issues that continue to reach into broader, often negative, conversations around cars and driving behaviours. Attention is paid to local newspaper stories that seem to reflect, and arguably magnify, anxieties around antisocial, criminal and, at times, deadly driving behaviour. Featuring throughout are elements that explain how racism, racial stereotypes and racialisation operate within discourses around specific forms of car cultural practice. Cross-referencing some of the earlier discussion points further reinforces the view that cars can be and are used as subtle code-making machines, often feeding into expressions of ethnic danger and difference.

How did I get here?

Nationally, there is robust regulation and control of driving through legal prohibition, road signage and speed cameras. Like other countries, the UK has driving tests that are passed through adequate demonstration of driving competence, but less formal are those culturally bound scripts that produce particular behaviours. In some countries, it is not unusual for pedestrians to wait at traffic lights even in the absence of traffic – a rare practice in the UK, arguably because personal agency overrides a pure but inefficient (and possibly inconsequential) obedience to the law, suggesting flexibility and discretion can trump formal rules of the road. This extends into expectations and interpretations of driving behaviour, and shores up ideas about the character, attributes and tendencies of particular types of driver. These expectations are operative in Bradford, but are amplified when ethnicity, as well as class, gender and age, become used as markers of identity that determine behaviours.

There are countless stereotypes of collectivities being constructed on the basis of perceived driving habits and lifestyles of specific vehicle users. More acutely, externally attributed characteristics come to be reified within the 'young Asian man' stereotype. For the most part, such framing processes produce identities that are problematic, and in some cases deviant and criminal.[1] This phenomenon is necessary to examine, not because it is both banal and spectacular, or because it is simply present, but rather, because neither driver nor car exists independently. What we encounter, therefore, is an amalgamation of car and driver and because of this, ascertaining the outcomes of car ownership and usage becomes possible. With this in mind, the car can be viewed as important in understanding the complexities of interethnic relations in Bradford and beyond.

What constitutes dangerous driving is not always widely shared; for many of us, driving with a seatbelt is framed through our appreciation of legal sanction as well as self-preservation. Similarly, ensuring our vehicles are in good working order reduces the risk of a breakdown and, again, ensures that we are not subject to fines or law enforcement interventions. This following field note extract, reflecting on a 'speed awareness' course, explores some of this:

So I turn up to this course, the venue's in Manningham, and there are a lot of people there.... There are two trainers leading the course. One's a bit of a comedian, the other one [TJ] ... is more to the point and drier in his delivery. Considering why we're all here, TJ asks a redundant question, 'How many people have ever broken the speed limit?', and then, without giving anyone a chance to answer, says 'I know I have.' What a rebel, this guy. But he qualifies that by saying we're all prone to lapses, but the big thing to remember is safety, and risk – not of being caught, but of doing harm.... We're shown a short film, and asked to note down any 'hazards'.... They also talked about the difference in outcomes at 30, and 40 miles per hour: if you hit someone at 30, they might live, but 40, no chance, really.... During the less demanding moments, some of the attendees blew off steam, about the injustice of having been caught speeding even though they never usually speed, or how the coppers should be out catching killers and muggers. (Field note, 30 January 2016)

Speeding can have economic impacts (fines, increased insurance premiums) and, of course, more serious consequences in terms of injury or death. Despite this, breaking speed limits seems fairly normative and widespread. This is not to say, however, that most drivers break speed limits consciously. As the following segment illustrates, driving is not always something that individuals, on reflection, appear to wholly commit:

> Sometimes you get to where you're going, and you can't remember how you got there. I'm like, *Oh my God! How did I get here? I don't even remember half the journey*. It's like they say about being auto-pilot. I wonder why or should I say how I didn't get into a smash. While I'm driving I think I'm concentrating but I might not be, you know what I mean? (SK, 27, female, 15 November 2016)

SK, however, was not alone in referencing 'auto-pilot' mode, with others being equally reflective of the possible outcomes of such journeys; for some, especially when in the company of others, driving feels incidental, with drivers taking part in conversations, listening to music or being distracted:

> When I first started driving, I couldn't listen to music or talk to someone sat next to me because it put me off. I couldn't concentrate on the road like that. I was really bad – if someone was sat next to me and they were talking, I'd be like, *please, be quiet, I'm driving*.... But now, now that I'm more experienced, it's not a problem – now it's easier.... When I drive, I listen to music even if I'm alone. With people, like my friends, then there's more noise, more laughs and more music – I'm more relaxed now when compared to how to I was. (RA, 23, male, 17 February 2017)

A lack of driver concentration connects with some elements of relevance, particularly the significance of what constitutes a distraction and, indeed, that most taken-for-granted of common practices – listening to music while driving – having an impact on mood, in turn influencing driving performance and driving behaviour. Brodsky, for example, informs us that

> 73% of drivers admit to having received a traffic fine for speeding, and that in 70% of the cases, the drivers were listening to 'pounding fast dance music'.... Drivers who listen to Rap or Hip-Hop music styles are most at risk for car accidents and road-rage incidents.... About half of the sample felt Classical music relaxes them when driving, and hence perceived that such music styles offer drivers the highest safety experience.[2]

Brodsky mentions how dance, classic rock, pop and even classical genres appear to induce aggression. As discussed in the previous chapter, beyond the car's occupants, the matter of being offended through sound is something that is loaded with cultural bias and can in turn lead to disproportionate outcomes: 'Many people feel violated when others impose their amplified music upon them. However, wider concerns emerge when one considers how cultural style may become criminalized as part of a questionable legal practice in fighting drugs.'[3]

Again, this ties in with the criminalisation of some elements of car culture. Car stereo noise, for example, impinges on desires for quieter neighbourhoods, but also helps reinforce, and construct, racialised narratives in which ethnicity and behaviour become concomitant. Following an analysis of statistical data in the US, Crawford notes that while motorists' 'race' was by no means a guaranteed predictor of arrest, black drivers were nearly three times as likely to be arrested as their white counterparts. For ethnic minorities in the UK, similar risk is a fact of life;[4] but for those who wish to announce their presence via the car, through visuals, sound or other enhancements, this risk is multiplied significantly.

Reference to the risks of being noticeable on the street were frequently rehearsed within the broader sample, with participants noting that in Bradford especially, law enforcement in relation to cars seems unusually active:

> Speed vans – you see them regular, sometimes hiding even. And random checks are not random, they happen regular and who do they randomly check? *Aapnay* [our] people more than white people. That's a fact. I tell you, that's a fact. (NH, 22, male, 7 June 2017)

This view was not unusual, with many participants referencing policing and other state apparatus that disproportionately impacts Muslims in general, and Bradfordian Pakistanis in particular. However, there was also acknowledgement that younger drivers with faster cars "tend" to drive irresponsibly – often at speed or with a seemingly brutal disregard for safety. Here, for example, SG, a driving instructor, elaborates:

> There are crazy drivers on the road … younger ones especially – they think they can handle the speed and the power, but the road, it's always changing, so many things that can change and the faster you move, the less you can take in and your brain isn't equipped to deal with it.… Then people get upset when one of them wraps his car round a lamp post and kills himself and maybe a passenger: *oh, he was a really good lad, hard working* and all this. Doesn't matter that he was a good lad because he just killed himself doing over a hundred miles an hour. (SG, 42, male, 11 March 2017)

Readings of younger drivers through risk and irresponsibility is demonstrably present in Bradford, and appeared frequently and often without solicitation, with interviewees citing irresponsibility, immaturity and naivety as central elements that constitute potential harm. While this sense of threat is real, it is also symbolic in that all young drivers are subject to its manifestation. This is given further substance through mass-mediated messages about driving in Bradford, discussed next.

Danger drivers

The city's local newspaper has been running a 'Stop the Danger Drivers' campaign since late 2015, with a ten-point plan including age and speed restrictions for new and younger drivers, greater police infrastructure, stronger sentences for those convicted of dangerous driving and more use of surveillance/CCTV. The campaign is premised with a public concern interest, with underpinning evidence drawn from national research and data:

> Many of those responsible [for dangerous driving] are young drivers: official statistics show more than a fifth of deaths on British roads in 2011 involved drivers aged 17 to 24 and our readers tell us that many of the people they see driving dangerously fall in this age group.[5]

Subsequent stories fuse car-related crime, driving violations and even death by car with road safety, driving as a social problem and criminality. Furthermore, the stories and especially the user and reader comments point strongly toward racialised concerns around young, Pakistani-heritage Bradfordian males. Beyond positive stories about a local classic car show or a thriving car business or entrepreneur, alternative and rich facets of car culture and practice barely feature. The voices, experiences or stories emanating from working-class identities are absent not only from this newspaper, but also from mainstream media more generally:

Story in the local paper a day or two ago. Some minister ... gives the paper a pat on the back.... '*T&A's Stop the Dang*er *Drivers* campaign has given authorities a "kick up the backside" says Chris Grayling' ... Not many of those I've met take this paper at all seriously; some even resent it and some have claimed it operates in a very biased, sensationalist and even racist way.... But this car thing ... it's not new but it's so basic, so simplistic – dangerous drivers running amok, law and order ignored, decency and civility a thing of the past, zombie apocalypse any day now. Like most other people, I do see some really bad driving on the road, and yes, we all know, there are some people who drive with no insurance, or with no road tax, or without a license, or all those things and more. But there's a difference between that and bad driving as a problem.... More often than not, it's where the bad driving is happening. Surprise! It's Manningham, West Bowling, Girlington, some parts of Keighley – those, and a few other demographically similar neighbourhoods, are the ones where most of the stories come from. Thing is, there are lots of different parts of Bradford you'll encounter bad driving, and they're not all 'Asian' areas. Too late for any of that, now: the links between neighbourhood, ethnicity and behaviour have become reasonable, common sense, embedded and made more real than ever.... You can see the attitude much more clearly in the comments sections, where Joe and Jolene Public get to throw in their tuppence worth (though it is usually males [indicated by usernames] who tend to get invested in these pointless little exercises in which being heard is perceived to be the same thing as having something to say). In the comments, some of them use code instead of allowing their racism to take full flight; being explicit might get them banned from the website, and maybe they genuinely believe what they're saying is fine. (Field note, 8 April 2016)

The same newspaper is the subject of another, originally much longer field note, over a year later. This time, the trigger for the reflection is a news story about how dashcam footage is helping pinpoint bad (possibly illegal) driving, often without necessary law enforcement action or punishment through relevant criminal justice mechanisms:[6]

The user comments, they really help you understand what people actually think.... One of the first is that there should be more cameras that can instigate fines and catch all these driving ne'er-do-wells.... That first comment, it's quite tame, really, but all you need is a spark.

The 'Brain dead' community drivers (mainly) who do this sort of illegal offence DONT have a licence, nor have insurance & these cars are usually 'POOL' cars ; so who does one send these fines to ?????????????? (Field note, 7 September 2017)

The word 'community' is used in a manner that is understood in the context of Bradford as a multi-ethnic city. This is not community in a more general and usual sense, but rather is coded language that says one thing, but means another:

> We all understand what it means and it means, you know, well, it means – them.... Asians. Not Asians. No. Pakistanis. Let's be honest, let's call a spade a spade: Muslims.... How can I make this statement? Well, because they're the ones who have a reputation for a. driving usually quite nice 'pool' cars and b. who else would he be talking about? Anyway, it gets better when someone else replies:
>
> *the owner simples.*
>
> Ah, yes: *simples*. Quoting an advertising catchphrase constitutes originality. Still, according to someone else ... it's not as 'simples' as it sounds:
>
> *You're not getting it ... these cars don't have an owner. They are collectively bought and used by a small band of Community drug dealing criminals that know the chance of a Police car seeing and stopping them is virtually nil and if that happens our pathetic not fit for purpose judges will not give effective sentences. This whole scenario is facilitated by bent, morally corrupt local & national politicians. Backed up by a pathetic PC, multicultural loving media.*

With the commenter referencing 'Community drug dealing criminals' (which could mean more than one thing), we see the operationalisation of stereotype that feeds into the creation of symbolic threat. In this case, however, the commenter forays into short but heavy swipes at the criminal justice system, politicians and the mass media, all of which have been undermined, possibly, through unfettered multicultural privileging. Where we are now is what happens when 'real' threat is enacted, or ignored; corruption, 'political correctness' and an over-appreciation of, or hypersensitivity to, ethnic diversity are all consequences of a failed multiculturalism. After some more posts and responses, the field note reflects on a much larger entry, one that the author probably drafted in Microsoft Word, worked on it over a weekend and got feedback from friends.... He's probably working on a gritty urban novel which explores interethnic romance and tension in a northern city called 'Haliford', 'Bradifax' or 'Huddersley'.

This commenter then ponders whether this kind of behaviour is linked more to one ethnic group than another, before calling for statistical openness from law enforcement and other agencies: how many bad drivers are caught; how many go unpunished; which crimes are recorded? Was the car owned or leased by the driver? At the time of the offence, was the driver the actual owner? How some people can afford to buy and run expensive cars is also raised:

Money, obviously, but more particularly, its source – is it good money or is it bad money? He calls for 'a thorough examination to establish if car crime has a clear link to other criminal activity – particularly drugs'. And then, he's also interested in having access to the ethnic heritage of violators. It's like a damned manifesto. At one level, it is impressive: you got to admire the commitment:

Because until this city and this country starts 'lifting the veil' on criminal activity in this country and starts addressing issues with a clear transparency and fairness, there will be continued cultural unrest, with citizens from one cultural backround [sic] *blaming citizens from another cultural background and genuinely believing that society is going 'soft' on perpetrators, for fear of accusations of racism... And to show where I stand on the matter, almost without exception, the 'idiots' I see driving erratically and stupidly, with a mobile phone clamped to their ear, or driving through red lights and at ridiculous speeds, are young asian* [sic] *males.*

So there it is: a reasonable, fine, upstanding, law abiding citizen contributing to the debate. The problem is the premise of the debate itself is flawed because it is founded on biased and partial information. You build on shaky foundations and you get shaky buildings: one way around it is to then knock them down and start again, the other is to buttress and reinforce the thing that shouldn't have been built in the

> first place. So yes, this guy's got something to say but he's bought into the narrative and that's why all his questions are equally problematic. How do we define bad driving behaviour? And why are you noticing particularly young Asian males as a problem? And here's another one: Does what we drive influence how others see us drive?... It's even more complex than that and it also includes how we, as a culture, value and validate some cultural artefacts, traditions and practices, and devalue, invalidate and resent others. It's not that this is about bad driving; it's more about who is driving, what they're driving as well as where and how they're driving; that's what's missing from, or is underneath, all this noise.

It is not coincidental that some of the themes raised in this extract were discussed with participants. The extract also closely aligns with my own identity as one who is, through various in-group memberships, being talked about in mainstream discourse. This is not mentioned to demonstrate insider credentials or a sense of 'ethnic' solidarity, but does reach into the broader remit of race and ethnic relations research, especially that which is ethnographic. As noted already, most of those involved in this research had very little sense of connection with or even appreciation of the local newspaper, or, indeed, faith in broader institutions including education, local government, and, more generally, work and culture initiatives that flowed through local and national state apparatus. In many cases, there was something close to alienation being experienced by virtue of how Pakistani- and Muslim-heritage identities, and communities, were perceived and discussed.

Invariably, those involved in this research perceived the local newspaper, and society in general, as Islamophobic, or anti-Muslim, in explicit and implicit ways. In the case of the local newspaper, for some, this view was formed through an active and critical appreciation of the types of stories the newspaper presented, but also through grounded understandings of news production processes and values in which the printed version of the truth is not necessarily shared by all. Indeed, as many have shown, the representation of non-whites within European/Western mass media has been, and still remains, racialised in various ways,[7] and this extends into news reporting also. Added to this, many among the sample, especially those interviewed during 2017 and 2018, explicitly referenced what was perceived to be an increasingly overzealous, draconian and often disproportionate policing and criminal justice interest:

> If you're like us, you know, Asian or Muslim, or even black, then you're in for it, really, I'd say.... Everything's against you: like now, there's a lot going on about driving, about bad driving and they're really clamping down which is fair enough. It's not fair enough, but let's say it is. Okay, so they're really going to town with this ... locking up these idiots for bad driving – and they are idiots. Alright, fair enough, go ahead and lock 'em up – but be consistent about it.... Where's the consistency and if you like equality? If you're not white, you'll get it worse, that's a fact.... What about all these bankers and big, big businesses that are screwing people over left, right and centre? They're respectable and they don't even call them criminals. They can't do anything wrong, do they? But the amount of damage they've done.... Where's their [prison] time? (LO, 26, male, 15 July 2018)

Similar points were echoed by others, especially males. For some, not only were they more likely to be stopped by police, but those involved in car accidents and found to be speeding would also inevitably experience a robust interpretation of the law, including heavy fines as well as custodial sentences for dangerous driving. LO's mention of consistency and equality also references disproportionality, in relation not just to white-collar crime, but to the difference between how white and non-white individuals are treated within the criminal justice system. Although written before the 'northern riots' of 2001, or the London bombings of 2005, Alexander's argument is cogent and relevant even now:

> Muslim masculinities are then positioned as outside, and in opposition to, hegemonic norms of male behaviour, defined through deviance and subject

> to increasingly stringent forms of social control.... The racialization of black young men, on the one hand, and the religio-ethnicization of Asian young men on the other, leaves Muslim youth visioned as twice disadvantaged and doubly dysfunctional, with apparently no space for difference, contestation or reimagination.[8]

It is precisely those latter points – of reimaginaton, contestation and difference – that are found to be active within car cultural practice, whether it is subcultural or mainstream in nature. However, as has been shown, this is challenging, especially when we account for the impact of car-derived life and death narratives, discussed next.

We gotta do summat

There have been a number of life-ending road traffic accidents on Bradford roads over several years, occasionally involving younger drivers losing control and harming themselves, their passengers, those in oncoming traffic and pedestrians. When this sort of event does occur, for reasons of decorum and appropriateness, idealised young male identity is rehearsed, but this is also accompanied by critical reflection and commentary, through local news media and social media, and through conversations within relevant neighbourhoods and beyond. In August 2018, for example, four young Pakistani-heritage men, while being pursued by an unmarked police car, died when their car crashed into a tree.[9] The story was subsumed within loss and tragedy, but also fed into the 'Stop the Danger Drivers' campaign. Subsequently, however, the local paper opened an online 'book of condolence', in which individuals offered sympathies, sometimes loaded with references to Islamic belief, custom and practice relating to death. Among the many comments around the tragic nature of the men's deaths, and the emotional turmoil for remaining family and friends, were some that also referenced dangerous driving:

> How terribly sad. Four lives lost. When will the young men of Bradford learn to stop driving so dangerously, putting everyone's lives at risk. The community, the police and the local council need to stop this once and for all.[10]

Although short, the message covers tragedy and potentially more tragedy to come, as well as recognition that this issue needs to be addressed at various levels. Similar questions and comments were raised by many participants, with some being perhaps less sympathetic, and others offering caveats around representation and disproportionality:

> Don't get me wrong, there are a lot of idiots about. No, not a lot: *some*. There are *some* people who should not be on the road.... It's a minority, course it is. The problem is, they are, and what these idiots do makes the rest of us look bad – don't forget, all it takes is one rotten apple to ruin the barrel, right? So I'm not saying there aren't *any*, what I am saying is there aren't as many as you think – they're not all hiring out cars and taking chases,[11] are they? A lot of times it's *aapnay* lads, that's worse.... With everything going on, they should know better. (QA, 30, male, 21 August 2018)

For QA, then, who works with younger people, the subject matter is negatively amplified, in turn having a disproportionate impact on how ethnic identity is perceived – "with everything going on" is an implicit reference to local, national and international discourses around the specific and intersecting facets of ethnicity, faith and also class. QA also mentioned the boredom and apathy of many of the young people he encounters professionally. These challenges are compounded by 'austerity' and shifting priorities within 'cohesion' work: "On the one hand, we have to engage them, but without the funding, it's impossible.... So what happens, these kids, they do whatever they do to fill up their days and some end up in bother because we miss them."

With over 20 years behind the wheel as a taxi driver, KH framed his reading of such events through the abilities of both car and driver:

> Obviously it's sad. Very sad but … what happened to them, it was their time *but* it didn't have to be. If one of them lads stayed home that night, he'd be alive today.… Like I was saying, it's all about the cars now – the cars are too quick, too fast for them. These were all young lads – been driving, two-three years – in a BMW: in a decent car and they're young, testosterone flowing, get in the car, *out for a drive, yeah yeah yeah* – it's exciting for them and they think they can handle it. Couldn't handle it as in knowing what the car can do and what it can't do. (KH, 50, male, 1 November 2018)

For KH, driver competence is only one part of the equation; modern cars are de facto designed to appeal in various ways – looks and performance being highly significant. We may believe we have agency when it comes to how we use such vehicles, but our driving practice is influenced in part by the spaces we occupy, mentally and physically, as well as our awareness of risk and hazard. Driving when angry, for example, invariably involves driving dangerously; driving if young, meanwhile, and of course generally speaking, can be characterised by deficits in experience, confidence or, conversely, fear.

Aggressive, fast or dangerous driving is not strictly limited to the young. For TA, a 43-year-old nurse, what the car was capable of doing *with* the driver resulted in ensuing driving behaviour: "Before this I had a T5 but had to get rid.… It was bit naughty" (TA, 43, male, 1 April 2015). Here, there seems to be a transference of agency and, as in other responses, mention was made of cars that "like to be driven hard", "need to be floored" or "are asking for a thrashing". A similar detachment of the driver from the car was mentioned when CK, a white 57-year-old male, described his company car: "Oh, it's got a bit of go in it; not a slouch when it wants to be" (CK, 57, male, 27 February 2015). The potential and capacity of the car, therefore, can be in and of itself an indispensable component when it is driven;

the driver, in some ways, becomes subject to the car's 'nature'. Clearly, this approach is entirely unreasonable in any rational, let alone legalistic, sense, but there was a discernible tendency for drivers, of whatever background, to elicit a similar causal relationship. Indeed, this tendency to narrate a car's identity, almost independently of the driver, also features in mass media. For example, in a relatively recent episode of the *Top Gear* television series, Renault's Megane RS Trophy-R was test driven by the presenter Chris Harris. The commentary included phrases such as: "this thing absolutely loves the corners", "it's bonkers", "a little monster", and, early on in the segment, the presenter tells us "the reason why this is the hottest of hot hatches, is it can do this...". "This" is demonstrated by the clunking of a dropped gear, roaring acceleration, screeching tyres, power sliding as well as Harris's enthusiastic verbal appreciation of the car's speed, handling and performance. Even the braking system is couched as existing independently of the driver: it is "immense" and "savage". While Harris weaves the car around a track, he tells us he is "just hanging on for dear life ... in a hatchback ... it's a complete hooligan".[12] Meanwhile, CK also narrated a story involving his wife, who, while sat in the passenger seat of their stationary vehicle, was asked to pick up an object located on the dashboard. As she attempted the task, CK accelerated: "The G-Force there, I tell you, she couldn't get close to it." Meanwhile, a younger participant discussed the appeal of such driving behaviours among some of his peers:

> I don't drive like that because I got a box[13] fitted [laughs].... No, if I didn't have a box I'd still drive … sensibly – ask anyone; safe driver me.... But for these [other] boys, it's like they get a thrill. Hire a car and giving it abuse, it's like fun. How else can you have fun in a car? Just driving is boring so they might take a chase and post videos and it's a big thing for them. (FP, 19, male, 11 October 2018)

FP's referencing of "fun", without which "just driving" becomes mundane, demonstrates how cars are social places, but also enable realisations of the symbolism conveyed through the media that service capitalism. In other words, using the car in a fun way is not surprising because happiness, enjoyment and 'fun' are key elements within processes that stimulate consumption. Part of the 'fun' extends into the contemporary practice of sharing aspects of our lives with the rest of the world. This is not to say that social media is a central, let alone fundamental, element within the generation of fun, but it does add another layer to social and cultural practice.

In several interviews undertaken after the accident mentioned earlier in this section, the question of alternatives and solutions surfaced frequently, often based on the following premise: *if this sort of driving behaviour among young males in particular was relatively common, and therefore a hazard to all road users, what could be done to change or subvert it?* Various suggestions were made: a clearer police presence; stronger punishments; barring younger drivers from owning, hiring or driving cars beyond a certain level of power and speed. However, there were also responses anchored in the difficulty in changing driver attitudes around safety. In several conversations, significant ground was covered in relation to this, as the following segments illustrate:

Must have talked to at least a dozen people over the last few months.... Someone sent me a video on WhatsApp, showing the car crashing into the tree; it looked like CCTV footage, taken from the vantage point of someone's house. I had to watch it a few times before I could actually see what had happened.... Thing of it all is that no one really knows what to do about this. Some people I talked to suggested restricted engines – so they can't be driven over however many miles an hour; but that's not impossible to hack, or get around. Others said maybe new drivers, or drivers under 25, should only be allowed to drive cars that align with their experience; the more years you drive, the more powerful the car you can control. That's kind of already in place, with insurance premiums being what they are but maybe it'd have an impact – but doubt it would ever get through – people would riot, car manufacturers would cry poverty. A few mentioned police and the law, saying sentencing is too soft: I doubt that is the case. (Field note, 28 December 2018)

It is not surprising that the themes of driver behaviour and road safety were articulated regularly. While the focus for many was on eradicating the behaviour through legal or other forms of sanction, for others, a more creative approach was forthcoming:

> I talked to these lads at a car meet – youngish, petrol heads, modifiers.... It's obviously something they've given a lot of thought to – kind of goes with the turf, given the cars they drive may as well have flashing neon signs saying 'look at me' on the roofs. The one with the Honda reckons people like me, as well as the more worried and anxious sorts, have got it all wrong. Instead of forcing this behaviour underground, it needs to be mainstreamed. Sounds crazy, right? But not really, not if you think about it. Like a few others have mentioned – in one way or another, it's just bodies full of piss and vinegar. And they need an outlet.... Why not move it out from the underground ... legitimise what they do? This is what happens when we're watching films, or *Top Gear* or whatever – the very same driving behaviours are aligned with heroes, or protagonists or nice men in corduroy trousers and Clarks shoes who appreciate speed, engineering and design.... The important thing is a controlled environment, not the streets.

The appeal of this sort of thinking is that it does cover more than one issue. If authorities, even at the local level, were to sanction and support subcultural car scenes as well as enable drivers to practise their driving prowess in controlled environments, trust and rapport could be built with those previously held in suspicion – the very same people who are usually couched as 'difficult' to reach or 'engage with':

> Give these young men an outlet – build a race track if that's what it takes because it'll be cheaper than arresting and policing your way out of it. And I know it sounds clichéd, it might even save a few lives.

This theme, of appreciating and validating a hitherto problematic feature of car culture, already touched upon previously, had some traction among many of those who engaged with the subject through interview or informal conversation:

> We gotta do summat – some of these kids you see, they need something – a release or something they can enjoy. If they like cars, then they can have cars but only if they're responsible about it.... We can't outlaw it, we can't make it impossible for them.... This is what we've got – them and their cars – and if it's already there, then obviously that's what we should work with. (RS, 36, male, 12 December 2018)

Given the overpowering force of consumption, furnished in part through notions of choice, agency and individuation, the idea of responsibility is not exactly irrelevant, but what constitutes responsibility for some may not apply to others. Indeed, on this point IZ, a motor mechanic, made reference to risk being enabled by parents:

> What I don't get – I don't understand is how these kids – and I do mean kids – 19, 20 year olds, get a hold of these cars. They come in, wanting some work done and they're in like a new – not brand new – but a decent car.... And not your bog-standard things, neither; these are proper cars, you get me? So, sometimes I might say, *Nice car – must be loaded, you.* And the first few times they told me, it shocked me. No word of a lie, I was like *Wow!* Gobsmacked.... *Uncle, my dad bought it me when I got married*, or *cos I got into uni* or *because I passed my A Levels*. I'm like *What?! Your dad bought you this?* I didn't say, but I thought, you know, *your dad, something wrong with him, kid. Something seriously wrong there.* (IZ, 42, male, 26 June 2015)

For IZ, irresponsibility is licensed, inadvertently, through parental support in buying expensive cars; in IZ's youth, he bought cars with money he had saved, and that placed a burden of responsibility on him, as the entitled owner. When cars are given as reward, or merely because they can be given, the same sense of responsibility does not exist. Such examples also illustrate, albeit implicitly, new modalities of consumption that are themselves linked to changes in economic class profile; where there is wealth, conspicuous consumption and materialism follow. Among the less affluent, however, an expensive and high-performance car may not be as common, but almost as a means of compensation, other ways of being seen have evolved.

Elite cars and their non-elite drivers

In Bradford, elite cars being driven by those of Pakistani ethnic heritage are prominent in their presence. Encountering such cars in neighbourhoods defined as deprived, or even 'working class', does at the very least seem counter-intuitive:

> I'm having a meal with friends. We're at a table by the window but I can see out, onto the main road.... I'm distracted by the number of high-end cars that I see.... I count two Lamborghinis (a Murcielago and a Gallardo [I think]), one Ferrari (unsure of model, but looks modern/newish), a Bentley (a coupe of some sort – probably a Continental), as well as Porsches and Audis (one RS8). As well as these 'exotics', there are numerous prestige cars.... BMWs (X6s, X5s, 7, 5 and 3 Series models are like dirt and I even notice an older [early 2000s model] convertible M3); Audi Q7s and S Line/RS variant A6s, A4s and A3s; some high spec VWs including Golfs and Sciroccos and also see a few large and well kitted out Mercedes Benz models; Range Rovers – again, high-end Vogues and Sport variants seem to be relatively common. Perhaps these cars are not that common, I wonder, but they are certainly noticeable and there are patches of time when there is at least one above average car passing through every minute or so. (Field note, 14 August 2012)

For many participants, the visibility of elite cars results in sense-making processes, often in the form of complementing stereotypes and associations through which understandings of the car, its driver and criminality can flow. To illustrate this, the following field note explores a meeting at which a number of Bradfordians were invited to a talk given by a senior law enforcement officer:

A bunch of people, maybe 40 or more altogether, attended this talk – it was billed as a meeting, but XXXX did most of the talking. The talk was supposed to be about law enforcement, recruitment of Muslims as coppers, some discussion of Prevent, some discussion of crime in the city, and, of course, the old 'community support' spiel. Flanked on each side of the main man were a couple of less senior coppers, both working in the city for years, I gather. At one point, somehow, the subject got on to drugs, and the amount of drug dealing going on in the city. Bradford, said XXXX, was a 'hub' for the drug trade. Okay, nothing really outlandish so far – maybe it is, maybe it isn't; I'm not a drug dealer so I don't move in those circles so wouldn't really know. Anyway, that's when he said:

'You only need to look around, and see some of the cars in some parts of Bradford, to know that.'

That was amazing.... I mean, who says that? As soon as he said it, the room became subject to one of those split second moments of dead, deadening silence, because every one of us was thinking the exact same thing: *did he just say that?* Hands went up: points made, questions asked, including something like:

'You do realise you've just offended most of the people in this room. Have you seen the cars in the car park?'

XXXX's counter was feeble and not very convincing – he'd made the comment in the hope of trying to provoke a discussion, apparently. The two coppers by his side, even they didn't believe it. Fact is, most of the people in the audience – most of them local, and most of them Muslim, I think – they were driving the same sorts of cars that XXXX was casually calling drug dealer cars. And why were these people – most of them professionals by the way – driving these gangsta-mobiles? Because they like them. Because they can afford them. Because they deserve them. Because they feel happy in them. Because they can. Because they want to. Because capitalism. (Field note, 4 August 2010)

While the speaker at the event may have demonstrated unfamiliarity with his audience, he certainly felt he knew enough to define Bradford as a drugs hub. This was evidenced by the hyper-visibility of 'drug dealer'-type cars, which, of course, require corresponding drivers – drug dealer cars are not going to drive themselves, or be driven by law-abiding citizens. When he specified where the drugs problem was especially noticeable, he was not talking about the middle-class zones of tranquillity, but inner-city, working-class areas, especially those with sizeable minority ethnic populations. In these neighbourhoods, expensive cars are present, but therein lies the rub: expensive cars in poor neighbourhoods call for a theory to explain their presence. This is not to say that Bradford has no drug dealers, or that drug dealers do not drive expensive cars. However, once unpicked, perceptions of place, cars, drivers and their behaviours are not isolated or peculiar, but are part of a much wider shared understanding: they fall short as they are built on assertion, aided by stereotype and perpetuated through becoming embedded, common sense, but inherently racialised wisdom.

Conflating a car type with criminality exists on the spectrum of associations that explain the car/driver hybrid. In the following segment, SJ acknowledged his car's 'presence' and what it might suggest to others, but stressed that for him its practical benefits outweigh the risk of labelling:

> All of the cars that belong to the company reflect the company in a way.... The company is trying to send out a message through its vehicles.... What I've found is the cars are a kind of a symbol, a sign to the rest of the community out there ... that you're dealing with somebody who's doing well; have confidence in this company and this company is going places. So for us, the cars are kind of a tool, a method to convey a certain message to a particular group of stakeholders.... When a supplier comes, and on purpose the car park is next to the reception, he'll walk past this fleet of cars. (SJ, 36, male, 19 July 2012)

Here, then, the car does important work: how others (clients and suppliers) perceive and interpret SJ's car also feeds into their subsequent perceptions of him and his business. More acutely, image, perception and meaning are given impact through the car.

It seems counter-intuitive, illogical, perhaps, that there appear to be many 'high-end' cars in Bradford, with inner-city locales consistently framed as being economically deprived and in perennial cycles of economic regeneration. Expensive cars are by nature hyper-visible, but when a minority ethnic driver is thrown into the mix, interesting responses and reactions result. For some, this signifies a glitch: an object of affluence in the hands of someone who is usually read as economically lacking seems incoherent. These interpretations feed into wider narratives around ethnicity and behaviour, particularly criminality:

> In Bradford, it [the Range Rover] does have that gangster image so a few people have said to me *Why you driving a gangster car for? You should have a respectable car.* I mean, what is a respectable car? The gangsters have them all! Everything what you drive in Bradford, above a certain price tag, it's a gangster car.... You can quite easily fall for that stereotype: it's the drug culture. The drug culture is minute and doesn't actually account for that much.... Whatever we do in Bradford, we're gonna be stereotyped, we can never do anything right. (SJ, 36, male, 19 July 2012)

Although arguably out of date in our contemporary shared and public discourse, again the category of *nouveaux riches* helps encapsulate the notion of the newly rich not quite being able to fit in. Stereotypically, they smoke expensive cigars, drink fine wines, live in mansions and eat at elite establishments, but their performances are incomplete because they lack the class-cultural competences through which inclusion into a distinctive class category would render more whole and authentic presentations of self. While working-class upward mobility can enable access to middle- and elite-class objects, their consumption is noticeably incomplete, or superficial, because the underlying work of a corresponding habitus is absent. For Bourdieu, consumer behaviour is linked with class position, but not only on the basis of income and resulting buying preferences. In addition to buying power, he situates the swirling elements of necessity, choice and space, constituting and flowing from habitus:

> As can be seen whenever a change in social position puts the habitus into new conditions, so that its specific efficacy can be isolated, it is taste – the taste of necessity or the taste of luxury – and not high or low income which commands the practices objectively adjusted to these resources.[14]

It is habitus, rather than active and conscious decision-making, that results in the consumption of objects that confer or enhance status. In relation to cars, for some participants, acquiring a nice vehicle is also symbolic, signifying success. Buying an expensive-looking car, therefore, is subsumed into the rehearsing of an agency liberated by economic power. Some vehicles in particular, however, are known to have very specific connotations and reputations, but these are operant only within given 'fields': those contexts in which class and its associations can be read and misread. Indeed, some owners of more expensive cars were mindful of this:

> I drive one myself and we do move a few on but no, usually normal – should I say ordinary – people buy them. Them and a few others, like X5s and what have you, they are seen as like drug dealer, gangster type cars but I don't think we've ever sold one to a proper like drug dealer.... Some people see one Asian guy driving a big car think we're all driving big cars.... They seem to think there is more of it going on than there is.... It's a bit like crime you know, all young Asian lads driving fast cars are all drug dealers. Well they can't all be drug dealers can they? (SR, 39, male, 1 September 2011)

The car, therefore, becomes a signifier of the driver's identity if the car/driver is occupying a certain (multi-ethnic) field in space and time, and if the driver is of a particular ethnicity. As a result, gaps are filled with detail and information: Pakistani driver + Range Rover + inner-city = gangster. A variation of this occurs even without the presence of the driver: Range Rover + inner-city = gangster-Pakistani driver; and here, gangster and Pakistani are interchangeable, one being read as the same as the other. Such general equations are now so embedded that their utterance is couched as social fact, used by the very same ethnicities that are subject to such readings. Here, stereotypes help form commonsense understandings, whether derived through symbolic or literal sources. Such phenomena, therefore, point to something less than legitimate. This is deemed reasonable because of what is 'known' about the area, its people and their likelihood of not succeeding through legitimate endeavour.

Ethnic minorities in the UK are evolving culturally, economically and attitudinally. Changes in consumption, therefore, are to be expected, but the potency of racial and class-based coding, in tandem with inner-city areas perceived as lacking in potential, helps ensure that more rounded and reasonable modes of analysis remain marginal. And yet there are numerous examples that demonstrate the power of individual agency, group solidarity and resistance. For SV, born and brought up in Manningham, an interest in cars was neither accidental nor avoidable:

> At the time we all wanted a supercar like the Ferraris. There weren't that many Ferraris back then, not as we are nowadays: you see one or two on a good day. Having a passion for having one of those cars stayed with me for a number of years.... My interest in cars stems from my childhood years – living in Manningham and seeing people with flashy cars. (SV, 32, male, 13 March 2013)

SV went on to discuss some other cars he had owned, including a number of Honda CRXs and some other 'old school', retro cars. He had also owned a Ferrari, an event that he couched as almost necessary:

> One of my dream cars that I got, going back a couple of years was to have a Ferrari.... My family knew this was always a lifetime passion for me to have a Ferrari from day one, and am always going on about it and I'm going to do it the right way. You can drive nice cars and not fund that through, you know, drugs. I was about 29. I bought this Ferrari, you know, dream accomplished kind of thing

> but after a bit you know the novelty wears off.... For me it was just something that was ticked off the list. I feel like I've achieved that now.

For SV, having an expensive car without illegal activity is possible, and although role modelling did not feature in his motivations to buy a Ferrari, it was clearly a consequence. Many participants were explicitly asked about their views on the presence of elite cars in the city. Responses varied, ranging from a familiar assertion around such cars being linked with criminal activity to responses that challenged this. For example, BS, a 40-year-old businessman, offered cogent input:

> People reckon it's all drugs money but I don't think it is. In fact I know it's not that, not that at all. People don't see, or maybe don't want to see, that for a start a lot of these cars aren't owned. They're not owned: they be hired or leased out.... I've hired cars out myself, so I know ... for weddings and things like that; a few of you chip in together, Lambo for the weekend. It's expensive, I won't say it's not, but if we can afford it, then there should be no problem. But no, it's *oh no, all these drug dealers blah-de-blah....* (BS, 40, male, 24 January 2019)

Meanwhile, LO, a much younger participant, offered a slightly different response that nevertheless countered the 'gangster'/drug dealer stereotype:

> My cousin, out-of-town cousin, he's doing really well. Really well: should see his house.... Big house, pool, everything you want.... Done really well, gets good – really good pay.... Looks after his whole family – pays for a lot, you know, cos he's the oldest as well. Everyone's looked after and then he looks after himself.... In his yard, he's got four cars: one's his wife's, one's his dad's and he's got two for himself. Last time I went up, he had a Murcielago for weekends and track days, and he's got his M5 for his runaround. (LO, 26, male, 15 July 2018)

Adding to this, PY, a 46-year-old male who had owned several sports and super cars over a number of years, was more reflective and perhaps understanding of how stereotypes develop:

> What you have to understand is that we, as a community, we're still not in, if you understand me … we're not quite there yet – we're not fully embraced. You might say that's our own fault because we don't do enough to belong.… I don't agree with that, but I would say that's where this comes from – that's what the root of it is.… So when a white person sees me driving my car – which, let's be honest, it does stand out and get attention – they'll already be ready to write it off: *oh, look, it's another Asian drug dealer, then.* That doesn't mean that for them it's a racist way to think – they don't think they're being racist when they think that.… No, because for them, it's obvious – obviously he's a dealer because he's driving a car that's worth more than their house. (PY, 46, male, 13 August 2018)

The theme in particular generated a lot of discussion, across most participants. Although statistical analysis is neither possible nor desirable, it is worth stating that, in broad terms, there were perhaps three types of view. As already mentioned, for some, elite cars were often bought through illegal revenue streams. Others felt this to be a significant minority whose criminality became emblematic of all such cars and their owners. A third view, however, straddled neither vantage point – and, in some ways, both. Here, there was an assertive, insistent and, at times, refreshingly brutal critique of consumption, identity and race:

> Why you're sat here now, talking to me about all this car hoo-haa is because of one reason and one reason only.… It's because we're Pakis, because we're Muslims.… If we're good or practising Muslims or if we're bad Muslims, doesn't matter – we're all the same.… We're not a threat, but what we are is different and they don't like that.… The they is white people, white society.… If they see us doing badly, it's all this stuff about dole scroungers, or scammers.… If they see us doing well, we're all drug dealers and drug

> lords.... Let me ask you this, what business is it of yours or anyone else's what car I drive? What gives anyone the right to think that I'm a drug dealer all because I've got a sports car parked outside? I work – worked since I was a kid, and I've done alright. I pay my taxes, feed and clothe myself and my family. I don't break any laws – never broken a single law – but now I'm a drug dealer? They can fuck off, think what they want to think.... There's nothing you or anyone else can do about it. If it's not cars, it's something else.... You do get sick of it but what can you do? It's how it is and how it is, is how it is.... (SN, 47, male, 21 May 2018)

In other parts of the interview, SN mentioned how his wife had stopped driving one of the family's more prestigious cars simply because of the unwarranted attention it received from other road users and law enforcement, and also because of the messages it sent out. Moreover, SN's view signals how the car conveys a middle-class, and racially couched, form of resistance as one further outcome: "They can fuck off, think what they want to think." Once again, and even though owners of elite cars are highly tuned into how they are perceived, the consumption they enact is not merely passive, vacuous, or in and of itself about commodities. Rather, by virtue of being subject to negative readings, elite car ownership can be seen as a political act because it functions in, and despite, a known and racialised context.

This final interview segment, although ambivalent at one level, points to the view that changes in consumer behaviour demonstrate a commitment to not only economic but also cultural integration:

> Let me tell you something, brother. When I started, which is a long time ago, I sold cars to white people.... I purposefully went for cars that I knew our people didn't want.... For our people, it was Japanese cars always, nearly always.... And the reason I did that was not because I couldn't get them cars – I could – but it was because it was always much easier selling to white people.... They didn't chip you [haggle] as much, they didn't come out with all this *my dad knows your dad now give some discount you bastard*

> [laughs].... And to be fair and to prove I'm not having a go, that was me as well – I still always try to chip something off: even at the supermarket! [laughs].... But now, that way of buying and selling cars isn't there any more. Our people, especially the younger ones, the professionals – they have a bit of money, and they're like what white people used to be like: *How much is it? It's x pounds. Can you do it for anything less? Go on then, I'll knock you 50 quid off.* And that's it – whereas before, you'd be arguing and going back and forwards for hours. And more and more, you can see this without even having to be in the trade – just look at the cars on the roads. There's probably more cars worth over a hundred grand in this city, sort of per square mile, than anywhere else, I bet.... To me, that shows you how much we've changed since our parents and grandparents first came. That's how much we've got on.... We've done what we need to do; if you like, we've integrated. (RK, 47, male, 19 January 2019)

As already mentioned in previous chapters, racial and class-biased coding remains pervasive and often comes to the fore through the car. Car-buying preferences of young, working-class Pakistanis today can also lead to stereotypical racial codes being reinforced and perpetuated. Cars that in some way stand out or are deemed unusual become active agents within commentary around criminality, and demonstrate a failure to 'integrate'. Absent is acknowledgement and appreciation of not only changes in consumption that enable the appreciation of cars, but also changes in sensibilities and tastes that are a consequence of being born and raised in the UK. There are complex, intersecting and, at times, contradictory features in the lives of especially young Pakistani-British males, particularly when the car is also a part of their lives. At the very least, the car presents opportunities in which the presentation of self has space to be articulated. In addition, cars enable forms of social integration that are so outside the conventional framings of community and 'cohesion' that they instead become instrumental in reinforcing skewed rehearsals of insular, segregated and deficient identities.

EIGHT

Conclusion

As personal and private, but also public-sphere objects, cars cannot be divorced from the enveloping automobile hegemony in which we find relations of dependence, collaboration and interaction in order to sustain ourselves and our vehicles. It has to be said, of course, that cars are also, in and of themselves, loaded with risks relating to the environment, or injury and death. At a more banal level, cars reference personal freedom, functioning as little more than a mode of transport and mobility, but for many, what they represent and signify are vital elements of consumption: some use cars as a way to confer status, while for others, being anonymous, or unnoticed, is more important.

Sociology offers opportunities for understanding and exploring aspects of everyday life, trivial and spectacular, some of which are problematic, while others problematise particular identities. Here, examining our relationships with cars helps situate identity as something that is lived, refined and developed in a relational, not necessarily transactional, manner. Through the dissection of the complex, intersecting and even conflicting aspects of a city's car culture and reputation, the car emerges as a means through which insights into human behaviours and attitudes can be gleaned, thus enabling individual and collective human identity to be explored. It follows, then, that cars can be seen as active and meaningful objects that impact and help crystallise notions of 'Us', 'Them' and 'the Other'. Here, the articulation of identity includes processes of car customisation as well as the more ordinary aspects of car usage. As a result, some dimensions of car culture are connected to particular sociologically grounded vantage points: taste, social class, consumption and conceptions of race continue to shape experience through the conduit of cars.

This book has produced discussions that tap into broader debates about how identity is worked on, projected and received. Despite the potential limitations linked with a relatively closed, or narrow, geographical site, the material has wider reach and appeal, not only within the realm of academic research, but especially within public discourse, in which ethnicity and class often feature as being self-evidently in need of repair. Although emblematic of youth in decline, the car enables us to see groups and individuals who are not atomised, segregated or lacking in 'cohesion'. This book therefore uncovers meanings and possibilities that reach beyond headlines, political discourse and myths that further essentialise and reduce identities to racially coded sound bites. Through an in-depth and focused analysis in which the car, identity and sociological inquiry are connected, we see overlaps with taste, culture and creativity on the one hand, and crime, racialisation and exclusion on the other.

Given the scope of and detail in the preceding chapters, it is apparent that for many young people, the car is an important element of their lived experience. It is a means and symbol of independence and freedom, but can be misread and interpreted in ways that refer back to existing stereotypes. At present, there are multi-strand accounts that locate ethnicity, masculinity and class within realms of criminality, unruliness and a failure to buy into whatever constitutes widely held norms and values. At best, these are partial and selective readings of inter- and intra-ethnic encounters on and off the road.

In popular culture, the car is used in varied and seemingly banal ways. Of course, we all know and understand that what we see on the screen is not always 'reality'. However, when it comes to 'factual' programming, we find that which we condemn in the real world is often validated, and, especially when it comes to speed, celebrated. In other media, particularly in some genres of popular music, the car is used to buttress masculinity, power and success, and to feed into the personae of the performers. However, the car's role here is not entirely consistent, with some songs charting the experience of racism – and, indeed, being used as a prop to symbolise resistance to, but at the same time investment in, whatever promises capitalism offers.

The ways in which the car is consumed open up the possibility of offering a positive perspective on agency, cultural vitality and identity in contemporary life. Here, critical means of self-, group and community expression are present. Often, however, instances of such highly finessed interplay between object and consumer are designated as either empty or worthless features of cultural practice. In order to more fully and coherently demarginalise, include and integrate those usually rendered insignificant, it is necessary to recognise and appreciate the car's role in the work of identities being formed, and performed.

Different cars do different things, and are bought for varied reasons, used through shifting modes of consumption not only linked with functionality, but also signifying class position, habitus and taste. There are widespread and mainstream sensibilities in which class-based consumption produces knowledge and understanding wherein cars and their consumers can be anchored relationally and rationally: crudely put, expensive cars for the wealthy; ordinary cars for the rest of us. Beyond this, cars still represent personal freedom and independence, but this is by no means experienced consistently or evenly. In Bradford, it is not unusual to see expensive cars, even in the most unlikely of places. When they appear in working-class neighbourhoods, some of which are deemed both 'mono-ethnic' and 'deprived', suspicion may be evoked due to the mismatch between what the car is, where it is and who is, or appears to be, driving it. When we experience a break from this, other more complex but casually accepted understandings are ascribed and assigned. And it is here, depending on the nature of such variables, that prominent racial stereotypes and the narratives in which they sit are given licence to be expressed. Expensive cars are owned and driven by those who do not *appear* to be able to afford them; therefore, some further, 'reasonable' information is introduced to make the encounter coherent.

Contemporary racialisation is not detached from deep-seated ways of seeing the world. Our understandings and practical implementations of race do, however, predate and preconfigure its place in relation to the car. In part, the idea of race and its corollaries still depends on the power of stereotype and prejudice, but it is additionally primed through a collective memory and experience. The historical legacies of economic, cultural and biological supremacy continue to influence our present-day understandings of ethnic groups. Myths, stereotypes and narratives in which minority ethnic drivers of expensive cars are perceived to be, for example, gangsters, drug dealers or dangerous drivers did not come into being with the car. Such embedded thinking has developed through centuries of ideological work, resulting in race having a normative, lingering presence in thought and behaviour. Our understandings of and attitudes toward ethnic minorities are therefore based on, and remain connected to, historical and structural contexts that helped produce, legitimise and perpetuate an ideology of race. In turn, racialisation connects with the processes that produce racial 'Others'; those who do not belong are problematic and need to be analysed, managed and resolved.

When it comes to how cars are read, signification points certainly to *the possible*, and arguably *the probable*. Interpreting information merely on the basis of the cars people drive falls within the parameters of how we make sense of what we observe. Our confidence in these connections produces a sense of security that is not restricted to us as individuals, but becomes part of a wider shared cultural repertoire. Noticing teenagers in expensive cars may elicit questions and especially answers that have little substantive basis; the driver may not be a teenager, nor the owner. Conversely, seeing a member of the royal family chauffeured in a 30-year-old Toyota Corolla with a noisy exhaust and faded red paintwork would require the work of imagination to explain the scene. The car therefore needs to be framed within this historical, economic and cultural continuum; how it is used and consumed evolves as we evolve, as agentic individuals or as members of specific groupings and communities.

Changing gears

In Bradford, and no doubt in other cities, cars are a potent shorthand in which ethnicity, age and class are translated as unruliness, deviance and danger, especially when associated with these intersecting markers of identity. Young, ethnic minority-heritage, working-class males driving certain cars yield certain types of responses: drug dealer, criminal, irresponsible and antisocial. Because the car is a salient, material means of cultural distinctiveness, there are highly positive, creative and otherwise hidden, unnoticed and, in some cases, quite rational behaviours flowing from car cultural practice. Some of these tie in closely with the formation or even the performance of class and ethnicity facets of identity. This is especially the case with those for whom the car represents something of their own identities and aspirations, but also helps negotiate, rebalance and confer status. For the more affluent, the car is also important as a means of performing identity, subject to distinct processes in which the layering of detail speaks to and from the self. The very fact that economically middle-class ethnic minority car owners are electing to own what seem to be disproportionately expensive cars points to the prerequisite of confidence in order to enact resistance, even if it is subtle and quiet in its form. As a result, the car can also be exploited as a means of subverting conventional, widely held, but class-dependent norms, values and articulations of identity.

The data, discussion and analyses offered in the preceding chapters provide an opportunity to revise existing approaches that have failed to integrate, connect and work with younger people in general, but especially those who may be enduring forms of discrimination based on class and ethnic markers of identity. Part of the overarching argument therefore goes beyond a peculiar, and outwardly discrete, interest. While cars are deeply sociological in more ways than this book could ever cover, what has been discussed can tangibly feed into the development of more rounded policy approaches that include, rather than further marginalise, those who are all too often talked about, rather than talked to. One facet of this is the need to challenge some of the powerful discourses that continue to circulate in the public sphere about young people and their cars, and particularly in relation to some of the pernicious understandings in which cars, class and race enable classist and racist modes of wisdom, and their impacts, to be transmitted.

Some of these knowledge deficits can be addressed through 'myth-busting' so that existing, and limited, understandings are challenged, or at the very least explained and the explanations acted upon. At present, and if the discourse remains as it is, there is a very real risk that younger car drivers, particularly those of working-class and minority ethnic backgrounds, will continue to be perceived and reified as suspect, their identities defined through threat and danger. In turn, it is just as likely that ignoring creative, emotional and financial investments in the car will do little to alleviate any pending or extant alienation – or, indeed, will give rise to more nihilistic activities, rather than the class-based practices in which creative resistance presently features.

One of the most compelling themes to have emerged in the course of this book is that of the capacity for some cultural practices to be discounted, or dismissed as insignificant or criminal. For car modifiers, their scenes are loaded with notions of taste, leisure and creativity. Despite their enthusiasm and modes of appreciation, there appears to be little legitimate space for them to express their identity. Indeed, in wider society the very appearance of modified cars evokes heightened anxieties based on expectations of behaviour, rather than a more grounded understanding of the richness and vitality within a culture that sits outside mainstream ideals. This phobia, if it can be called that, is fairly widespread, all the more surprisingly given that modified car scenes cut across age, gender and ethnicity.

The principle, cohesive force, then, is the car itself, rather than those markers of identity that are more generally deemed to be in need of rebalancing or integration. So, yes, instead of being seen as precarious and unworthy, this sort of car cultural practice could quite easily be exploited within the terrain of social cohesion and integration. More importantly and more widely still, in order for roads to become safer, dangerous driving behaviours need to be eradicated, or at the very least reduced; a partnership, rather than an adversarial and arguably counterproductive approach, could prove fruitful. As a number of participants especially noted, working with younger drivers, particularly those with high-performance cars, might not only demonstrate an appreciation of class-based car cultures, but also further validate and value articulations of taste, creativity and identity while simultaneously enabling opportunities for more organic, fulsome and real engagements with notions of belonging, community and citizenship. Certainly at the local level, formal institutions could be much more open to engaging with those who deeply appreciate this element of *social* life that is otherwise deemed empty or negative. Legitimising the creative aspects of car culture might enable identities to be appreciated more fully, rather than being rehearsed as problems to be addressed. In concrete terms, reducing dangerous driving through policing and criminalisation is not a particularly effective, long-term approach. What is certainly worth exploring is the possibility of relevant actors setting about resourcing collaborative, shared, safe spaces and opportunities through which speed, risk and danger are facilitated in controlled environments. This would not only enable greater levels of trust with and access to the same authorities and institutions that are presently held in suspicion, but also demonstrate that those labelled as problematic are more than this.

A further but central element in this book is the significance of the car within the cultural life of ethnic minority communities in general. While cars help us read something of the person in the driving seat, in Bradford, the car is a flexible and taken-for-granted signifier of identity and difference, often prompting the performance of race thinking to become embodied, further reinforcing processes of racialisation. Although the focus has been on Bradfordians of Pakistani heritage, many of the issues apply in other multi-ethnic spaces, especially where meanings of race conflate with danger, threat or even, at more mundane levels, merely 'ethnic' difference.

Postscript

This postscript is being written in the midst of the widespread social lockdown, the seemingly universal response to the COVID-19 pandemic. Over the past few months, things we've previously taken for granted have been viewed with fresh eyes and, occasionally, through perspectives laced with fear, insecurity and an increasing sense of trepidation. There are banal and perhaps ridiculous behaviours (for some reason, the panic buying of toilet paper, milk, and bread started almost as suddenly as it stopped), but more pressing are questions around how we support and care for those who are most vulnerable to the virus. For those who are consigned to some form of medical quarantine, there is a lingering possibility of an impending, and solitary, period of illness and even death. For those in mourning, the process of grieving no longer comes with some form of limited closure to which we may have been previously accustomed. We are all subject, in our own ways, to this new reality. The impacts of these new elements of life, of course, are partly financial but also emotional and psychological.

Worryingly, we still don't really know what it is that we're living through, and what the world will look like in the months and years to come. One thing seems indisputable: for most of us, the world and our place in it will change. We know this because we have already made adaptations to the everyday; from the rituals and practices of greeting one another, to how we work, make leisure and consume media; there have been spikes in sales of games consoles, streaming media services, as well as consumption of user-created media, via YouTube.com, for example, some of which explores alternatives to the pandemic source and alternative treatments. More generally in mainstream mass media, there seems to be a paucity of views which challenge or provide alternatives to guidelines, policies and statements about the state, or phase, we are in, and how we will come out of it. On this note, it is curious, and possibly quite annoying for some of us, that Piers Morgan, through a particular form of populism, has emerged as one of the most consistently critical commentators of the UK government's response to COVID-19.

It is interesting, though perhaps not surprising, that many of the news stories that predated the pandemic – in the UK, Brexit and its delivery had a strong visibility for months – appear to be no longer relevant, or important. Similarly, stories around youth in decline, migration, terrorism, the economy, and even the arguably polarising discourse around gender identity all seem to have subsided. This is unsurprising because we are all, across the world, facing a similar existential threat – we are all likely to know someone who has either been directly infected, or we know someone who is vulnerable to the virus. This pandemic, while mass-mediated and arguably indiscriminate, resonates with us personally. In turn, this enables us to invest in its trajectory and narrative; once the narrative ends, or the storyline becomes more optimistic with an end in sight, some of those other stories and issues that we were previously asked to engage with will resurface. Here, at the local level, the negative discourse around cars has similarly quietened but again, this will not last. Already, but further afield, there are reports of some drivers continuing to ignore guidance on social gathering and social distancing through organising and attending car meets. Panic buying toilet paper aside, Bradford, however, seems to currently be demonstrating arguably surprising restraint when it comes to minimising the risk of spreading infection; this is partly borne out by the statistic that Bradford has one of the lowest COVID-19 death/infection rates in Yorkshire, despite having some areas of high population density and multiple indicators of deprivation.

Of course, throughout our encounters with television, social media and other forms of mass communication, we do come across an understandable levels of support and sympathy for key workers, the infected, their families, and, of course, the NHS – an institution that has suddenly become something it was not until COVID-19: appreciated, valuable and, for the moment, off-limits in terms of critique, funding and significance. It is possible that once this current situation subsides, the NHS will be once again subject to overhaul. Indeed, some of the failings or shortcomings of the response will be attributed to NHS inefficiencies, the dominance of overpaid employees and the ideological need for systemised healthcare to enter the twenty-first century more wholly, in part rationalised with the purported benefits of free-market capitalism.

Contrary to what some commentators and politicians have claimed, however, this pandemic, like others before it, is not a social leveller. We already know that some minority-ethnic and working-class heritage groups are much more vulnerable to the COVID-19 virus. A post-virus world, if we ever get there, is unlikely to magically evolve us into beings for whom inequalities – borne of centuries-old prejudices, quasi-scientific reasoning and plain old economics – are recognised, prioritised and eradicated. Of course, we're all more vulnerable, regardless of our heritage, class, income and status. However, it's also the case that our resilience is built on social, as well as physical and biological, determinants. Even what I'm doing now, typing these words while working from home, and yes, still in paid work, is a privilege that hinges on my class capital that in part comes through my professional identity: I'm an academic, and universities were quick to respond to the needs of the sector by enabling staff to work from home, and students to take part in online and technology-mediated teaching and learning encounters. Even within universities, however, there are different categories of employee, some of which do not have the same privilege as academics, managers and those who can labour remotely.

For many of us, however, remote working is only viable because of the nature of the work that we do; for those whose presence is physically required at a place of work, their labour is impractical and may become simply redundant. Even being isolated to our homes and aiming to limit our movements outside is not something experienced evenly across a given, but diverse, population. As usual, social and economic class markers help ensure differential outcomes will prevail and probably increase. The less well-off are more likely to be subject to deeper levels of vulnerability than the more affluent simply because economic wealth and income has a profound, and proven, influence on health outcomes. Even how the infected are being assessed and treated has connection with their social background; in the process of triage, age, employment and underlying health conditions all feed into viability scores which in turn determine the nature of treatment. There is a plethora of factors that could be mentioned here, each of which has the potential to form long-lasting scars across families, generations, sectors and places. These are difficult times, producing fundamental insecurity for many of us not only in relation to how we live and die, but everything in between, including work, family, leisure and movement.

In relation to the car, there are obvious changes. All over the country, and despite the occasional instance of a high-ranking prime ministerial advisor seeming not to follow his government's own guidance, drivers are tending to follow 'essential' travel guidelines, making roads significantly quieter. Meanwhile, those with a pronounced subcultural interest in the car are instead spending time lavishing attention on their vehicles: the lull in motorised mobility has, no doubt, also given rise to an escalation in gardening, home improvement/repairs and 'quality' (and quantity) time spent with loved ones. The car industry has, for the most part, ground to halt – with many manufacturers closing down production, and some repurposing plants in order to produce medical equipment. The second-hand car market, meanwhile, is in an unusual position in which disruption cascades through every level of transaction. With car auctions being closed or switching to online formats until further notice, supply to meet the needs of retailers is drying up. But these retailers can't sell to buyers; and buyers may be unable or unwilling to buy cars given the lack of personal, and widespread, longer-term financial stability. At present, then, demand seems to be reduced, but still outstripping supply. Cars are therefore 'holding'; that is, maintaining strong market value/price. Some car traders, whose showrooms are presently off limits, are confident that, in time, things will go back to 'normal'. However, for many, not being able to sell cars means not being able to earn, and that again has not only economic consequences for households, but can induce stress, anxiety and other impacts on well-being. However, there remain some who work in the car trade – repair garages, valeters, car washes, and so on – who, despite the risks, continue to stay open for business as a matter of financial necessity.

Beyond and above all this and more, it seems that the car is not as vital as we may have thought. People are driving less, fewer cars are being bought and sold, and the economic significance of the car-related industry is worth noticeably less than it was two months ago. However, generally speaking, there remains a sense of faith in the idea that things will go back to how they were. Of course, there may be tweaks in social, cultural and economic practice, but once this episode of human history blurs into the next, we will probably resume where we left off. If the past gives us lessons for the future, then we know that big corporations, not exclusively those in the financial sector, will be bailed out through state intervention. Perhaps some will simply be allowed to fail, but if the economic fallout grows more intense and we experience a large economic crash, then of course there is a colossal risk to the global economic system in which we are all embedded. Even if things go relatively well, and a global depression is avoided, the long-term economic impact of this pandemic will almost certainly produce a significant shift in the distribution and scale of disposable income that will have direct consequences for us all, and not especially within the domain of conspicuous consumption.

The scale and depth of the pandemic is far-reaching, and traverses every aspect of contemporary society; nothing is immune, and what we do as part of our social, cultural and economic life requires thought and a variance in practice; hygiene, travel, diet, and how we greet and treat others are already elements of life that have undergone change. While state rhetoric and intervention aims to inspire some confidence and signpost the idea that 'everything will be alright', it's reasonable to suggest that 'everything will be different'. This is not to suggest we are heading for an extreme, year-zero type global level reset, but the learning from this event will feed into how we restart and thus define us and future generations. Already, however, universities and their researchers are rightly seeking to develop work exploring all facets of the pandemic – and here, there is research interest around causes/sources and cures/ vaccines, the efficacy of interventions and, of course, the social impacts of not only the virus, but its responses: social, cultural and economic change remain core features of not only helping us to understand these impacts, but how we can better manage any future outbreaks. Against this context, then, sociology of course has a role to play in not only mapping social change, but also tapping into the human impact of life after the pandemic. And here, class, ethnicity and other markers of identity will continue to figure heavily in understanding the reality of differential outcomes in relation to health specifically, and how lives are lived relationally through the intersection points in our communities, at the places we call home, and with the people we encounter, regardless of where, and how. Despite the urgent, life-changing and distressing fallout from this global event, unfortunately, the presence of discriminations – direct, indirect, overt, covert and institutional – will prevail.

May 2020

Notes

Preface

1 Said, E.W. (1977) *Orientalism*, London: Penguin; Ansari, H. (2004) *'The Infidel Within': Muslims in Britain Since 1800*, London: Hurst; Fekete, L. (2009) *A Suitable Enemy: Racism, Migration and Islamophobia in Europe*, London: Pluto Press.

Chapter One

1 The terms 'mobility' and 'automobility' have come to refer to a diverse range of themes (migration, communications, design and engineering, as well as transport). Because the research that this book is built on is specifically about cars and their owners, using 'cars' is more appropriate in most contexts.

2 Redshaw, S. (2008) *In the Company of Cars: Driving as a Social and Cultural Practice*, Aldershot: Ashgate.

3 Urry, J. (2000) *Sociology Beyond Societies: Mobilities for the Twenty-First Century*, London: Routledge; Urry, J. (2008) 'Moving on the mobility turn', in W. Canzler, V. Kaufmann and S. Kesselring (eds) *Tracing Mobilities: Towards a Cosmopolitan Perspective*, Aldershot: Ashgate, pp 13–24.

4 Paterson, M. (2007) *Automobile Politics: Ecology and Cultural Political Economy*, Cambridge: Cambridge University Press, p 96.

5 Paterson (2007), p 92.

6 Parry, T. (2019) 'Statistical Release: Vehicle Licensing Statistics: Annual 2018', *Department for Transport* [online], 11 April, available from: https://assets.publishing.service.gov.uk/government/uploads/system/uploads/attachment_data/file/800502/vehicle-licensing-statistics-2018.pdf [Accessed 11 February 2020].

7 Hirst, D. (2020) *Briefing Paper, Number CBP07480: Electric Vehicles and Infrastructure*, London: House of Commons.

8 Department for Transport (2018) *Transport Energy Model Report: Moving Britain Ahead*, London: Department for Transport.

9 Hirst (2020), p 11.

10 Department for Transport (2018), p 90.

11 Cuthbertson, A. (2019) 'Driverless cars to be rolled out on UK roads by end of 2019, government announces', *The Independent* [online], 6 February, available from: https://www.independent.co.uk/news/uk/

home-news/driverless-cars-uk-roads-2019-self-driving-hacking-cyber-security-a8766716.html [Accessed 24 April 2019].

12 Urry, J. (2004) 'The "system" of automobility', *Theory, Culture & Society*, 21(4–5): 25–39.

13 This idea did surface especially amongst slightly older participants. There was a tendency to situate their decision to buy a relatively expensive car on the grounds of deserving; to argue that they worked and that an expensive car was not selfish, but actually quite important as a means of enhancing self-esteem. Note: the term 'participant' reflects the diversity of encounters with those who took part or somehow influenced the research. For example, some were formally interviewed, but others explored various aspects of car culture, consumption and practice through more informal, and in some cases, unplanned or opportunistic conversations. See also Chapter 2 for more detail relating to research methodology.

14 Miller, D. (ed.) (2001) *Car Cultures*, Oxford: Berg; Packer, J. (2008) *Mobility Without Mayhem: Safety, Cars, and Citizenship*, Durham, NC: Duke University Press; Lumsden, K. (2013) *Boy Racer Culture: Youth, Masculinity and Deviance*, London: Routledge; Redshaw (2008); Conley, J. and McLaren, A.T. (eds) (2016) *Car Troubles: Critical Studies of Automobility and Auto-Mobility*, London: Routledge; Alam, Y. (2014) 'The car, the streetscape and inter-ethnic dynamics', in C. Husband, Y. Alam, J. Hüttermann and J. Fomina, *Lived Diversities: Space, Place and Identities in the Multi-Ethnic City*, Bristol: Policy Press, pp 149–200.

15 Urry (2000; 2004); Urry, J. (2006) 'Inhabiting the car', in S. Böhm, C. Jones, C. Land and M. Paterson (eds) *Against Automobility*, Oxford: Blackwell, pp 17–31; Urry, J. (2007) *Mobilities*, Cambridge: Polity; Urry (2008); Canzler, W., Kaufmann, V. and Kesselring, S. (eds) (2008) *Tracing Mobilities: Towards a Cosmopolitan Perspective*, Aldershot: Ashgate; Dennis, K. and Urry, J. (2009) *After the Car*, Cambridge: Polity; Ohnmacht, T., Maksim, H. and Bergman, M.M. (eds) (2009) *Mobilities and Inequality*, Farnham: Ashgate.

16 Warren, A. and Gibson, C. (2011) 'Blue-collar creativity: reframing custom-car culture in the imperilled industrial city', *Environment and Planning A: Economy and Space*, 43(11): 2705–22.

17 Sheller, M. (2004) 'Automotive emotions: feeling the car', *Theory, Culture & Society*, 21(4–5): 221–42.

18 Urry (2000).

19 Sheller, M. and Urry, J. (2000) 'The city and the car', *International Journal of Urban and Regional Research*, 24(4): 737–57.

20 A relatively small number of (male and female) 'white' heritage individuals were also featured as research participants.

21 Alam, M.Y. (ed.) (2006) *Made in Bradford*, Pontefract: Route; Alam, M.Y. and Husband, C. (2006) *British-Pakistani Men From Bradford: Linking Narratives to Policy*, York: Joseph Rowntree Foundation.

22 Berger, P.L. and Luckmann, T. (1966) *The Social Construction of Reality: a Treatise in the Sociology of Knowledge*, London: Penguin.

[23] Here, I am referring particularly to cultural changes in UK universities, which, by and large, tend to put measurable value on most things academics do; the push toward the monetisation of knowledge continues unabated, with exceptions usually being examples of individual goodwill.

[24] Back, L. (2007) *The Art of Listening*, Oxford: Berg; Husband, C. (ed.) (2015) *Research and Policy in Ethnic Relations: Compromised Dynamics in a Neoliberal Era*, Bristol: Policy Press.

[25] Gunaratnam, Y. (2003) *Researching 'Race' and Ethnicity: Methods, Knowledge and Power*, London: Sage; Kalra, V.S. (2006) 'Ethnography as politics: a critical review of British studies of racialized minorities', *Ethnic and Racial Studies*, 29(3): 452–70; Husband (2015).

[26] Gane, N. and Back, L. (2012) 'C. Wright Mills 50 years on: the promise and craft of sociology revisited', *Theory, Culture & Society*, 29(7–8): 399–421.

[27] Giddens, A. (1998) *The Third Way: the Renewal of Social Democracy*, Cambridge: Polity.

[28] Barlow, A., Duncan, S., James, G. and Park, A. (2005) *Cohabitation, Marriage and the Law: Social Change and Legal Reform in the 21st Century*, Oxford: Hart.

[29] Abridged field note extracts are taken from diaries written soon after an interaction or experience. In many cases, the originals have also been subject to my own censoring; in some instances, the frank language used in the originals might have detracted from the points being presented.

[30] Alam (2006); Husband, C. and Alam, Y. (2011) *Social Cohesion and Counter-Terrorism: a Policy Contradiction?*, Bristol: Policy Press; Alam (2014); Alam, Y. (2015) 'In-group identity and the challenges of ethnographic research', in C. Husband (ed.) *Research and Policy in Ethnic Relations: Compromised Dynamics in a Neoliberal Era*, Bristol: Policy Press, pp 79–104.

[31] Fieldhouse, J. (1978) *Bradford*, Bradford: Watmoughs Financial Print; Husband, C., Alam, Y., Hüttermann, J. and Fomina, J. (2014) *Lived Diversities: Space, Place and Identities in the Multi-Ethnic City*, Bristol: Policy Press.

[32] Pearce, J. and Milne, E-J. (2010) *Participation and Community on Bradford's Traditionally White Estates*, York: Joseph Rowntree Foundation.

[33] For example, even today, friends, neighbours and families rely on interest-free loans through cooperative saving schemes, and through the pooling of resources in order to establish and develop businesses, pay for weddings, and buy homes.

[34] Husband et al (2014).

[35] The phrase 'ethnic difference', as opposed to 'ethnic diversity', is used quite consciously; 'diversity' is arguably a more recent and vacuous intervention within the lexicon of ethnic relations discourse, certainly when compared with more helpful and concrete framing words ('inequality', 'discrimination' or even 'relations' come to mind).

[36] Husband and Alam (2011); Alam (2014; 2015).

[37] Ruthven, M. (1991) *A Satanic Affair: Salman Rushdie and the Rage of Islam*, London: Hogarth; Solomos, J. (2003) *Race and Racism in Britain* (3rd edn), Houndmills: Palgrave Macmillan, pp 104–5.

38 Thatcher, quoted in Ansell, A.E. (1997) *New Right, New Racism: Race and Reaction in the United States and Britain*, Houndmills: Macmillan, p 234.

39 Palat, R.A. (2015) 'Empire, food and the diaspora: Indian restaurants in Britain', *South Asia*, 38(2): 171–86.

40 Lewis, R. (2015) *Muslim Fashion: Contemporary Style Cultures*, Durham, NC: Duke University Press.

41 Husband, C. and Alam, Y. (2012) 'Ethnic diversity and creative urban practice: the case of Bradford's Mughal garden', *COLLeGIUM*, 13, 93–114; Barker, A., Manning, N. and Sirriyeh, A. (2014) *'The Great Meeting Place': a Study of Bradford's City Park*, Bradford: University of Bradford.

42 A more recent variation of this theme can be found in Holmwood, J. and O'Toole, T. (2018) *Countering Extremism in British Schools? The Truth About the Birmingham Trojan Horse Affair*, Bristol: Policy Press. Holmwood and O'Toole offer an enlightening overview of a 'plot' to 'Islamicise' British schools, also known as the 'Trojan Horse Affair'.

43 Lasting from 8 June until 11 June 1995, the incident has various origin narratives, including police officers mistreating a heavily pregnant woman while attempting to arrest a suspect. The riots lasted for three days, and at one point, large groups of local residents congregated outside the relatively newly built Lawcroft House police station. See also Anwar, M. (1998) *Between Cultures: Continuity and Change in the Lives of Young Asians*, London: Routledge, pp 91, 157.

44 Conway, G. (1997) *Islamophobia: a Challenge for Us All*, London: Runnymede Trust.

45 Kundnani, A. (2001) 'From Oldham to Bradford: the violence of the violated', *Race and Class*, 43(2): 105–10; Amin, A. (2003) 'Unruly strangers? The 2001 urban riots in Britain', *International Journal of Urban and Regional Research*, 27(2): 460–3; Meer, N. (2006) '"GET OFF YOUR KNEES": Print media public intellectuals and Muslims in Britain', *Journalism Studies*, 7(1): 35–59; Ramji, H. (2007) 'Dynamics of religion and gender amongst young British Muslims', *Sociology*, 41(6): 1171–89; Bagguley, P. and Hussain, Y. (2008) *Riotous Citizens: Ethnic Conflict in Multicultural Britain*, Aldershot: Ashgate; Husband and Alam (2011); Meer, N. (2012) 'Complicating "radicalism" – counter-terrorism and Muslim identity in Britain', *Arches Quarterly*, 5(9): 10–20.

46 Cantle, T. (2001) *Community Cohesion: a Report of the Independent Review Team, Chaired by Ted Cantle*, London: Home Office; Clarke, T. (2001) *Burnley Speaks, Who Listens?*, Burnley: Burnley Borough Council; Ouseley, H. (2001) *Community Pride Not Prejudice: Making Diversity Work in Bradford*, Bradford: BradfordVision; Ritchie, D. (2001) *Oldham Independent Review: One Oldham One Future*, Manchester: Government Office for the North West; Denham, J. (2002) *Building Cohesive Communities: a Report of the Ministerial Group on Public Order and Community Cohesion*, London: Home Office.

47 Simpson, L. (2004) 'Statistics of racial segregation: measures, evidence and policy', *Urban Studies*, 41(3): 661–81; Phillips, D. (2006) 'Parallel lives?

Challenging discourses of British Muslim self-segregation', *Environment and Planning D: Society and Space*, 24(1): 25–40; Husband and Alam (2011).

48 Amin, A. (2010) 'The remainders of race', *Theory, Culture & Society*, 27(1): 1–23; Elahi, F. and Khan, O. (eds) (2017) *Islamophobia: Still a Challenge for Us All*, London: Runnymede Trust; Tariq, M. and Syed, J. (2018) 'An intersectional perspective on Muslim women's issues and experiences in employment', *Gender, Work & Organization*, 25(5): 495–513.

49 Casey, L. (2016) *The Casey Review: a Review Into Opportunity and Integration*, London: Ministry of Housing, Communities & Local Government.

50 In terms of ethnic diversity, Bradford is home to residents of Eastern European, South Asian, African and African Caribbean heritage, as well as those from parts of the Middle East. Within these broad categories, of course, there is further diversity.

51 Husband et al (2014).

52 Alam (2006); Back (2007), p 148; Phillips, R. (ed.) (2009) *Muslim Spaces of Hope: Geographies of Possibility in Britain and the West*, London: Zed Books; Alam, M.Y. (ed.) (2011) *The Invisible Village: Small World, Big Society*, Pontefract: Route; Husband et al (2014).

53 'Race' is used frequently in this book, despite its contentious meaning, and indeed, in the knowledge that it has been anything but a useful, let alone neutral, means of categorising human beings according to variances in physical, cultural or political markers of identity. Despite its provenance and continuing impact, the term remains meaningful and is used where alternatives seem insufficient.

Chapter Two

1 Gane, N. and Back, L. (2012) 'C. Wright Mills 50 years on: the promise and craft of sociology revisited', *Theory, Culture & Society*, 29(7–8): 399–421.

2 Burawoy, M. (2005) '2004 American Sociological Association presidential address: for public sociology', *British Journal of Sociology*, 56(2): 259–94; Burawoy, M. (2007) 'For public sociology', in D. Clawson, R. Zussman, J. Misra, N. Gerstel, R. Stokes, D.L. Anderton and M. Burawoy (eds) *Public Sociology: Fifteen Eminent Sociologists Debate Politics and the Profession in the Twenty-First Century*, Berkeley: University of California Press, pp 23–64.

3 Bhattacharyya, G. and Murji, K. (2013) 'Introduction: race critical public scholarship', *Ethnic and Racial Studies*, 36(9): 1359–73; Husband, C. (ed.) (2015) *Research and Policy in Ethnic Relations: Compromised Dynamics in a Neoliberal Era*, Bristol: Policy Press.

4 Madden, R. (2010) *Being Ethnographic: a Guide to the Theory and Practice of Ethnography*, London: Sage.

5 Fine, G.A. (1999) 'Field labor and ethnographic reality', *Journal of Contemporary Ethnography*, 28(5): 532–9.

6 This does not mean ethnography is unsystematic, but because it is perceived to be an organic, free-flowing and reflexive mode of inquiry, rather than one that has rigid, fixed boundaries of practice, it does often receive criticism around the centrality of subjectivity.

7 Lumsden, K. (2013) '"You are what you research": researcher partisanship and the sociology of the "underdog"', *Qualitative Research*, 13(1): 3–18.

8 Jeffrey, B. and Troman, G. (2004) 'Time for ethnography', *British Educational Research Journal*, 30(4): 535–48.

9 Tillmann-Healy, L.M. (2003) 'Friendship as method', *Qualitative Inquiry*, 9(5): 729–49.

10 See, for example, Malinowski, B. (1922) *Argonauts of the Western Pacific: an Account of Native Enterprise and Adventure in the Archipelagoes of Melanesian New Guinea*, London: Routledge & Kegan Paul; Chagnon, N.A. (1968) *Yanomamo: the Fierce People*, New York: Holt, Rinehart and Winston.

11 See, for instance, Bennett, A. (1999) 'Rappin' on the Tyne: white hip hop culture in northeast England: an ethnographic study', *Sociological Review*, 47(1): 1–24; Westmarland, L. (2001) 'Blowing the whistle on police violence: gender, ethnography and ethics', *British Journal of Criminology*, 41(3): 523–35.

12 Madden (2010), p 39.

13 See, for example, Saifullah Khan, V. (1977) 'The Pakistanis: Mirpuri villagers at home and in Bradford', in J.L. Watson (ed.) *Between Two Cultures: Migrants and Minorities in Britain*, Oxford: Blackwell, pp 57–89; Bhatti, G. (1999) *Asian Children at Home and at School: an Ethnographic Study*, London: Routledge; Bolognani, M. (2007) 'Islam, ethnography and politics: methodological issues in researching amongst West Yorkshire Pakistanis in 2005', *International Journal of Social Research Methodology*, 10(4): 279–93.

14 Van Maanen, J. (ed.) (1995) *Representation in Ethnography*, Thousand Oaks, CA: Sage.

15 Madden (2010), p 15.

16 See, for example, Alam, M.Y. (ed.) (2006) *Made in Bradford*, Pontefract: Route; Alam, M.Y. (ed.) (2011) *The Invisible Village: Small World, Big Society*, Pontefract: Route.

17 Ali, S. (2006) 'Racializing research: managing power and politics?', *Ethnic and Racial Studies*, 29(3): 471–86, p 476.

18 Some field notes demonstrate observation being incidental and unplanned.

19 While there are differences between literary and semiotic representation, either applies in this context, but Hall's use of the term is especially useful (see Chapter 3).

20 Denscombe, M. (2003) *The Good Research Guide for Small-Scale Social Research Projects* (2nd edn), Buckingham: Open University Press, pp 84–5.

21 Saifullah Khan (1977); Wacquant, L. (2004) *Body & Soul: Notebooks of an Apprentice Boxer*, Oxford: Oxford University Press; Alam (2006).

22 Brannick, T. and Coghlan, D. (2007) 'In defense of being "native": the case for insider academic research', *Organizational Research Methods*, 10(1): 59–74; Nayak, A. (2006) 'Displaced masculinities: chavs, youth and class in the post-industrial city', *Sociology*, 40(5): 813–31; de Andrade, L.L. (2000) 'Negotiating from the inside: constructing racial and ethnic identity in qualitative research', *Journal of Contemporary Ethnography*, 29(3): 268–90.

23 Sanghera, G.S. and Thapar-Björkert, S. (2008) 'Methodological dilemmas: gatekeepers and positionality in Bradford', *Ethnic and Racial Studies*, 31(3): 543–62.
24 Sanghera and Thapar-Björkert (2008), p 558.
25 This term refers not only to ethnic groups who are smaller in terms of numbers, but also to the relative lack of political power they hold.
26 Taylor, J. (2011) 'The intimate insider: negotiating the ethics of friendship when doing insider research', *Qualitative Research*, 11(1): 3–22.
27 Bhattacharyya and Murji (2013), p 1362.
28 Jeffrey and Troman (2004).

Chapter Three

1 Bramwell, R. (2015) *UK Hip-Hop, Grime and the City: the Aesthetics and Ethics of London's Rap Scenes*, London: Routledge.
2 Hodkinson, P. and Deicke, W. (eds) (2007) *Youth Cultures: Scenes, Subcultures and Tribes*, Abingdon: Routledge; Buckingham, D., Bragg, S. and Kehily, M.J. (eds) (2014) *Youth Cultures in the Age of Global Media*, Houndmills: Palgrave Macmillan; Hodkinson, P. (2016) 'Youth cultures and the rest of life: subcultures, post-subcultures and beyond', *Journal of Youth Studies*, 19(5): 629–45.
3 Back, L. and Solomos, J. (eds) (2000) *Theories of Race and Racism: a Reader*, Abingdon: Routledge; Cottle, S. (ed.) (2000) *Ethnic Minorities and the Media: Changing Cultural Boundaries*, Buckingham: Open University Press; Messer, M., Schroeder, R. and Wodak, R. (eds) (2012) *Migrations: Interdisciplinary Perspectives*, Vienna: Springer.
4 Hall, S. (1997) (ed.) *Representation: Cultural Representations and Signifying Practices*, London: Sage, p 15.
5 Barker, M. and Petley, J. (eds) (2001) *Ill Effects: the Media/Violence Debate* (2nd edn), London: Routledge.
6 Usually, when it comes to mainstream Hollywood 'action' genre films in which cars feature significantly, gender especially is realised through hegemonic understandings of masculinity. In the context of cars used by younger, working-class males, see Walker, L., Butland, D. and Connell, R.W. (2000) 'Boys on the road: masculinities, car culture, and road safety education', *Journal of Men's Studies*, 8(2): 153–69, for connections with hegemonic masculinity that works to exclude females, while enhancing male traits, including risk-taking.
7 Also known as the 'Keatonmobile', and designed by Anton Furst, this vehicle appeared in the Tim Burton-directed 1989 *Batman* feature film.
8 Conley, J. (2016) 'Automobile advertisements: the magical and the mundane', in J. Conley and A.T. McLaren (eds) *Car Troubles: Critical Studies of Automobility and Auto-Mobility*, London: Routledge, pp 37–57.
9 Urry, J. (2004) 'The "system" of automobility', *Theory, Culture & Society*, 21(4–5): 25–39.

[10] Soron, D. (2016) 'Driven to drive: cars and the problem of "compulsory consumption"', in J. Conley and A.T. McLaren (eds) *Car Troubles*, pp 181–96.

[11] The concept has also been developed through combining works originated by other theorists, including Freud and Lacan; see Böhm, S. and Batta, A. (2010) 'Just doing it: enjoying commodity fetishism with Lacan', *Organization*, 17(3): 345–61.

[12] Billig, M. (1999) 'Commodity fetishism and repression: reflections on Marx, Freud and the psychology of consumer capitalism', *Theory & Psychology*, 9(3): 313–29.

[13] For a focus on the emotional effects of contemporary capitalism, see, for example, Burkitt, I. (2019) 'Alienation and emotion: social relations and estrangement in contemporary capitalism', *Emotions and Society*, 1(1): 51–66.

[14] Marx, K. (1867) *Capital: a Critique of Political Economy: Vol. 1*, edited by F. Engels, reprint, New York: Cosimo Classics, 2007, pp 81–2.

[15] White, M.V. (2002) 'Doctoring Adam Smith: the fable of the diamonds and water paradox', *History of Political Economy*, 34(4): 659–83.

[16] Marx (1867), p 85.

[17] Böhm and Batta (2010), p 354.

[18] Böhm and Batta (2010), p 354.

[19] Veblen, T. (1899) *The Theory of the Leisure Class: an Economic Study in the Evolution of Institutions*, reprint, Boston, MA: Adamant Media Corporation, 2000.

[20] Goffman, E. (1969) *The Presentation of Self in Everyday Life*, London: Allen Lane.

[21] Conley, J. (2016) 'Automobile advertisements: the magicaland the mundane', in J. Conley and A.T. McLaren (eds) *Car Troubles*, London: Taylor and Francis, pp 37-57.

[22] Campbell, C. (1987) *The Romantic Ethic and the Spirit of Modern Consumerism*, Oxford: Blackwell.

[23] Tragos, P. (2009) 'Monster masculinity: honey, I'll be in the garage reasserting my manhood', *Journal of Popular Culture*, 42(3): 541–53, p 542.

[24] Herman, E.S. and Chomsky, N. (1988) *Manufacturing Consent: the Political Economy of the Mass Media*, New York: Pantheon.

[25] See billybobworddog (2007) 'Chop Shop: London Garage Episode 2', *You Tube* [online], 10 October, available from: https://www.youtube.com/watch?v=Da5JkEOowxk [Accessed 17 June 2019].

[26] Best, A.L. (2006) *Fast Cars, Cool Rides: the Accelerating World of Youth and Their Cars*, New York: New York University Press; Warren, A. and Gibson, C. (2011) 'Blue-collar creativity: reframing custom-car culture in the imperilled industrial city', *Environment and Planning A: Economy and Space*, 43(11): 2705–22.

[27] Jeremy Clarkson, one of the show's former presenters (the BBC decided not to renew his contract in 2015), is known for having made racially problematic comments. See also Meadows, B. and Sayer, P. (2013) 'The Mexican sports car controversy: an appraisal analysis of BBC's *Top Gear*

and the reproduction of nationalism and racism through humor', *Discourse, Context & Media*, 2(2): 103–10.

28 Miller, D. (2012) *Consumption and Its Consequences*, Cambridge: Polity, pp 39–40.

29 Hebdige, D. (2012) 'Contemporizing "subculture": 30 years to life', *European Journal of Cultural Studies*, 15(3): 399–424, p 399; Debies-Carl, J.S. (2013) 'Are the kids alright? A critique and agenda for taking youth cultures seriously', *Social Science Information*, 52(1): 110–33.

30 George, N. (1998) *Hip Hop America*, New York: Penguin; Rose, T. (2008) *The Hip Hop Wars: What We Talk About When We Talk About Hip Hop – and Why It Matters*, New York: Basic Books; Belle, C. (2014) 'From Jay-Z to Dead Prez: examining representations of black masculinity in mainstream versus underground hip-hop music', *Journal of Black Studies*, 45(4): 287–300; Bramwell (2015).

31 For example, the former US President, Barack Obama, has mentioned the culture's significance in his own life, and has also 'performed' hip-hop gestures; see DailyTrix (2010) 'Obama brushes dirt off his shoulders', *YouTube* [online], 10 April, available from: https://www.youtube.com/watch?v=1Hq8awi9Oaw [Accessed 21 March 2018].

32 Rose, T. (1994) *Black Noise: Rap Music and Black Culture in Contemporary America*, Hanover, NH: Wesleyan University Press; Watkins, S.C. (2005) *Hip Hop Matters: Politics, Pop Culture, and the Struggle for the Soul of a Movement*, Boston, MA: Beacon; Rose (2008).

33 Wise, T. (2010) *Colorblind: the Rise of Post-Racial Politics and the Retreat From Racial Equity*, San Francisco, CA: City Lights Books.

34 Alexander, M. (2010) *The New Jim Crow: Mass Incarceration in the Age of Colorblindness*, New York: New Press.

35 Of course, over the last two decades, there has been a rising black presence in Hollywood. However, a noticeable proportion of black British actors seem to find more opportunities in the US than the UK. For a discussion of ethnicity and casting within film, see Okafor, K. (2018) 'Let's not punish black British actors like Cynthia Erivo for playing roles like Harriet Tubman – it's the TV and film industry's fault', *The Independent* [online], 17 September, available from: https://www.independent.co.uk/voices/harriet-tubman-casting-british-black-actors-cynthia-martin-luther-king-selma-a8541276.html [Accessed 17 May 2019].

36 Mastro, D.E., Blecha, E. and Seate, A.A. (2011) 'Characterizations of criminal athletes: a systematic examination of sports news depictions of race and crime', *Journal of Broadcasting & Electronic Media*, 55(4): 526–42; Colburn, A. and Melander, L.A. (2018) 'Beyond black and white: an analysis of newspaper representations of alleged criminal offenders based on race and ethnicity', *Journal of Contemporary Criminal Justice*, 34(4): 383–98. For more UK-oriented work, see Bhatia, M., Poynting, S. and Tufail, W. (eds) (2018) *Media, Crime and Racism*, Cham: Palgrave Macmillan.

[37] See Fiske, J. (1989) *Understanding Popular Culture*, London: Routledge, p 88; Gelder, K. and Thornton, S. (eds) (1997) *The Subcultures Reader*, London: Routledge.

[38] Storey, J. (2010) *Cultural Studies and the Study of Popular Culture* (3rd edn), Edinburgh: Edinburgh University Press, p 143.

[39] Fiske (1989), p 46.

[40] George (1998), p 161.

[41] There are countless examples of rappers aligning themselves with or, at the very least, validating particular brands, some of which are evidenced in song lyrics: Eminem/The Notorious BIG's 'Dead Wrong' (1999; Northface); Brandy and Mase's 'Top of the World' (1998; Helly Hansen); and Mobb Deep's 'Drink Away the Pain' (1995; Boss, Hilfiger, Northface, Donna Karan, Nike, Helly Hansen).

[42] See Bourdieu, P. (1984) *Distinction: a Social Critique of the Judgment of Taste*, translated by R. Nice, Cambridge, MA: Harvard University Press. See also Chapter 4.

[43] For example, complimenting custom-designed in-car entertainment (ICE) systems, compositions are arranged to rigorously test bass reflex, volume and clarity.

[44] 'Rocket 88', by Jackie Brenston and Ike Turner, was released in 1951. In 1946, Nat King Cole performed '(Get Your Kicks On) Route 66'. During the 1960s, The Beach Boys had several songs explicitly mentioning a car. In the 1970s, the band War released 'Low Rider', and toward the end of that decade, Gary Numan's 'Cars', perhaps emblematic of the shift toward electronic music, charted highly. In the 1980s, Prince, Madness and Tracy Chapman all released songs based on the car or driving. It was not until the 1990s, however, that hip-hop car songs, with artists such as Will Smith, Coolio and LL Cool J, became prevalent.

[45] This includes 'Top 100' list-style television shows, such as Channel 4's *100 Greatest* series, in which songs are listed and presented as successful in whatever category is designated significant.

[46] Rosenbaum, J. and Prinsky, L. (1987) 'Sex, violence and rock 'n' roll: youths' perceptions of popular music', *Popular Music and Society*, 11(2): 79–89.

[47] Portelli, A. (2019) *Bruce Springsteen's America: a Dream Deferred*, Newcastle upon Tyne: Cambridge Scholars.

[48] Brodsky, W. (2016) *Driving With Music: Cognitive-Behavioural Implications*, Abingdon: Routledge, pp 329–32. Ostensibly, Brodsky's text explores a range of psychological and behavioural aspects of driving with music, some of which may feed into driver error and traffic violations, but it also offers some relevant discussion around car driving and popular music, particularly in relation to how music makes us feel when we are driving.

[49] Also, for many of the younger participants especially, hip-hop and its various genres were particularly favoured.

[50] SBTV: Music (2013) 'Meridian Dan ft Big H & JME | German Whip [Music Video]: SBTV', *YouTube* [online], 29 September, available from:

https://www.youtube.com/watch?v=OHZRHEJHS2k [Accessed 12 April 2019].

51 BBC Radio 1Xtra (2014) 'Hugh Jackman & Meridian Dan - German Whip (Wolverine Remix) feat. JME & Bossman Birdie', *YouTube* [online], 17 May, available from: https://www.youtube.com/watch?v=f2_ibidGpKc [Accessed 19 June 2019].

52 Bramwell (2015).

53 Guy, M. (2017) 'Why is a car called a whip?', *The Drive* [online], 15 February, available from: https://www.thedrive.com/opinion/7495/why-is-a-car-called-a-whip [Accessed 23 June 2019].

54 Hall (1997).

55 The lyrics are available from: https://genius.com/Meridian-dan-german-whip-lyrics.

56 Bowling, B. and Phillips, C. (2007) 'Disproportionate and discriminatory: reviewing the evidence on police stop and search', *Modern Law Review*, 70(6): 936–61.

57 Link Up TV (2014) 'German Whip Parody | Link Up TV', *YouTube* [online], 14 April, available from: https://www.youtube.com/watch?v=3WeQrrexlHM [Accessed 12 April 2019].

58. At the time of writing, the lyrics for this song are not available on a public lyrics database, but can be heard on the source video: Link Up TV (2014).

59 Gilroy, P. (2001) 'Driving while black', in D. Miller (ed.) *Car Cultures*, Oxford: Berg, pp 81–104.

60 jerudoriginal91 (2011) 'The Pharcyde- Officer', *YouTube* [online], 19 April, available from: https://www.youtube.com/watch?v=JUqdrkpsIho [Accessed 12 April 2019]; spectrotoons (2017) 'The Pharcyde - OFFICER (Unofficial Animated Music Video)', *YouTube* [online], 22 January, available from: https://www.youtube.com/watch?v=IpbQh4jYfXI [Accessed 12 April 2019].

61 See, for example, 'Regulate' by Nate Dogg and Warren G (1994), 'The Rain' by Missy Elliott (1997), 'Return of the Mack' by Mark Morrison (1997), 'Dilemma' by Nelly ft. Kelly Rowland (2002), 'Still D.R.E.' by Dr. Dre ft. Snoop Dogg (1999), 'X Gon' Give It To Ya' by DMX (2003), and 'Poppin' Them Thangs' by G-Unit (2003).

62 Hall, S., Critcher, C., Jefferson, T., Clarke, J. and Roberts, B. (1978) *Policing the Crisis: Mugging, the State, and Law and Order*, London: Macmillan; Smith, M.R. and Petrocelli, M. (2001) 'Racial profiling? A multivariate analysis of police traffic stop data', *Police Quarterly*, 4(1): 4–27; Bowling, B. and Weber, L. (2011) 'Stop and search in global context: an overview', *Policing and Society*, 21(4): 480–8.

63 Darder, A. and Torres, R.D. (2004) *After Race: Racism After Multiculturalism*, New York: New York University Press; Gillborn, D. (2005) 'Education policy as an act of white supremacy: whiteness, critical race theory and education reform', *Journal of Education Policy*, 20(4): 485–505.

[64] mike1519 (2007) 'Big Tymers - #1 Stunna Uncensored', *YouTube* [online], 7 December, available from: https://www.youtube.com/watch?v=KEB274xvzvg [Accessed 31 December 2019].

[65] Brodsky (2016), p 188.

[66] Among the many songs and videos that share some similarity are 504 Boyz' 'Tight Whips' (2002), Gucci Mane and Waka Flocka Flame's 'Ferrari Boyz' (2011) and 'Beamer, Benz, or Bentley' by Lloyd Banks ft. Juelz Santana (2010).

[67] In a scene in which the artists are in the process of buying jewellery, we see a pile of items on the counter. "All that," says Baby to the salesperson (Steve Harvey), followed by, "And what's on your wrist." Steve Harvey takes off his own wristwatch upon request and, as he closes the briefcase full of money, states, "That's really how you do business." Everything can be bought because everything has a price.

[68] Hayes, R.M. and Luther, K. (2018) *#Crime: Social Media, Crime, and the Criminal Legal System*, New York: Palgrave Macmillan.

[69] hooks, b. (1994) *Outlaw Culture: Resisting Representations*, New York: Routledge.

[70] Peterson, J.B. (2014) *The Hip-Hop Underground and African American Culture: Beneath the Surface*, Houndmills: Palgrave Macmillan, p 67.

[71] Peterson (2014), p 67.

[72] Mist (2020) 'MIST - Savage [Official Video]', *YouTube* [online], 3 January, available from: https://www.youtube.com/watch?v=9aRk5tCk48k&feature=youtu.be [Accessed 16 January 2020].

[73] Call me Ham (2019) 'WELCOME TO BRADFORD - Ham ft. Shotta Shah | Aaja Nachle (Official Music Video)', *YouTube* [online], 16 April, available from: https://www.youtube.com/watch?v=CpeG-uxx1SY [Accessed 16 January 2020].

[74] FirstMediaTV (2018) 'Faisal x Fatts - 100 Riders [Music Video] | First Media TV', *YouTube* [online], 28 December, available from: https://www.youtube.com/watch?v=P4DETDFT9Rg&feature=youtu.be [Accessed 16 January 2020]; GRM Daily (2018) 'EO - German [Music Video] | GRM Daily', *YouTube* [online], 22 March, available from: https://www.youtube.com/watch?v=YQziAomUCT4&feature=youtu.be [Accessed 16 January 2020].

[75] BBCC - BAD BOY CHILLER CREW OFFICIAL MUSIC CHANNEL (2019) 'BBCC - Bad Boy Chiller Crew - BOYS & TOYS', *YouTube* [online], 11 December, available from: https://www.youtube.com/watch?v=oBlL_ZDko5k [Accessed 16 January 2020].

Chapter Four

[1] Husband, C., Alam, Y., Hüttermann, J. and Fomina, J. (2014) *Lived Diversities: Space, Place and Identities in the Multi-Ethnic City*, Bristol: Policy Press.

[2] BBC (2018) 'Women talking about cars', *BBC Radio 4* [online], 12 December, available from: https://www.bbc.co.uk/programmes/b00clsbk [Accessed 30 April 2019].

3 Bourdieu, P. (1984) *Distinction: a Social Critique of the Judgment of Taste*, translated by R. Nice, Cambridge, MA: Harvard University Press.

4 Bourdieu (1984), p 372.

5 Bourdieu (1984), pp 101–2.

6 Bourdieu (1984), p 466.

7 Bourdieu (1984), p 16.

8 During, S. (ed.) (1999) *The Cultural Studies Reader* (2nd edn), London: Routledge; Shuker, R. (2002) *Understanding Popular Music* (2nd edn), London: Routledge.

9 Bourdieu (1984), p 56.

10 Gronow, J. (1997) *The Sociology of Taste*, London: Routledge; Stewart, S. (2010) *Culture and the Middle Classes*, Farnham: Ashgate; Stewart, S. (2014) *A Sociology of Culture, Taste and Value*, Houndmills: Palgrave Macmillan; Warde, A. (2014) 'After taste: culture, consumption and theories of practice', *Journal of Consumer Culture*, 14(3): 279–303; Vercelloni, L. (2016) *The Invention of Taste: a Cultural Account of Desire, Delight and Disgust in Fashion, Food and Art*, translated by K. Singleton, London: Bloomsbury Academic; Ferrant, C. (2018) 'Class, culture, and structure: stratification and mechanisms of omnivorousness', *Sociology Compass*, 12(7): e12590.

11 Bourdieu (1984), p 68.

12 Bourdieu (1984), p 243.

13 Bourdieu (1984), p 2.

14 Miller, D. (2012) *Consumption and Its Consequences*, Cambridge: Polity.

15 Miller (2012), p 44.

16 Gilroy, P. (2001) 'Driving while black', in D. Miller (ed.) *Car Cultures*, Oxford: Berg, pp 81–104; Thacker, A. (2006) 'Traffic, gender, modernism', in S. Böhm, C. Jones, C. Land and M. Paterson (eds) *Against Automobility*, Oxford: Blackwell, pp 175–89; Paterson, M. (2007) *Automobile Politics: Ecology and Cultural Political Economy*, Cambridge: Cambridge University Press.

17 On the significance of extended family, family culture and *biraderi*, for example, see Werbner, P. (1990) *The Migration Process: Capital, Gifts and Offerings Among British Pakistanis*, Oxford: Berg.

18 Huq, R. (2007) *Beyond Subculture: Pop, Youth and Identity in a Postcolonial World*, Abingdon: Routledge; Gilliat-Ray, S. (2010) *Muslims in Britain: an Introduction*, Cambridge: Cambridge University Press.

19 Gilroy (2001), p 84.

20 Watson, J.L. (ed.) (1977) *Between Two Cultures: Migrants and Minorities in Britain*, Oxford: Blackwell.

21 BBC (2010) 'Toyota recalls "up to 1.8m" cars', *BBC News* [online], 30 January, available from: http://news.bbc.co.uk/1/hi/business/8487984.stm [Accessed 15 May 2019]; Finch, J. (2010) 'Toyota sudden acceleration: a case study of the National Highway Traffic Safety Administration – recalls for change', *Loyola Consumer Law Review*, 22(4): 472–96.

22 AE86 and AE82 are manufacturer codes, which yield common meaning only to those who are familiar with the code: the use of such codes reinforces

and legitimises in-group (subcultural) identity and boundary maintenance. AE86s and AE82s are also known, somewhat affectionately, as 'twinnys' amongst enthusiasts (derived from 'twin cam').

23 Also known as 'controlled skidding'. 'Power sliding', however, is performed with front-wheel drive cars. The Scandinavian or Finnish 'flick', developed during the 1960s by Scandinavian rally car drivers, involves sliding the car around bends and corners using steering, acceleration and braking.

24 See, for example, the *Fast and Furious* film franchise, one entry in which is subtitled *Tokyo Drift*.

25 Drifting has been showcased in the television programme *Top Gear* and others, including the Netflix series *Hyperdrive*, in which drifting is central. Reviewers and commentators will often use the words 'sideways' or 'drifting' when describing a car's ability to corner with a skid. Even in the 1990s, however, *Initial D*, a manga (comic book) series featuring illegal street racing, with particular emphasis on drifting, gained popularity in Japan and beyond; this manga was later made into an animated television series.

26 *Assetto Corsa*, *Forza Motorsport* and *Gran Turismo* are three of many car/racing games.

27 Warren, A. and Gibson, C. (2011) 'Blue-collar creativity: reframing custom-car culture in the imperilled industrial city', *Environment and Planning A: Economy and Space*, 43(11): 2705–22, pp 2711–15.

28 Warren and Gibson (2011), p 2705.

29 There are also a relatively small number of females, as well as a few white ethnic heritage enthusiasts who visit car meets, and are self-evidently invested in car enhancement as a personal, leisure and creative pursuit.

30 Warren and Gibson (2011), p 2710.

31 Hoggart, R. (1957) *The Uses of Literacy: Aspects of Working-Class Life*, London: Chatto & Windus; Williams, R. (1958) *Culture and Society, 1780–1950*, London: Chatto & Windus.

32 Warren and Gibson (2011), p 2708.

33 Skeggs, B. (2004) *Class, Self, Culture*, London: Routledge, p 175.

34 Warren and Gibson (2011), p 2706.

35 Department for Transport (2018) *Transport Energy Model Report: Moving Britain Ahead*, London: Department for Transport.

Chapter Five

1 Lansley, G. (2016) 'Cars and socio-economics: understanding neighbourhood variations in car characteristics from administrative data', *Regional Studies, Regional Science*, 3(1): 264–85, p 264.

2 Lansley (2016), pp 280–3.

3 Lansley (2016), p 283.

4 Parry, T. (2019) 'Statistical Release: Vehicle Licensing Statistics: Annual 2018', *Department for Transport* [online], 11 April, available from: https://assets.publishing.service.gov.uk/government/uploads/system/uploads/

attachment_data/file/800502/vehicle-licensing-statistics-2018.pdf [Accessed 11 February 2020].

5 Husband, C., Alam, Y., Hüttermann, J. and Fomina, J. (2014) *Lived Diversities: Space, Place and Identities in the Multi-Ethnic City*, Bristol: Policy Press.

6 Ayres, I. and Siegelman, P. (1995) 'Race and gender discrimination in bargaining for a new car', *American Economic Review*, 85(3): 304–21.

7 Phillips, T. and Webber, R. (2016) 'Ethnic penalties in motor insurance premiums', *WebberPhillips* [online], available from: http://www.actuarialpost.co.uk/downloads/cat_1/Ethnic-Penalties.pdf [Accessed 25 February 2019], p 11.

8 Liberty and StopWatch (2017) '"Driving while black": Liberty and Stopwatch's briefing on the discriminatory effect of stop and search powers on our roads', *Liberty* [online], available from: https://www.libertyhumanrights.org.uk/sites/default/files/Liberty%20Driving%20While%20Black.pdf [Accessed 12 February 2020].

9 Balkmar, D. (2014) 'Negotiating the "plastic rocket": masculinity, car styling and performance in the Swedish modified car community', *NORMA*, 9(3): 166–77.

10 Urry, J. (2004) 'The "system" of automobility', *Theory, Culture & Society*, 21(4–5): 25–39.

11 Sennett, R. (1998) *The Corrosion of Character: the Personal Consequences of Work in the New Capitalism*, New York: Norton; Sennett, R. (2006) *The Culture of the New Capitalism*, New Haven: Yale University Press.

12 Featherstone, M. (2004) 'Automobilities: an introduction', *Theory, Culture & Society*, 21(4–5): 1–24, p 14.

13 Later, I would turn up as a car enthusiast, after I acquired a 1990 'vintage' Toyota. Arguably, at this point, I may have gone 'even more native', but in concrete, everyday terms, that car had an impact on my identity as a member of an in-group in which ownership of such a car seemed significant.

14 Alam, Y. (2017) '7/5/17: Bradford Modifiers Club Car meet – Tesco car park, Great Horton Road, Bradford', *sociologyofcars* [online], 9 May, available from: https://sociologyofcars.wordpress.com/2017/05/09/7517-bradford-modifiersclub-car-meet-tesco-car-park-great-horton-road-bradford/ [Accessed 20/03/2019].

15 Carrabine, E. and Longhurst, B. (2002) 'Consuming the car: anticipation, use and meaning in contemporary youth culture', *Sociological Review*, 50(2): 181–96; Warren, A. and Gibson, C. (2011) 'Blue-collar creativity: reframing custom-car culture in the imperilled industrial city', *Environment and Planning A: Economy and Space*, 43(11): 2705–22, pp 2705–6.

16 Fiske, J. (1989) *Understanding Popular Culture*, London: Routledge, pp 27–8.

17 Pronounced 'tee-pee', this is established informal shorthand, used principally by British-born Pakistanis as a derogatory term for non-British-born Pakistanis, with various applications connecting to signifiers of taste, including dress/fashion and, in this context, cars.

18 For reportage relating to research conducted by onepoll.com, the findings of which, to some extent, echo the points in this section, see, for example,

Bailey, G. (2017) 'British drivers still believe in motoring stereotypes like Subaru boy racer and smug BMW businessman, study finds', *The Independent* [online], 13 December, available from: https://www.independent.co.uk/life-style/cars-popular-driving-stereotypes-subaru-boy-racer-bmw-businessman-white-van-man-motoring-survey-a8107196.html [Accessed 21 June 2019].

[19] Back, L. (2007) *The Art of Listening*, Oxford: Berg, p 56.

[20] The statement, or myth, does occasionally appear online. For not only evidence of the claim, but for the discourse around Bradford and its cars, see for example, toyotagtturbo.com (2009) 'Its not Jap but..', *Toyota GT Turbo* [online], 5 January, available from: http://www.toyotagtturbo.com/community/index. php?threads/its-not-jap-but.32416/#post-404883 [Accessed 9 January 2020].

Chapter Six

[1] On social identity and intergroup dynamics, see Capozza, D. and Brown, R. (eds) (2000) *Social Identity Processes: Trends in Theory and Research*, London: Sage.

[2] Turkle, S. (ed.) (2007) *Evocative Objects: Things We Think With*, Cambridge, MA: MIT Press, p 5.

[3] Donath, J. (2007) '1964 Ford Falcon', in S. Turkle (ed.) *Evocative Objects*, pp 153–61.

[4] Michael, M. (2001) 'The invisible car: the cultural purification of road rage', in D. Miller (ed.) *Car Cultures*, Oxford: Berg, pp 59–80.

[5] Tajfel, H. (1981) *Human Groups and Social Categories: Studies in Social Psychology*, Cambridge: Cambridge University Press; Abrams, D. and Hogg, M.A. (eds) (1999) *Social Identity and Social Cognition*, Oxford: Blackwell.

[6] Swanton, D. (2010) 'Flesh, metal, road: tracing the machinic geographies of race', *Environment and Planning D: Society and Space*, 28(3): 447–66, p 447.

[7] Katz, J. (1999) *How Emotions Work*, Chicago: University of Chicago Press; Sheller, M. (2004) 'Automotive emotions: feeling the car', *Theory, Culture & Society*, 21(4–5): 221–42.

[8] Webster, L. (2012) 'The rise of the fake engine roar', *Popular Mechanics* [online], 2 August, available from: https://www.popularmechanics.com/cars/a7923/the-rise-of-the-fakeengine-roar-11291754/ [Accessed 14/07/2019].

[9] Bourdieu, P. (1984) *Distinction: a Social Critique of the Judgment of Taste*, translated by R. Nice, Cambridge, MA: Harvard University Press, p 56.

[10] Crawford, C. (2006) 'Car stereos, culture and criminalization', *Crime, Media, Culture*, 2(1): 85–92, p 85.

[11] O'Connell, S. (1998) *The Car in British Society: Class, Gender and Motoring, 1896–1939*, Manchester: Manchester University Press; Best, A.L. (2006) *Fast Cars, Cool Rides: the Accelerating World of Youth and Their Cars*, New York: New York University Press; Bengry-Howell, A. and Griffin, C. (2007) 'Self-made motormen: the material construction of working-class masculine identities through car modification', *Journal of Youth Studies*, 10(4): 439–58.

[12] Gilroy, P. (2001) 'Driving while black', in D. Miller (ed.) *Car Cultures*, pp 81–104. See also Böhm, S., Jones, C., Land, C. and Paterson, M. (eds) (2006) *Against Automobility*, Oxford: Blackwell, p 8.

[13] For a much more developed discussion of this, and other features of race and racialisation, see for example, Fanon, F. (1986) *Black Skin, White Masks,* translated by C.L.Markmann, London: Pluto.

[14] Back, L. (2007) *The Art of Listening*, Oxford: Berg, p 51.

[15] Katz (1999), p 29.

[16] Stephan, W.G. and Stephan, C.W. (1996a) *Intergroup Relations*, Boulder, CO: Westview Press; Stephan, W.G. and Stephan, C.W. (1996b) 'Predicting prejudice', *International Journal of Intercultural Relations*, 20(3–4): 409–26.

[17] Alam, M.Y. (ed.) (2006) *Made in Bradford*, Pontefract: Route; Bagguley, P. and Hussain, Y. (2008) *Riotous Citizens: Ethnic Conflict in Multicultural Britain*, Aldershot: Ashgate; Husband, C., Alam, Y., Hüttermann, J. and Fomina, J. (2014) *Lived Diversities: Space, Place and Identities in the Multi-Ethnic City*, Bristol: Policy Press.

[18] Swanton (2010), p 447.

[19] Stephan and Stephan (1996b).

Chapter Seven

[1] Alexander, C.E. (2000) *The Asian Gang: Ethnicity, Identity, Masculinity*, Oxford: Berg; Alexander, C. (2004) 'Imagining the Asian gang: ethnicity, masculinity and youth after "the riots"', *Critical Social Policy*, 24(4): 526–49; Alexander, C. (2008) *(Re)Thinking 'Gangs'*, London: Runnymede Trust.

[2] Brodsky, W. (2016) *Driving With Music: Cognitive-Behavioural Implications*, Abingdon: Routledge, p 262.

[3] Crawford, C. (2006) 'Car stereos, culture and criminalization', *Crime, Media, Culture*, 2(1): 85–92, p 90.

[4] Bowling, B. and Phillips, C. (2007) 'Disproportionate and discriminatory: reviewing the evidence on police stop and search', *Modern Law Review*, 70(6): 936–61; Hargreaves, J. (2018) 'Police stop and search within British Muslim communities: evidence from the crime survey 2006–11', *British Journal of Criminology*, 58(6): 1281–302; Lennon, G. and Murray, K. (2018) 'Under-regulated and unaccountable? Explaining variation in stop and search rates in Scotland, England and Wales', *Policing and Society*, 28(2): 157–74.

[5] Austin-Clarke, P. (2015) 'Stop the danger drivers: new campaign launched by Telegraph & Argus today', *Telegraph & Argus* [online], 30 November, available from: https://www.thetelegraphandargus.co.uk/news/14111344.stop-the-danger-drivers-new-campaign-launched-by-telegraph-argus-today/ [Accessed 16 April 2019].

[6] Lowson, R. (2017) 'Warning after dashcam footage captures drivers ignoring red lights at some of Bradford's busiest junctions', *Telegraph & Argus* [online], 4 September, available from: https://www.thetelegraphandargus.co.uk/news/15512085.warning-after-dashcam-footage-captures-drivers-

ignoring-red-lights-at-some-of-bradfords-busiest-junctions/ [Accessed 21 June 2019].

7 Cottle, S. (ed.) (2000) *Ethnic Minorities and the Media: Changing Cultural Boundaries*, Buckingham: Open University Press; Hall, S. (2003) 'The whites of their eyes: racist ideologies and the media', in G. Dines and J.M. Humez (eds) *Gender, Race, and Class in Media: a Text-Reader* (2nd edn), Thousand Oaks, CA: Sage, pp 89–93; Downing, J. and Husband, C. (2005) *Representing 'Race': Racisms, Ethnicity and the Media*, London: Sage; Meer, N., Dwyer, C. and Modood, T. (2010) 'Beyond "angry Muslims"? Reporting Muslim voices in the British press', *Journal of Media and Religion*, 9(4): 216–31.

8 Alexander (2000), pp 236–7.

9 Macnamara, F. (2018) 'Four men killed in crash on Bingley Road after police chase', *Telegraph & Argus* [online], 2 August, available from: https://www.thetelegraphandargus.co.uk/news/16393196.four-men-killed-in-crash-on-bingley-road-after-police-chase/?ref=mrb&lp=4 [Accessed 13 August 2018].

10 *Telegraph & Argus* (2018) 'Toller Lane car crash book of condolence', *Telegraph & Argus* [online], 2 August, available from: https://www.thetelegraphandargus.co.uk/news/16394879.toller-lane-car-crash-book-of-condolence/ [Accessed 18 August 2018].

11 'Taking a chase' is a phrase used when a driver initiates, perhaps inadvertently, a police pursuit.

12 BBC 2 (2020) *Top Gear*, Series 24, Episode 4. First aired 16/02/2020. Available from: https://www.bbc.co.uk/iplayer/episode/m000fjpt/top-gear-series-28-episode-4 [Accessed 21/02/2020].

13 Sometimes called a 'black box', a term borrowed presumably from the aviation sector, this is a standard piece of 'telematics' technology that monitors driving style and speed, either increasing or decreasing subsequent insurance premiums.

14 Bourdieu, P. (1984) *Distinction: a Social Critique of the Judgment of Taste*, translated by R. Nice, Cambridge, MA: Harvard University Press, p 175.

References

Abrams, D. and Hogg, M.A. (eds) (1999) *Social Identity and Social Cognition*, Oxford: Blackwell.

Alam, M.Y. (ed.) (2006) *Made in Bradford*, Pontefract: Route.

Alam, M.Y. (ed.) (2011) *The Invisible Village: Small World, Big Society*, Pontefract: Route.

Alam, Y. (2014) 'The car, the streetscape and inter-ethnic dynamics', in C. Husband, Y. Alam, J. Hüttermann and J. Fomina, *Lived Diversities*, pp 149–200.

Alam, Y. (2015) 'In-group identity and the challenges of ethnographic research', in C. Husband (ed.) *Research and Policy in Ethnic Relations*, pp 79–104.

Alam, Y. (2017) '7/5/17: Bradford Modifiers Club Car meet – Tesco car park, Great Horton Road, Bradford', *sociologyofcars* [online], 9 May, available from: https://sociologyofcars.wordpress.com/2017/05/09/7517-bradford-modifiers-club-car-meet-tesco-car-park-great-horton-road-bradford/ [Accessed 20 March 2019].

Alam, M.Y. and Husband, C. (2006) *British-Pakistani Men From Bradford: Linking Narratives to Policy*, York: Joseph Rowntree Foundation.

Alexander, C.E. (2000) *The Asian Gang: Ethnicity, Identity, Masculinity*, Oxford: Berg.

Alexander, C. (2004) 'Imagining the Asian gang: ethnicity, masculinity and youth after "the riots"', *Critical Social Policy*, 24(4): 526–49.

Alexander, C. (2008) *(Re)Thinking 'Gangs'*, London: Runnymede Trust.

Alexander, M. (2010) *The New Jim Crow: Mass Incarceration in the Age of Colorblindness*, New York: New Press.

Ali, S. (2006) 'Racializing research: managing power and politics?', *Ethnic and Racial Studies*, 29(3): 471–86.

Amin, A. (2003) 'Unruly strangers? The 2001 urban riots in Britain', *International Journal of Urban and Regional Research*, 27(2): 460–3.

Amin, A. (2010) 'The remainders of race', *Theory, Culture & Society*, 27(1): 1–23.

Ansari, H. (2004) *'The Infidel Within': Muslims in Britain Since 1800*, London: Hurst.

Ansell, A.E. (1997) *New Right, New Racism: Race and Reaction in the United States and Britain*, Houndmills: Macmillan.

Anwar, M. (1998) *Between Cultures: Continuity and Change in the Lives of Young Asians*, London: Routledge.

Austin-Clarke, P. (2015) 'Stop the danger drivers: new campaign launched by Telegraph & Argus today', *Telegraph & Argus* [online], 30 November, available from: https://www.thetelegraphandargus.co.uk/news/14111344.stop-the-danger-drivers-new-campaign-launched-by-telegraph-argus-today/ [Accessed 16 April 2019].

Ayres, I. and Siegelman, P. (1995) 'Race and gender discrimination in bargaining for a new car', *American Economic Review*, 85(3): 304–21.

Back, L. (2007) *The Art of Listening*, Oxford: Berg.

Back, L. and Solomos, J. (eds) (2000) *Theories of Race and Racism: a Reader*, Abingdon: Routledge.

Bagguley, P. and Hussain, Y. (2008) *Riotous Citizens: Ethnic Conflict in Multicultural Britain*, Aldershot: Ashgate.

Bailey, G. (2017) 'British drivers still believe in motoring stereotypes like Subaru boy racer and smug BMW businessman, study finds', *The Independent* [online], 13 December, available from: https://www.independent.co.uk/life-style/cars-popular-driving-stereotypes-subaru-boy-racer-bmw-businessman-white-van-man-motoring-survey-a8107196.html [Accessed 21 June 2019].

Balkmar, D. (2014) 'Negotiating the "plastic rocket": masculinity, car styling and performance in the Swedish modified car community', *NORMA*, 9(3): 166–77.

Barker, A., Manning, N. and Sirriyeh, A. (2014) *'The Great Meeting Place': a Study of Bradford's City Park*, Bradford: University of Bradford.

Barker, M. and Petley, J. (eds) (2001) *Ill Effects: the Media/Violence Debate* (2nd edn), London: Routledge.

Barlow, A., Duncan, S., James, G. and Park, A. (2005) *Cohabitation, Marriage and the Law: Social Change and Legal Reform in the 21st Century*, Oxford: Hart.

BBC 2 (2020) *Top Gear*, Series 24, Episode 4. First aired 16/02/2020. Available from: https://www.bbc.co.uk/iplayer/episode/m000fjpt/top-gear-series-28-episode-4 [Accessed 21/02/2020].

BBC (2010) 'Toyota recalls "up to 1.8m" cars', *BBC News* [online], 30 January, available from: http://news.bbc.co.uk/1/hi/business/8487984.stm [Accessed 15 May 2019].

Belle, C. (2014) 'From Jay-Z to Dead Prez: examining representations of black masculinity in mainstream versus underground hip-hop music', *Journal of Black Studies*, 45(4): 287–300.

Bengry-Howell, A. and Griffin, C. (2007) 'Self-made motormen: the material construction of working-class masculine identities through car modification', *Journal of Youth Studies*, 10(4): 439–58.

Bennett, A. (1999) 'Rappin' on the Tyne: white hip hop culture in northeast England: an ethnographic study', *Sociological Review*, 47(1): 1–24.

Berger, P.L. and Luckmann, T. (1966) *The Social Construction of Reality: a Treatise in the Sociology of Knowledge*, London: Penguin.

Best, A.L. (2006) *Fast Cars, Cool Rides: the Accelerating World of Youth and Their Cars*, New York: New York University Press.

Bhatia, M., Poynting, S. and Tufail, W. (eds) (2018) *Media, Crime and Racism*, Cham: Palgrave Macmillan.

Bhattacharyya, G. and Murji, K. (2013) 'Introduction: race critical public scholarship', *Ethnic and Racial Studies*, 36(9): 1359–73.

Bhatti, G. (1999) *Asian Children at Home and at School: an Ethnographic Study*, London: Routledge.

Billig, M. (1999) 'Commodity fetishism and repression: reflections on Marx, Freud and the psychology of consumer capitalism', *Theory & Psychology*, 9(3): 313–29.

Böhm, S. and Batta, A. (2010) 'Just doing it: enjoying commodity fetishism with Lacan', *Organization*, 17(3): 345–61.

Böhm, S., Jones, C., Land, C. and Paterson, M. (eds) (2006) *Against Automobility*, Oxford: Blackwell.

Bolognani, M. (2007) 'Islam, ethnography and politics: methodological issues in researching amongst West Yorkshire Pakistanis in 2005', *International Journal of Social Research Methodology*, 10(4): 279–93.

Bourdieu, P. (1984) *Distinction: a Social Critique of the Judgment of Taste*, translated by R. Nice, Cambridge, MA: Harvard University Press.

Bowling, B. and Phillips, C. (2007) 'Disproportionate and discriminatory: reviewing the evidence on police stop and search', *Modern Law Review*, 70(6): 936–61.

Bowling, B. and Weber, L. (2011) 'Stop and search in global context: an overview', *Policing and Society*, 21(4): 480–8.

Bramwell, R. (2015) *UK Hip-Hop, Grime and the City: the Aesthetics and Ethics of London's Rap Scenes*, London: Routledge.

Brannick, T. and Coghlan, D. (2007) 'In defense of being "native": the case for insider academic research', *Organizational Research Methods*, 10(1): 59–74.

Brodsky, W. (2016) *Driving With Music: Cognitive-Behavioural Implications*, Abingdon: Routledge.

Buckingham, D., Bragg, S. and Kehily, M.J. (eds) (2014) *Youth Cultures in the Age of Global Media*, Houndmills: Palgrave Macmillan.

Burawoy, M. (2005) '2004 American Sociological Association presidential address: for public sociology', *British Journal of Sociology*, 56(2): 259–94.

Burawoy, M. (2007) 'For public sociology', in D. Clawson et al (eds) *Public Sociology*, pp 23–64.

Burkitt, I. (2019) 'Alienation and emotion: social relations and estrangement in contemporary capitalism', *Emotions and Society*, 1(1): 51–66.

Campbell, C. (1987) *The Romantic Ethic and the Spirit of Modern Consumerism*, Oxford: Blackwell.

Cantle, T. (2001) *Community Cohesion: a Report of the Independent Review Team, Chaired by Ted Cantle*, London: Home Office.

Canzler, W., Kaufmann, V. and Kesselring, S. (eds) (2008) *Tracing Mobilities: Towards a Cosmopolitan Perspective*, Aldershot: Ashgate.

Capozza, D. and Brown, R. (eds) (2000) *Social Identity Processes: Trends in Theory and Research*, London: Sage.

Carrabine, E. and Longhurst, B. (2002) 'Consuming the car: anticipation, use and meaning in contemporary youth culture', *Sociological Review*, 50(2): 181–96.

Casey, L. (2016) *The Casey Review: a Review Into Opportunity and Integration*, London: Ministry of Housing, Communities & Local Government.

Chagnon, N.A. (1968) *Yanomamo: the Fierce People*, New York: Holt, Rinehart and Winston.

Clarke, T. (2001) *Burnley Speaks, Who Listens?*, Burnley: Burnley Borough Council.

Colburn, A. and Melander, L.A. (2018) 'Beyond black and white: an analysis of newspaper representations of alleged criminal offenders based on race and ethnicity', *Journal of Contemporary Criminal Justice*, 34(4): 383–98.

Conley, J. (2016) 'Automobile advertisements: the magical and the mundane', in J. Conley and A.T. McLaren (eds) *Car Troubles*, London: Taylor and Francis, pp 37–57.

Conley, J. and McLaren, A.T. (eds) (2016) *Car Troubles: Critical Studies of Automobility and Auto-Mobility*, London: Routledge.

Conway, G. (1997) *Islamophobia: a Challenge for Us All*, London: Runnymede Trust.

Cottle, S. (ed.) (2000) *Ethnic Minorities and the Media: Changing Cultural Boundaries*, Buckingham: Open University Press.

Crawford, C. (2006) 'Car stereos, culture and criminalization', *Crime, Media, Culture*, 2(1): 85–92.

Cuthbertson, A. (2019) 'Driverless cars to be rolled out on UK roads by end of 2019, government announces', *The Independent* [online], 6 February, available from: https://www.independent.co.uk/news/uk/home-news/driverless-cars-uk-roads-2019-self-driving-hacking-cyber-security-a8766716.html [Accessed 24 April 2019].

Darder, A. and Torres, R.D. (2004) *After Race: Racism After Multiculturalism*, New York: New York University Press.

de Andrade, L.L. (2000) 'Negotiating from the inside: constructing racial and ethnic identity in qualitative research', *Journal of Contemporary Ethnography*, 29(3): 268–90.

Debies-Carl, J.S. (2013) 'Are the kids alright? A critique and agenda for taking youth cultures seriously', *Social Science Information*, 52(1): 110–33.

Denham, J. (2002) *Building Cohesive Communities: a Report of the Ministerial Group on Public Order and Community Cohesion*, London: Home Office.

Dennis, K. and Urry, J. (2009) *After the Car*, Cambridge: Polity.

Denscombe, M. (2003) *The Good Research Guide for Small-Scale Social Research Projects* (2nd edn), Buckingham: Open University Press.

Department for Transport (2018) *Transport Energy Model Report: Moving Britain Ahead*, London: Department for Transport.

Donath, J. (2007) '1964 Ford Falcon', in S. Turkle (ed.) *Evocative Objects*, pp, 153–61.

Downing, J. and Husband, C. (2005) *Representing 'Race': Racisms, Ethnicity and the Media*, London: Sage.

During, S. (ed.) (1999) *The Cultural Studies Reader* (2nd edn), London: Routledge.

Elahi, F. and Khan, O. (eds) (2017) *Islamophobia: Still a Challenge for Us All*, London: Runnymede Trust.

Fanon, F. (1986) *Black Skin, White Masks*, translated by C.L.Markmann, London: Pluto.

Featherstone, M. (2004) 'Automobilities: an introduction', *Theory, Culture & Society*, 21(4–5): 1–24.

Fekete, L. (2009) *A Suitable Enemy: Racism, Migration and Islamophobia in Europe*, London: Pluto Press.

Ferrant, C. (2018) 'Class, culture, and structure: stratification and mechanisms of omnivorousness', *Sociology Compass*, 12(7): e12590.

Fieldhouse, J. (1978) *Bradford*, Bradford: Watmoughs Financial Print.

Finch, J. (2010) 'Toyota sudden acceleration: a case study of the National Highway Traffic Safety Administration – recalls for change', *Loyola Consumer Law Review*, 22(4): 472–96.

Fine, G.A. (1999) 'Field labor and ethnographic reality', *Journal of Contemporary Ethnography*, 28(5): 532–9.

Fiske, J. (1989) *Understanding Popular Culture*, London: Routledge.

Gane, N. and Back, L. (2012) 'C. Wright Mills 50 years on: the promise and craft of sociology revisited', *Theory, Culture & Society*, 29(7–8): 399–421.

Gelder, K. and Thornton, S. (eds) (1997) *The Subcultures Reader*, London: Routledge.

George, N. (1998) *Hip Hop America*, New York: Penguin.

Giddens, A. (1998) *The Third Way: the Renewal of Social Democracy*, Cambridge: Polity.

Gillborn, D. (2005) 'Education policy as an act of white supremacy: whiteness, critical race theory and education reform', *Journal of Education Policy*, 20(4): 485–505.

Gilliat-Ray, S. (2010) *Muslims in Britain: an Introduction*, Cambridge: Cambridge University Press.

Gilroy, P. (2001) 'Driving while black', in D. Miller (ed.) *Car Cultures*, pp 81–104.

Goffman, E. (1969) *The Presentation of Self in Everyday Life*, London: Allen Lane.

Gronow, J. (1997) *The Sociology of Taste*, London: Routledge.

Gunaratnam, Y. (2003) *Researching 'Race' and Ethnicity: Methods, Knowledge and Power*, London: Sage.

Guy, M. (2017) 'Why is a car called a whip?', *The Drive* [online], 15 February, available from: https://www.thedrive.com/opinion/7495/why-is-a-car-called-a-whip [Accessed 23 June 2019].

Hall, S. (1997) (ed.) *Representation: Cultural Representations and Signifying Practices*, London: Sage.

Hall, S. (2003) 'The whites of their eyes: racist ideologies and the media', in G. Dines and J.M. Humez (eds) *Gender, Race, and Class in Media: a Text-Reader* (2nd edn), Thousand Oaks, CA: Sage, pp 89–93.

Hall, S., Critcher, C., Jefferson, T., Clarke, J. and Roberts, B. (1978) *Policing the Crisis: Mugging, the State, and Law and Order*, London: Macmillan.

Hargreaves, J. (2018) 'Police stop and search within British Muslim communities: evidence from the crime survey 2006–11', *British Journal of Criminology*, 58(6): 1281–302.

Hayes, R.M. and Luther, K. (2018) *#Crime: Social Media, Crime, and the Criminal Legal System*, New York: Palgrave Macmillan.

Hebdige, D. (2012) 'Contemporizing "subculture": 30 years to life', *European Journal of Cultural Studies*, 15(3): 399–424.

Herman, E.S. and Chomsky, N. (1988) *Manufacturing Consent: the Political Economy of the Mass Media*, New York: Pantheon.

Hirst, D. (2020) *Briefing Paper, Number CBP07480: Electric Vehicles and Infrastructure*, London: House of Commons.

Hodkinson, P. (2016) 'Youth cultures and the rest of life: subcultures, post-subcultures and beyond', *Journal of Youth Studies*, 19(5): 629–45.

Hodkinson, P. and Deicke, W. (eds) (2007) *Youth Cultures: Scenes, Subcultures and Tribes*, Abingdon: Routledge.

Hoggart, R. (1957) *The Uses of Literacy: Aspects of Working-Class Life*, London: Chatto & Windus.

Holmwood, J. and O'Toole, T. (2018) *Countering Extremism in British Schools? The Truth About the Birmingham Trojan Horse Affair*, Bristol: Policy Press.

hooks, b. (1994) *Outlaw Culture: Resisting Representations*, New York: Routledge.

Huq, R. (2007) *Beyond Subculture: Pop, Youth and Identity in a Postcolonial World*, Abingdon: Routledge.

Husband, C. (ed.) (2015) *Research and Policy in Ethnic Relations: Compromised Dynamics in a Neoliberal Era*, Bristol: Policy Press.

Husband, C. and Alam, Y. (2011) *Social Cohesion and Counter-Terrorism: a Policy Contradiction?*, Bristol: Policy Press.

Husband, C. and Alam, Y. (2012) 'Ethnic diversity and creative urban practice: the case of Bradford's Mughal garden', *COLLeGIUM*, 13, 93–114.

Husband, C., Alam, Y., Hüttermann, J. and Fomina, J. (2014) *Lived Diversities: Space, Place and Identities in the Multi-Ethnic City*, Bristol: Policy Press.

Jeffrey, B. and Troman, G. (2004) 'Time for ethnography', *British Educational Research Journal*, 30(4): 535–48.

Kalra, V.S. (2006) 'Ethnography as politics: a critical review of British studies of racialized minorities', *Ethnic and Racial Studies*, 29(3): 452–70.

Katz, J. (1999) *How Emotions Work*, Chicago: University of Chicago Press.

Kundnani, A. (2001) 'From Oldham to Bradford: the violence of the violated', *Race and Class*, 43(2): 105–10.

Lansley, G. (2016) 'Cars and socio-economics: understanding neighbourhood variations in car characteristics from administrative data', *Regional Studies, Regional Science*, 3(1): 264–85.

Lennon, G. and Murray, K. (2018) 'Under-regulated and unaccountable? Explaining variation in stop and search rates in Scotland, England and Wales', *Policing and Society*, 28(2): 157–74.

Lewis, R. (2015) *Muslim Fashion: Contemporary Style Cultures*, Durham, NC: Duke University Press.

Liberty and StopWatch (2017) '"Driving while black": Liberty and Stopwatch's briefing on the discriminatory effect of stop and search powers on our roads', *Liberty* [online], available from: https://www.libertyhumanrights.org.uk/sites/default/files/Liberty%20Driving%20While%20Black.pdf [Accessed 12 February 2020].

Lowson, R. (2017) 'Warning after dashcam footage captures drivers ignoring red lights at some of Bradford's busiest junctions', *Telegraph & Argus* [online], 4 September, available from: https://www.thetelegraphandargus.co.uk/news/15512085.warning-after-dashcam-footage-captures-drivers-ignoring-red-lights-at-some-of-bradfords-busiest-junctions/ [Accessed 21 June 2019].

Lumsden, K. (2013a) *Boy Racer Culture: Youth, Masculinity and Deviance*, London: Routledge.

Lumsden, K. (2013b) '"You are what you research": researcher partisanship and the sociology of the "underdog"', *Qualitative Research*, 13(1): 3–18.

Macnamara, F. (2018) 'Four men killed in crash on Bingley Road after police chase', *Telegraph & Argus* [online], 2 August, available from: https://www.thetelegraphandargus.co.uk/news/16393196.four-men-killed-in-crash-on-bingley-road-after-police-chase/?ref=mrb&lp=4 [Accessed 13 August 2018].

Madden, R. (2010) *Being Ethnographic: a Guide to the Theory and Practice of Ethnography*, London: Sage.

Malinowski, B. (1922) *Argonauts of the Western Pacific: an Account of Native Enterprise and Adventure in the Archipelagoes of Melanesian New Guinea*, London: Routledge & Kegan Paul.

Marx, K. (1867) *Capital: a Critique of Political Economy: Vol. 1*, edited by F. Engels, reprint, New York: Cosimo Classics, 2007.

Mastro, D.E., Blecha, E. and Seate, A.A. (2011) 'Characterizations of criminal athletes: a systematic examination of sports news depictions of race and crime', *Journal of Broadcasting & Electronic Media*, 55(4): 526–42.

Meadows, B. and Sayer, P. (2013) 'The Mexican sports car controversy: an appraisal analysis of BBC's *Top Gear* and the reproduction of nationalism and racism through humor', *Discourse, Context & Media*, 2(2): 103–10.

Meer, N. (2006) '"GET OFF YOUR KNEES": Print media public intellectuals and Muslims in Britain', *Journalism Studies*, 7(1): 35–59.

Meer, N. (2012) 'Complicating "radicalism" – counter-terrorism and Muslim identity in Britain', *Arches Quarterly*, 5(9): 10–20.

Meer, N., Dwyer, C. and Modood, T. (2010) 'Beyond "angry Muslims"? Reporting Muslim voices in the British press', *Journal of Media and Religion*, 9(4): 216–31.

Messer, M., Schroeder, R. and Wodak, R. (eds) (2012) *Migrations: Interdisciplinary Perspectives*, Vienna: Springer.

Michael, M. (2001) 'The invisible car: the cultural purification of road rage', in D. Miller (ed.) *Car Cultures*, pp 59–80.

Miller, D. (ed.) (2001) *Car Cultures*, Oxford: Berg.

Miller, D. (2012) *Consumption and Its Consequences*, Cambridge: Polity.

Nayak, A. (2006) 'Displaced masculinities: chavs, youth and class in the post-industrial city', *Sociology*, 40(5): 813–31.

O'Connell, S. (1998) *The Car in British Society: Class, Gender and Motoring, 1896–1939*, Manchester: Manchester University Press.

Ohnmacht, T., Maksim, H. and Bergman, M.M. (eds) (2009) *Mobilities and Inequality*, Farnham: Ashgate.

Okafor, K. (2018) 'Let's not punish black British actors like Cynthia Erivo for playing roles like Harriet Tubman – it's the TV and film industry's fault', *The Independent* [online], 17 September, available from: https://www.independent.co.uk/voices/harriet-tubman-casting-british-black-actors-cynthia-martin-luther-king-selma-a8541276.html [Accessed 17 May 2019].

Ouseley, H. (2001) *Community Pride Not Prejudice: Making Diversity Work in Bradford*, Bradford: Bradford Vision.

Packer, J. (2008) *Mobility Without Mayhem: Safety, Cars, and Citizenship*, Durham, NC: Duke University Press.

Palat, R.A. (2015) 'Empire, food and the diaspora: Indian restaurants in Britain', *South Asia*, 38(2): 171–86.

Parry, T. (2019) 'Statistical Release: Vehicle Licensing Statistics: Annual 2018', *Department for Transport* [online], 11 April, available from: https://assets.publishing.service.gov.uk/government/uploads/system/uploads/attachment_data/file/800502/vehicle-licensing-statistics-2018.pdf [Accessed 11 February 2020].

Paterson, M. (2007) *Automobile Politics: Ecology and Cultural Political Economy*, Cambridge: Cambridge University Press.

Pearce, J. and Milne, E-J. (2010) *Participation and Community on Bradford's Traditionally White Estates*, York: Joseph Rowntree Foundation.

Peterson, J.B. (2014) *The Hip-Hop Underground and African American Culture: Beneath the Surface*, Houndmills: Palgrave Macmillan.

Phillips, D. (2006) 'Parallel lives? Challenging discourses of British Muslim self-segregation', *Environment and Planning D: Society and Space*, 24(1): 25–40.

Phillips, R. (ed.) (2009) *Muslim Spaces of Hope: Geographies of Possibility in Britain and the West*, London: Zed Books.

Phillips, T. and Webber, R. (2016) 'Ethnic penalties in motor insurance premiums,' *WebberPhillips* [online], available from: http://www.actuarialpost.co.uk/downloads/cat_1/Ethnic-Penalties.pdf [Accessed 25 February 2019].

Portelli, A. (2019) *Bruce Springsteen's America: a Dream Deferred*, Newcastle upon Tyne: Cambridge Scholars.

Ramji, H. (2007) 'Dynamics of religion and gender amongst young British Muslims', *Sociology*, 41(6): 1171–89.

Redshaw, S. (2008) *In the Company of Cars: Driving as a Social and Cultural Practice*, Aldershot: Ashgate.

Ritchie, D. (2001) *Oldham Independent Review: One Oldham One Future*, Manchester: Government Office for the North West.

Rose, T. (1994) *Black Noise: Rap Music and Black Culture in Contemporary America*, Hanover, NH: Wesleyan University Press.

Rose, T. (2008) *The Hip Hop Wars: What We Talk About When We Talk About Hip Hop – and Why It Matters*, New York: Basic Books.

Rosenbaum, J. and Prinsky, L. (1987) 'Sex, violence and rock 'n' roll: youths' perceptions of popular music', *Popular Music and Society*, 11(2): 79–89.

Ruthven, M. (1991) *A Satanic Affair: Salman Rushdie and the Rage of Islam*, London: Hogarth.

Said, E.W. (1977) *Orientalism*, London: Penguin.

Saifullah Khan, V. (1977) 'The Pakistanis: Mirpuri villagers at home and in Bradford', in J.L. Watson (ed.) *Between Two Cultures*, pp 57–89.

Sanghera, G.S. and Thapar-Björkert, S. (2008) 'Methodological dilemmas: gatekeepers and positionality in Bradford', *Ethnic and Racial Studies*, 31(3): 543–62.

Sennett, R. (1998) *The Corrosion of Character: the Personal Consequences of Work in the New Capitalism*, New York: Norton.

Sennett, R. (2006) *The Culture of the New Capitalism*, New Haven: Yale University Press.

Sheller, M. (2004) 'Automotive emotions: feeling the car', *Theory, Culture & Society*, 21(4–5): 221–42.

Sheller, M. and Urry, J. (2000) 'The city and the car', *International Journal of Urban and Regional Research*, 24(4): 737–57.

Shuker, R. (2002) *Understanding Popular Music* (2nd edn), London: Routledge.

Simpson, L. (2004) 'Statistics of racial segregation: measures, evidence and policy', *Urban Studies*, 41(3): 661–81.

Skeggs, B. (2004) *Class, Self, Culture*, London: Routledge.

Smith, M.R. and Petrocelli, M. (2001) 'Racial profiling? A multivariate analysis of police traffic stop data', *Police Quarterly*, 4(1): 4–27.

Solomos, J. (2003) *Race and Racism in Britain* (3rd edn), Houndmills: Palgrave Macmillan.

Soron, D. (2016) 'Driven to drive: cars and the problem of "compulsory consumption"', in J. Conley and A.T. McLaren (eds) *Car Troubles*, pp 181–96.

Stephan, W.G. and Stephan, C.W. (1996a) *Intergroup Relations*, Boulder, CO: Westview Press.

Stephan, W.G. and Stephan, C.W. (1996b) 'Predicting prejudice', *International Journal of Intercultural Relations*, 20(3–4): 409–26.

Stewart, S. (2010) *Culture and the Middle Classes*, Farnham: Ashgate.

Stewart, S. (2014) *A Sociology of Culture, Taste and Value*, Houndmills: Palgrave Macmillan.

Storey, J. (2010) *Cultural Studies and the Study of Popular Culture* (3rd edn), Edinburgh: Edinburgh University Press.

Swanton, D. (2010) 'Flesh, metal, road: tracing the machinic geographies of race', *Environment and Planning D: Society and Space*, 28(3): 447–66.

Tajfel, H. (1981) *Human Groups and Social Categories: Studies in Social Psychology*, Cambridge: Cambridge University Press.

Tariq, M. and Syed, J. (2018) 'An intersectional perspective on Muslim women's issues and experiences in employment', *Gender, Work & Organization*, 25(5): 495–513.

Taylor, J. (2011) 'The intimate insider: negotiating the ethics of friendship when doing insider research', *Qualitative Research*, 11(1): 3–22.

Telegraph & Argus (2018) 'Toller Lane car crash book of condolence', *Telegraph & Argus* [online], 2 August, available from: https://www.thetelegraphandargus.co.uk/news/16394879.toller-lane-car-crash-book-of-condolence/ [Accessed 18 August 2018].

Thacker, A. (2006) 'Traffic, gender, modernism', in S. Böhm et al (eds) *Against Automobility*, pp 175–89.

Tillmann-Healy, L.M. (2003) 'Friendship as method', *Qualitative Inquiry*, 9(5): 729–49.

toyotagtturbo.com (2009) 'Its not Jap but..', *Toyota GT Turbo* [online], 5 January, available from: http://www.toyotagtturbo.com/community/index.php?threads/its-not-jap-but.32416/#post-404883 [Accessed 9 January 2020].

Tragos, P. (2009) 'Monster masculinity: honey, I'll be in the garage reasserting my manhood', *Journal of Popular Culture*, 42(3): 541–53.

Turkle, S. (ed.) (2007) *Evocative Objects: Things We Think With*, Cambridge, MA: MIT Press.

Urry, J. (2000) *Sociology Beyond Societies: Mobilities for the Twenty-First Century*, London: Routledge.

Urry, J. (2004) 'The "system" of automobility', *Theory, Culture & Society*, 21(4–5): 25–39.

Urry, J. (2006) 'Inhabiting the car', in S. Böhm et al (eds) *Against Automobility*, pp 17–31.

Urry, J. (2007) *Mobilities*, Cambridge: Polity.

Urry, J. (2008) 'Moving on the mobility turn', in W. Canzler et al (eds) *Tracing Mobilities*, pp 13–24.

Van Maanen, J. (ed.) (1995) *Representation in Ethnography*, Thousand Oaks, CA: Sage.

Veblen, T. (1899) *The Theory of the Leisure Class: an Economic Study in the Evolution of Institutions*, reprint, Boston, MA: Adamant Media Corporation, 2000.

Vercelloni, L. (2016) *The Invention of Taste: a Cultural Account of Desire, Delight and Disgust in Fashion, Food and Art*, translated by K. Singleton, London: Bloomsbury Academic.

Wacquant, L. (2004) *Body & Soul: Notebooks of an Apprentice Boxer*, Oxford: Oxford University Press.

Walker, L., Butland, D. and Connell, R.W. (2000) 'Boys on the road: masculinities, car culture, and road safety education', *Journal of Men's Studies*, 8(2): 153–69.

Warde, A. (2014) 'After taste: culture, consumption and theories of practice', *Journal of Consumer Culture*, 14(3): 279–303.

Warren, A. and Gibson, C. (2011) 'Blue-collar creativity: reframing custom-car culture in the imperilled industrial city', *Environment and Planning A: Economy and Space*, 43(11): 2705–22.

Watkins, S.C. (2005) *Hip Hop Matters: Politics, Pop Culture, and the Struggle for the Soul of a Movement*, Boston, MA: Beacon.

Watson, J.L. (ed.) (1977) *Between Two Cultures: Migrants and Minorities in Britain*, Oxford: Blackwell.

Webster, L. (2012) 'The rise of the fake engine roar', *Popular Mechanics* [online], 2 August, available from: https://www.popularmechanics.com/cars/a7923/the-rise-of-the-fake-engine-roar-11291754/ [Accessed 14/07/2019].

Werbner, P. (1990) *The Migration Process: Capital, Gifts and Offerings Among British Pakistanis*, Oxford: Berg.

Westmarland, L. (2001) 'Blowing the whistle on police violence: gender, ethnography and ethics', *British Journal of Criminology*, 41(3): 523–35.

White, M.V. (2002) 'Doctoring Adam Smith: the fable of the diamonds and water paradox', *History of Political Economy*, 34(4): 659–83.

Williams, R. (1958) *Culture and Society, 1780–1950*, London: Chatto & Windus.

Wise, T. (2010) *Colorblind: the Rise of Post-Racial Politics and the Retreat From Racial Equity*, San Francisco, CA: City Lights Books.

Young, C. (2016) 'T&A's Stop the Danger Drivers campaign has given authorities a "kick up the backside" says Chris Grayling', *Telegraph & Argus* [online], 16 April, available from: https://www.thetelegraphandargus.co.uk/news/14431472 [Accessed 16 March 2019].

Audiovisual sources

BBC (2018) 'Women talking about cars', *BBC Radio 4* [online], 12 December, available from: https://www.bbc.co.uk/programmes/b00clsbk [Accessed 30 April 2019].

BBC Radio 1Xtra (2014) 'Hugh Jackman & Meridian Dan - German Whip (Wolverine Remix) feat. JME & Bossman Birdie', *YouTube* [online], 17 May, available from: https://www.youtube.com/watch?v=f2_ibidGpKc [Accessed 19 June 2019].

BBCC - BAD BOY CHILLER CREW OFFICIAL MUSIC CHANNEL (2019) 'BBCC - Bad Boy Chiller Crew - BOYS & TOYS', *YouTube* [online], 11 December, available from: https://www.youtube.com/watch?v=oBlL_ZDko5k [Accessed 16 January 2020].

billybobworddog (2007) 'Chop Shop: London Garage Episode 2', *YouTube* [online], 10 October, available from: https://www.youtube.com/watch?v=Da5JkEOowxk [Accessed 17 June 2019].

Call me Ham (2019) 'WELCOME TO BRADFORD - Ham ft. Shotta Shah | Aaja Nachle (Official Music Video)', *YouTube* [online], 16 April, available from: https://www.youtube.com/watch?v=CpeG-uxx1SY [Accessed 16 January 2020].

DailyTrix (2010) 'Obama brushes dirt off his shoulders', *YouTube* [online], 10 April, available from: https://www.youtube.com/watch?v=1Hq8awi9Oaw [Accessed 21 March 2018].

FirstMediaTV (2018) 'Faisal x Fatts - 100 Riders [Music Video] | First Media TV', *YouTube* [online], 28 December, available from: https://www.youtube.com/watch?v=P4DETDFT9Rg&feature=youtu.be [Accessed 16 January 2020].

GRM Daily (2018) 'EO - German [Music Video] | GRM Daily', *YouTube* [online], 22 March, available from: https://www.youtube.com/watch?v=YQziAomUCT4&feature=youtu.be [Accessed 16 January 2020].

jerudoriginal91 (2011) 'The Pharcyde - Officer', *YouTube* [online], 19 April, available from: https://www.youtube.com/watch?v=JUqdrkpsIho [Accessed 12 April 2019].

Link Up TV (2014) 'German Whip Parody | Link Up TV', *YouTube* [online], 14 April, available from: https://www.youtube.com/watch?v=3WeQrrexlHM [Accessed 12 April 2019].

mike1519 (2007) 'Big Tymers - #1 Stunna Uncensored', *YouTube* [online], 7 December, available from: https://www.youtube.com/watch?v=KEB274xvzvg [Accessed 31 December 2019].

Mist (2020) 'MIST - Savage [Official Video]', *YouTube* [online], 3 January, available from: https://www.youtube.com/watch?v=9aRk5tCk48k&feature=youtu.be [Accessed 16 January 2020].

SBTV: Music (2013) 'Meridian Dan ft Big H & JME | German Whip [Music Video]: SBTV', *YouTube* [online], 29 September, available from: https://www.youtube.com/watch?v=OHZRHEJHS2k [Accessed 12 April 2019].

spectrotoons (2017) 'The Pharcyde - OFFICER (Unofficial Animated Music Video)', *YouTube* [online], 22 January, available from: https://www.youtube.com/watch?v=IpbQh4jYfXI [Accessed 12 April 2019].

Index

Note: Page numbers in *italic* type refer to figures; page numbers followed by 'n' refer to notes.